THE TRACKER
Tom Brown's classic true story—the most powerful and magical high-spiritual adventure since *The Teachings of Don Juan.*

THE SEARCH
The continuing story of *The Tracker*, exploring the ancient art of the new survival.

THE VISION
Tom Brown's profound, personal journey into an ancient mystical experience, the Vision Quest.

THE QUEST
The acclaimed outdoorsman shows how we can save our planet.

THE JOURNEY
A message of hope and harmony for our earth and our spirits—Tom Brown's vision for healing our world.

GRANDFATHER
The incredible true story of a remarkable Native American and his lifelong search for peace and truth in nature.

AWAKENING SPIRITS
For the first time, Tom Brown shares the unique meditation exercises used by students of his personal Tracker classes.

THE WAY OF THE SCOUT
Tom Brown's newest, most empowering work—a collection of stories illustrating the advanced tracking skills taught to him by Grandfather.

**AND THE BESTSELLING SERIES
OF TOM BROWN'S FIELD GUIDES**

About the Author

At the age of eight, Tom Brown, Jr., began to learn tracking and hunting from Stalking Wolf, a displaced Apache Indian. Today Brown is an experienced woodsman whose extraordinary skill has saved many lives, including his own. He manages and teaches one of the largest wilderness and survival schools in the U.S. and has instructed many law enforcement agencies and rescue teams.

THE SEARCH

THE CONTINUING STORY OF THE TRACKER

TOM BROWN, JR.

WITH WILLIAM OWEN

POSSUM

BERKLEY BOOKS, NEW YORK

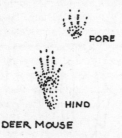

FORE

HIND

DEER MOUSE

This Berkley book contains the complete
text of the original hardcover edition.
It has been completely reset in a typeface
designed for easy reading and was printed
from new film.

THE SEARCH

A Berkley Book / published by arrangement with
Prentice-Hall, Inc.

PRINTING HISTORY
Prentice-Hall edition published 1980
Berkley trade paperback edition / May 1982

ISBN: 0-425-10251-3

A BERKLEY BOOK ® TM 757,375
Berkley Books are published by The Berkley Publishing Group,
200 Madison Avenue, New York, New York 10016.
The name "BERKLEY" and the "B" logo
are trademarks belonging to Berkley Publishing Corporation.
PRINTED IN THE UNITED STATES OF AMERICA

20 19 18 17 16

To Judy, the greatest inspiration in my life and through whose wisdom this book was made possible. To my kids, Kelly, Paul, Tommy III, and Richard, who stood by me and put up with my mud fights, wild edible dinners, and my strange profession.

The making of a book requires not only a writer and an editor, but also supporters. I would like to acknowledge the many people who made this book possible.

My mom and dad and my brother Jim, whose understanding and love allowed me the freedom to enter the wilderness. My writer, William Owen, for his ability to understand my thoughts. Bob and Betty Kapke, who insulated me from the business world and whose wisdom and friendship enabled me to see my dream come true. My friends and brothers who provided photographs, work, and the spiritual backing I needed to make this book possible: Gary and Maryann Eiff, Aubrey and Diane Harless, Fred Smeiser, Wayne and Linda Blais, Damien Emerics, Steve Lee, John McCoy, Dick and Vikki Mills, John Friedlander, King Golding, John Spiridon, Mike Burke, Marie Harbourn, Rob Hall, Bud Ward, Denny Every, Jon Young and Brian Kennedy. My daughter Kelly whose sketches reflect her deep love for the natural.

Finally, I would like to acknowledge my gratitude to Stalking Wolf and Rick, whose spirits are always with me.

All Good Medicine,
Tom

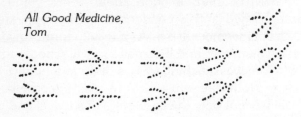

SPARROW
To Mr. Robert Kapke, the person who made this entire adventure possible.

I would like to express my appreciation to the following people for their support and contributions toward the completion of this work.

Kelly Brown for her inspiring work.

Lois Silva and Debbie Shenberger for their tireless hours of typing and proofing.

The families Brown, Kapke, and Culton for their patience and support throughout the entire process.

The congregation of the Frenchtown Presbyterian Church for their understanding and inspiration.

My wife, Kendel, and our children, Aaron and Leah, for the time and space amidst an understanding love they gave to me during this adventure.

Our editor, Oscar Collier, for his constant direction and encouragement.

Tom Brown, Jr., whose life and spirit provided the inspiration and information to make this book possible.

Love
William Owen

Foreword: An Interview with Tom Brown, Jr.

Tom Brown, Jr., is an outdoorsman who was raised in southern New Jersey. The Pine Barrens, an enormous natural wilderness, was his backyard during his boyhood. When he was eight years old, Tom met another young boy, named Rick, who was to become his closest friend. Rick's grandfather, Stalking Wolf, an Apache Indian, took on the task of teaching these two young boys the ways of the Indian. They were taught to track, hunt, fish, build, and survive off the land as the Indian had for thousands of years. They acquired skills long neglected, and as a result of ten years of Stalking Wolf's tutoring, they became almost unique individuals in the modern world.

In the fall of 1978 a book about Tom's youth, *The Tracker*, was published and a condensed version appeared in *Reader's Digest* in November 1978. As a result, Tom Brown, Jr., received national attention, and his small survival school began to grow. By 1980 Tom was teaching classes of up to a hundred students in three- and four-day seminars from coast to coast the year around. He teaches not only the basic skills of survival and tracking, but also an approach, a philosophy toward the Earth, which he feels is as important as the skills themselves.

This new book deals with the philosophy Tom has garnered and fostered from the American Indian as well as with his unique relationship with nature. The interview with Tom Brown, Jr., that follows attempts to answer many questions readers of his first book have had, and to anticipate many you, the reader of this book, may have concerning Tom and his life and thought.

Following the interview, "Tom's World" offers insight into his interaction with the environment, and the parts and chapters of the book tell of his experiences of the past ten years.

William: What happened to Stalking Wolf and Rick?

Tom: Stalking Wolf died in the Southwest in 1970, after Rick and his family moved overseas. Rick died in Europe in a horseback riding accident.

William: How do you feel about them being gone?

Tom: They're physically gone, but their spirits are with me. They are with me whenever I walk in the woods. Did you ever get the feeling that you are not alone? Every time I find an animal's skull, Rick is there. Every time I follow a track to its conclusion, Stalking Wolf is there.

William: You are married now, and have come out of the woods into society. How has the adjustment been for you?

Tom: The first two years were hard. It has just been recently that I have found, even during my teaching, that I should just be myself and do what I want to do. Every day, I get off by myself in the woods to reorient myself and sort of reaffirm who I am. Even when I'm teaching, I have the opportunity, while traveling to and from the classes, to see some of the most beautiful land in the country. About having a family, you know that the woman I married, Judy, had two children, Paul and Kelly, and we have since had little Tommy. What I used to do alone, we now do as a family. We love to go into the Pine Barrens, especially Kelly. My family is an extension of myself. The other day, I was up in the mountains, impressed with their beauty; I found myself saying out loud, "Hey, Judy, look at that snowshoe track!" Then I realized that she wasn't even there. The Great Spirit has given me, to replace my friend Rick, an entire family. As for reorienting to society, I try to stay clear of its influences as much as possible. I still forage to add to the family diet. As a family, we sit around in the evenings, when I'm not across the continent teaching a class on survival, and practice the old Indian crafts and skills. We have time then as a family to talk.

William: You mentioned the Pine Barrens. What do you think of what is happening to them?

Tom: Well, like everything else, they are being destroyed, slowly but surely. Recently a cease-and-desist order was passed by the state legislature to halt development there until proper studies can be made. But if we lose the Pine Barrens, we will lose the largest watershed area on the East Coast.

William: I know that you are very interested in ecology. You are interested in man's relation to the earth. Is this how you were led into teaching survival?

Tom: Just after Tommy was born, I was daydreaming in

the Barrens about bringing him to the places where Rick and I had spent so much of our time. I realized that one of those areas had been made into a development. The clear river that ran through it is polluted, and there is garbage everywhere. I decided then that as long as I could, I was going to teach people the ways that would leave the earth unscarred.

William: Had you ever thought of teaching your skills before this?

Tom: Stalking Wolf told me that I would teach. Before we parted, he said that Rick would take a spirit trip, and I was going to teach. I understand now that he was referring to Rick's death, although that didn't occur to either of us then.

William: When did Stalking Wolf tell you of these things?

Tom: In the last few weeks we were together. Rick and I asked him what he thought about the future and the chances of us ever coming back together. He answered that he, Stalking Wolf, was going to take a walk to the mountain. That, I know now, meant death. Rick was going to take a journey with the spirits, and I was going to journey and teach man the old ways.

William: You seem very comfortable with an expression that is unfamiliar to most of us. By that I mean the acceptance you seem to have of the Indian philosophy. How have you come to accept this thought process?

Tom: My personal philosophy and what you might call "Indian philosophy" are two different things. The Indians called God the Great Spirit. I also chose that terminology. I believe that all life is sacred. I don't question a lot of things like, "Is God real?" I see God in nature. John Muir said, "If I have to worship God, it's going to be in a temple that His hands made," and that's what I think of the woods. When I walk through the woods, like an Indian, my walk is a prayer. All life is precious to me—from the mushroom to the oak, from the beetle to the eagle. What is important is truth and being a just man. If I can live in truth, then I will be taken care of.

William: Do you mean taken care of in this life or in some afterlife?

Tom: Both. But I was referring to whatever life comes after this.

William: Your reward then would be in direct relation to how you have related to the world around you?

Tom: Yes, I think so.

William: Well, it's obvious that we are not relating to the world as the Indian did. You must have some deep feelings about this.

Tom: Stalking Wolf said that the farther man's feet were removed from the earth, the less respect he has for living, growing things, and sooner or later it will mean less respect for mankind. He was quoting from an old Apache saying that originated over 150 years ago. The interesting thing is that as man has taken on boots and removed his feet from the ground, and has made chairs instead of sitting on the ground, as he has made sidewalks of concrete and roads of asphalt and shut himself up in cars when he travels, he has separated himself from the earth. He has lost touch with living, growing, beautiful things, and he has lost touch with humanity. He has no respect for humanity. Look at the conditions all around us. It is because we have lost touch with our roots.

William: If it is true that man is getting even more and more removed from the earth, then what future does he have? What do you think of man's future?

Tom: I think that there are an awful lot of people—and I see this in people who have gone through my school—who are searching for more than just money or power. There is a desire to return to the earth, to get out in the woods and get in touch with themselves. There is a lot more awareness about how we are destroying what little we have left. I think that man is searching for something more spiritual from life. He just goes out into the woods right now, and he doesn't understand what he sees or feels. The course I teach tries to help the searcher see a little more deeply into the life around us and such people get more out of their relation to the earth. So, a five-minute walk through a vacant lot or the park will have regenerating qualities about it. They'll be able to see more and feel more and, therefore, realize their aliveness.

As for man's future, if we don't continue to turn things around, and if we don't take some drastic measures, we can forget life as it used to be. We can forget the wilderness. All that will be pictures and memories because we will have destroyed it all. Our streams will run dirty and our fields foul and we will perish—not from nuclear war but from our own poisons.

William: I know that you've done a lot of work with young people with drug habits. Do you care to make a comment about this work?

Tom: If I can have a young person with me in the woods for a weekend and can show him/her that there is another way to look at life, the chances are that person will stay off drugs from that time on. You can get high on nature, high on your own surroundings—more up than you've ever been. Like John Muir said, "There is no upness like the mountains." Kids say to me all the time, "I thought you could only get this way when you're high!" I try to redirect them toward the wonders of nature. Our young people have little to believe in. They look around them, and everything is polluted and dirty. There's crime in the streets. There's embezzlement. People are constantly trying to rip each other off. The government is so big it can't be trusted. They're tired of it. They're looking for something more. I'm just doing with them what the Indians pointed out. I'm getting their feet back on the earth. When they do this, they gain respect for the earth around them and for mankind. This is what shocks them and gets them back onto a path that's a little bit better. They have gone a long time without respect for anything, and now they can see something to respect, and it gives them hope and that all-important self-respect they need.

William: You seem to think that these young people are looking for something when they get involved in their drug habits.

Tom: Well, I think that goes for anybody. The doctors and other professionals who go through my classes are looking for something more. They're tired of the way they're living. They don't see anything anymore. The one comment that I get when people are done with my school is not "Gee, Tom, I loved the course." They say that all the way through. But they'll say, "I'll never go outside and look at it the same way I did before. Thank you! It's just such a spiritual high, realizing all the life I've missed until now."

William: With your definite reactions to pollution and the way the world is going, did you ever get the urge just to take your family and run off into the wilderness and stay there?

Tom: There's no such thing as running away. I mean that two ways. First, no matter where you go, no matter how far back you go, within two years, they'll put up a development. That's what I tell my students. "If you ever get lost, just stick it out long enough, and I guarantee you they'll put a skyscraper up right next to you." Secondly, somebody has to do something about the state of affairs. If I have to dedicate the rest of my life to that, I will. The first part of my life I spent in the woods. I could easily go back in. But I feel I owe it to the earth to stay out and do something to save her from destruction.

William: Many of us also want to do something to help save the earth, but we often feel incapable or insignificant in the face of this great task. What can we do to be a positive influence ecologically?

Tom: When a man steps, the ripple of his steps can be felt across the earth. Everything man touches is affected. If we walk through nature as a prayer, if we respect everything we have left and stop going after money and profit and ripping apart our landscapes, we can stop the destruction and possibly save what we have left. We can do that by being aware of what is really going on. When we have found out, we have to get others involved.

William: I know what you're saying, but it just doesn't happen. We feel our voices are too small. Why?

Tom: Inactivity! We are too lazy. We would rather sit in front of a television set and watch *Wild Kingdom* than go outside in our yards and view it firsthand. We think, "What's one letter to a Congressman? No one will listen to me." We have to understand that one voice multiplied can shake things and turn them around.

William: What do you mean when you speak of the wilderness?

Tom: Wilderness as a modern term is relative. To the white man when he first came to this country, wilderness was anything that wasn't directly under his control. The wilderness was full of savages and wild beasts. When I use the term "wilderness," I use it as a convenient reference but I don't believe that land uninhabited by man is "wild." That kind of land is actually "natural." To me, the real wilderness in our country is our inner cities. There's more that can hurt you there than in the woods.

William: Can you enjoy nature without going five hundred miles from the nearest man? Can I enjoy the wonders of nature in my own backyard?

Tom: Sure. John Burroughs said that it would take a lifetime to explore your own backyard, and it does. I do something in my classes called "A Closer Look." What we do is bury our heads in the earth and everything that is growing or crawling on a square foot of it for one solid hour. In that time, we have to draw or name everything we see. We have found out that an hour is not enough. Some of my students mark off a piece of earth and are observing it every spare moment of the week during their course. There's a lot to see that's alive on every square inch of our world. You could be busy for a lifetime in your own backyard.

William: Busy, yes. But also bored. How can you sit for hours and look at one piece of earth?

Tom: I can sit for an entire day under a tree and observe and never get bored. Everything that I see is "real" and alive. There are mice, the grasses, the plants, the birds, squirrels, chipmunks, rabbits, ants, beetles, leaves, sunlight. I could go on and on. All these things are constantly changing and speaking to me. They are constantly affirming my aliveness, my reality. The question I ask is how can anyone sit in front of a machine for hours on end, viewing an unreal world, and not get bored?

William: Could you survive off the land anywhere in the world? I mean, could you survive in Africa or South America or the outback of Australia as easily as you would in the Pine Barrens?

Tom: Let's put some parameters on that question. You couldn't just be plopped down anywhere and told to survive on a ten-square-foot plot. I could if I were allowed free range and could roam as far as I wanted. There are many areas I am completely unfamiliar with, such as Africa. In places like that, I would be confined to eating meat until I figured out what plants were edible. But in most of the United States, I would have no trouble, provided I had room to forage and wasn't confined. You see, survival isn't survival.

William: It isn't? What is survival?

Tom: Too much emphasis is put on the difficulty of survival. It's as easy as living in your own home. Nature provides everything. All you have to do is look and take it. Nature takes very good care of you. All you have to do is respect her, but she'll eat you alive if you don't. Survival is a term I use purely for communication! It is living off the land. What I really mean by survival is prospering. It is. It is the easiest state for man to be in because there are no troubles or worries. It is all provided there for you.

William: I like that, Tom. I know that an entire chapter of this book deals with what you call prospering. You also write about fasting. Is fasting something for everyone?

Tom: No. Fasting can be used for cleansing the body—getting out all the poisons, which is a three- to four-day fast. It can also be used for separating oneself from the physical aspects of life to concentrate on the spiritual. It's not for everybody. The Indians used it for vision quests, but I wouldn't recommend that. It entails more than simply not eating. Fasting is good, but it is not for everybody. That's not to say that there aren't a lot of people who could use it. To most people, a fast is missing lunch. Let's face it, we overindulge. When I take a survival class into the Pine Barrens, we fast for two days just to shrink our stomachs. We can survive on half the amount of food we consume daily.

William: Who is your favorite naturalist?

Tom: John Muir. The father of our park systems, the father of the Sierra Club.

William: What's your favorite quote from him?

Tom: It is something like this, "Climb the mountains and get their good tidings. Let nature flow into you like sunshine and flowers. Let the storms blow their energy into you. Your cares will drop off like autumn leaves." The fastest way to God is through the forest wilderness.

William: Do you consider yourself more Indian than white?

Tom: Oh, yes. My spirit is. It's not a color of skin or the blood or even your upbringing that makes you an Indian. It's how you feel spiritually. It's how attuned you are to all of creation. It is a kinship with the earth.

William: Why do the Indian ways and philosophy appeal to you so much?

Tom: Mainly because of the way I was brought up. I was brought up by an Indian. But also because I enjoy their life-style. They are, or were, so close to the earth, so reverent toward the earth. Every one of them seemed to be a spirit of the earth. They knew what was going on around them, could blend in with their surroundings and live in perfect harmony with them. By this I mean their natural surroundings.

William: You were taught in a unique way by Stalking Wolf. How do you compare that to the way you were taught in the public schools, or the way they teach in the schools today?

Tom: Stalking Wolf taught me how to think. They don't teach that in school. Stalking Wolf would never answer our questions directly. He would ask us another question or point us in a direction. We would have to seek out ourselves the answers to our questions. He would also teach by example. He would say, in so many words, "Look at the way I am." Many people today can't think for themselves. Living in the woods, you have to think constantly. Being a tracker, you have to think constantly.

William: Tell me about your survival school.

Tom: I'm trying to teach something that is not found in other schools in the United States today. Not only survival, but a huge dose of Indian philosophy, nature observation, tracking, looking, and feeling—both physically and spiritually—things that go on in the woods that most people don't see. I want to teach the old ways and show how to exist on this earth in harmony.

William: Can a person like myself really learn this? Can the average person really learn to become what you call "one with the earth"?

Tom: I think so. Many of my students who were regular, run-of-the-mill, blind, unfeeling, unmotivated people before are now saying that there is more to life.

William: How can I learn to know my surroundings the way you know yours?

Tom: Get into nature by going out and emptying yourself. Forget your troubles and problems. Look out into nature and don't classify it or figure it out. Just accept it and let it flow into you. It will come to you. There is a saying that holds true for those who really want to enjoy nature. "Empty your cup before it can be filled." That's what you have to do.

William: What was your most challenging track?

Tom: Caribe Island.* Because of the heat and the landscape. There were only partial tracks, and they were so old and it was on very hard ground.

William: What animal would you be most frightened of and why?

Tom: Man. He has the power to destroy anything he comes in contact with. With one gesture, he can wipe out a hundred acres.

William: What is the spirit that moves in all things that you so often mention?

Tom: The life flow, the Great Spirit. It's like finding part of the creator in all things—rocks, trees, soil. To the Indians, everything had a spirit, even the rocks.

William: You've learned to survive. You're teaching people to survive. You've learned to live off the land, and you're teaching others to live off the land. You've learned about the ways of animals. How did you learn what you know? By reading?

Tom: By watching. Reading is becoming an armchair naturalist. The only way you can experience is to watch. The only way you can learn to track is to watch an animal make a track and know what gesture causes that track and then go over and see what that track looks like. John Muir says, "Books are but stepping stones to show you where other minds have been."

William: All of this takes patience. Where did you learn your patience?

Tom: Stalking Wolf. Stalking Wolf. You see the Indians had a lot of virtues. One of them was patience. They were time rich. I learned this time richness from Stalking Wolf.

William: Why are you so interested in tracking?

Tom: I don't know why I'm so fascinated by the woods. All I know is that at the age of seven, when Stalking Wolf read those tracks to me, I knew right then and there that this was what I wanted to do with my life. I have not swayed from that in the twenty-one years that I have been doing it.

William: Patience is important to all that you do, isn't it?

Tom: You can't exist with nature without patience be-

*See Chapter 5

cause everything in nature happens with such an easy, flowing manner. You get out of step, and you miss it. It's gone. And with it, your understanding.

William: What do you think about trapping and hunting?

Tom: Trapping and hunting would be okay, provided that the animal was killed humanely and if every part of the animal was used because all life is so precious. If you kill a fly, it should be for some form of use. If the people who hunt would use everything from the bones to the fur to the flesh, then I could see some purpose in it. But I would like to see those hunters go out and kill a deer as I had to with a knife so they could feel that last ounce of life move from the body. If they kill from a distance with a shotgun or a bow, they are not there. They are not even killing it, really. The bullet is. But if you drive the life from a body with your own hands, you get a totally different reverence for it as I did.

William: In your first book, *The Tracker*, you got very angry at some hunters for butchering some deer in the Pine Barrens. Would you ever do that again?

Tom: They were killing deer to sell and taking only certain parts, leaving the rest to rot. It was bad medicine. At that time, I considered myself the guardian of that part of the woods. The Great Spirit had put me there to protect the animals. They were my deer. But I guess my days of being a warrior are over, and I've gotten more into being a teacher. Instead of using violence to teach as I did then, I try to teach with words and example.

William: If you had one thing you could say to people, what is it that you would say?

Tom: Seek the wilderness, for there is peace.

W.O.

Preface: Tom's World

There is a place I know where everything lives in harmony. Nothing is envied, stolen, or killed. Instead, everything is shared. The land is everyone's and no one's. Life is sacred there. A dweller in this place thinks highly of human life because he lives so close to the earth. He understands his part in the scheme of nature and is not lost or searching for himself.

In this place, man sleeps easily, without fear, and rises to greet the day with praises instead of with curses. He wanders the land at times, but never without purpose. Sometimes he hunts, fishes, farms, gathers, and sometimes he just sits and watches and listens.

Everything is valued in this place. The smallest insect is as important as the largest bear. Each has its purpose and is respected. The water runs clear in the streams. The lakes are alive with fish. The paths are clean and covered only with the tracks of life. The trees grow uncut, and the vines untrimmed—homes for the thousands of forms of wildlife created to live within their protection.

The birds, the wind, and the rushing water are the only music except the songs that spring spontaneously from man's heart. The eyes and hands and mouths and bodies are the only form of communication. In this place a man must face another in order to speak. There is no falsehood there, no deceit, no envy. There is only brotherhood and truth.

Pain and death are there because they are part of life. Only there the pain is natural. It is not inflicted by man, but by the natural order of life. It does not debilitate, but teaches. It does not depress, but frees. Death there is the natural end and the supernatural beginning.

There is a God in this place, for without the Great Spirit, there could be no harmony. It is the force which exists both outside creating and within, relating all living forms. The Great Spirit created this place. The Great Spirit made it good and enables all its creatures to live full lives there.

This is a place I know, where man is naked and unashamed, naked and neither hot from the sun nor cold from the wind. There is serenity for man in this place and a oneness with all of creation. There man neither hates nor envies, for everything is his, and he belongs to everything. There man feels his part of the whole and is not anxious.

There is a place I know where the seasons change, but mildly . . . with a splendor beyond description. Where summer rises on the waving lines of heat out of a spring so lush and green and full of excitement that it drips with life. In this place, summer goes on forever like a meandering river, and all of its life is caught up and caressed in its dry warmth. Fall sneaks up on you in this place, discerned only by its color and the frost that replaces the dew. Winter there is white and crisp and sleepy . . . promising beneath its blanket the key to eternity.

There is change in this place I know. The seasons change, the trees grow tall, and man is born, grows old, and dies with a smile on his lips and peace in his heart.

Where is this place? Does it really exist? Yes. It is within me and can be within you. It is a state of mind; it is an awareness; it is an appreciation; it is an understanding; it is a commitment to life. It is the realization that everything I described is all about us every day of our lives, but we miss it. We are blind to the beauty of a sunset, deaf to the music of the wind, callous to rough bark and soft grass. We speak of salaries and war instead of singing songs of life. We taste the bitterness of pollution and miss the sweetness of wild honeysuckle. We smell bus fumes but never the apple blossoms or clover flower.

We are trapped by our conditioning in a world of steel and plastic, asphalt and concrete. We are removed from the earth and getting farther and farther from it daily. We worry, fret, strive, slave, and accumulate. We see life as a treadmill, a production plant, a honkytonk, a garage. We see it as early American or neo-classical, or nouveau or modern or ancient. But we never see it as natural. Life is manufactured and marketed. It is, for many of us, something to be bought or sold, and the more we pay the better off we feel we are.

In my world, there is nothing artificial, nothing sterile. In my world, the closer I can get to the dirt and the mud, the more alive I become. I neither worry nor fret nor strive nor slave. Whatever happens happens, and I learn from it. I accumulate only what I can carry, and I see life as a great banquet at which I'm the honored guest, along with my brothers the deer and the bear and the raccoon and the salamander and the eagle and the fly. My world has no time except the seasons and the perspectives of youth and old age. My world is natural, designed by hands that are universal in nature. It is neither American nor Chinese. Its differences are high and low, wet and dry, cold and warm, and it makes little difference to me which one I'm in. In my world, life is a gift to be accepted and returned. Life is a celebration, it is a learning, it is a gift. We cannot buy it or sell it, because it is not ours. It is the Great Spirit's, given to us to enjoy. . . . That is the word that best explains this place: *joy.* That is what I feel in my world. Joy. and I sincerely believe that you can feel that same joy in your world because they are the same place, only seen through different eyes.

I once asked my old Apache friend and teacher, Stalking Wolf, why he would not be cold in the winter or hot in the summer. His answer was, "I am both, but I am not bothered by them."

"Why?" I asked.

He looked for a long time at me, trying to decide, I feel, if I was ready to receive his answer, to accept what he was about to tell me. Then he said, "Because they are real."

I've spent a long time trying to understand those words the only way I know how—by living them. By being as real as I can and appreciating all real things in this world.

We are a part of everything real and natural, and therefore they are a part of us. If we don't fight them, but let them flow through us, they will never bother us, only enrich us. It is such a simple principle that most of us miss it. But by missing it, we miss most of what life is all about. What I am saying is that to be a part of this real world, you need to see things differently . . . that's all. Listen with your feelings, see with your heart. Read the earth, listen to the wind as it speaks to you. Gather in its fragrances and touch its differences. Taste it, and see that it is good. This earth is a garden, this life a banquet, and it's time we realized that it was given to all life, animal and man, to enjoy.

T.B., Jr.

Contents

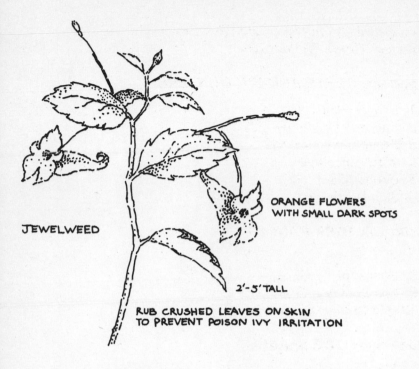

JEWELWEED

ORANGE FLOWERS
WITH SMALL DARK SPOTS

2'-5' TALL

RUB CRUSHED LEAVES ON SKIN
TO PREVENT POISON IVY IRRITATION

part one

TESTS AND ENCOUNTERS

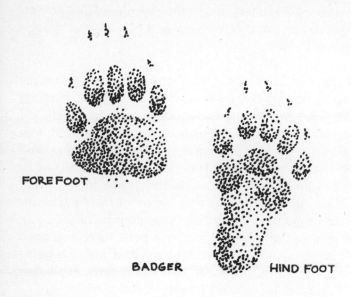

FORE FOOT

BADGER   HIND FOOT

1/Badger Play

Youth is a time of testing. It is a time when we test our bodies and our ideas. It is an exciting time. It is a fearful time.

I turned eighteen in 1968. It was, for most young people, a year of conflict. Our country was embroiled in Viet Nam, and the pressure to take sides was awesome. For me, it was a year of decisions.

I had graduated from high school and was feeling the pressure from some of my friends and my parents to settle down and get a job or go to college. This would mean that I would have to come out of the woods and live like the white man.

I was confused. The white man's world was at war. This war caused movements to be born that sought members from the youth of our nation. There was the group which refused to trust or work for anyone who supported the war. There was the group who took drugs, thumbed their noses at society and "dropped out." There was the group who trusted the government's judgment and saw the war as a way to test their manhood and patriotism. I belonged to none of these groups and didn't feel as though I fit in anywhere.

I had the highest of ideals as a young man—ideals that were taught to me by one of the earth's wisest individuals, Stalking Wolf. Stalking Wolf was the grandfather of my best childhood friend, Rick. He was a displaced Apache Indian who lived with his son, an officer in the U.S. Air Force. That's how Stalking Wolf came to be in the Pine Barrens of New Jersey. I was privileged to spend ten years under his tutelage, learning how to track and stalk and survive, using the ways and beliefs of the Apache Indians. I was privileged to live every boy's dream to be raised by an Indian—and an Apache at that. Up to this point there had been no real pressure to change. My youth protected me. Everyone considered my wild lifestyle a phase that would pass. My father told my mother many times not to worry.

I could imagine the kind of conversation that might have gone on between my father and mother.

Dad: He'll be all right when he gets a little older.

Mom: You're always saying that, Dad. You've been saying that since the boy was eight years old.

Dad: Mom, I know what I'm talking about. All boys dream a little.

Mom: You call an eighteen-year-old spending months naked in the woods by himself, eating God knows what, a dream?

Dad: There aren't many men who can do that, you know. (My father with his slight Scottish brogue would probably sound a little proud when he said it, and that would rouse Mom.)

Mom: There you go again, defending him.

Dad: What do you want me to do?

My father always wanted to keep peace in the home, and was willing to go against some of his instincts in order to do so. I believed that, if he went along with my mother's wishes, it was sometimes against his will. When he had little talks with me, they would go something like this:

Dad: Tom, do you have a minute?

Tom: Sure, Dad, that's about all I do have, time. What's up?

Dad: I'd like to talk to you about something.

Tom (regretfully): I know.

Dad: No, son, you don't know. There's a real world out there that has to be met. You can't keep avoiding it by staying in the woods like some hermit.

Tom: What I've met, I don't like.

Dad: You're too young to know what you don't like. You haven't seen enough to judge. Why, I'm forty-five, and I haven't seen a fraction of this world, and I understand less.

Tom: So that's you, it isn't me.

I had seen more of the world in the Barrens than most people have seen in a lifetime of travel. I was sure of myself, but would avoid at all costs being disrespectful. My father, after all, is my father, and I am bound to respect that fact and act accordingly. But statements like this last one bordered on a challenge, and my father would wait a few moments and even clench his fists before answering me.

Dad: So that's it, huh? You think you know more than your father. I don't know what's happening to the kids today! Flag burning, antieverything, pot-smoking directionless kids!

We were in the midst of the Viet Nam conflict. I remember it as a time of great personal confusion. I knew that I could be effective in war, up to a point. I could track, stalk, camouflage, and evade—but I couldn't kill. When men kill, it should be for survival. Man should kill for no other reason, and he should never kill another human being. I couldn't imagine myself taking a life when I didn't know if I believed in the conflict. I was spared the agony that so many of my peers had to undergo—whether to go when drafted, or run off to Canada.

There is in every eighteen-year-old boy the desire to face death. We all want to be tested. We all want to know for sure whether or not we are cowards or heroes, and our youth puts us at a disadvantage. We think the only way we can prove our manhood is through some life-or-death situation on the battlefield. It isn't until we are more mature that we realize that manhood has little or nothing to do with physical prowess or cowardice, with our ability or inability to kill. Our manhood can be understood through our relation to the earth and its creatures, and survival is not to kill or be killed, but to understand our place, our part in nature, and play it out.

I saw Father as upset by the number of young people who were dropping out of what he considered the productive mainstream of society. Possibly he was even slightly concerned that I, too, might become involved in the drug scene. Not because my physical appearance (loincloth, bare feet, and headband) was unusual, but because my habits could be mistaken or confused with the habits of the hippie drug culture. Here was a group which seemed lost and confused to my father. I also seemed to him confused and ready to drop out of society. Perhaps I had more in common with my peers than I thought at the time, but you couldn't convince me of that. I was not accepted by members of the drug culture (and I don't claim to understand them, either), because I didn't do drugs. And a person who didn't was suspect. I was not understood by my parents because I looked like a hippie. I was dropping out like a hippie, but I claimed not to be.

These were very lonely years in my life. Stalking Wolf had gone back to the Southwest, and his son and grandson, my best friend Rick, had been sent to Spain. I desperately needed someone who could understand me, and there was no one. I would retreat, or advance, to my true home, the wilderness of the Pine Barrens and be reassured that life was good and worth living. I didn't feel too close to my fellow human beings at that time of my life, but I felt very close to nature, and that comforted me. I grew up under the shadow of Fort Dix and McGuire Air Force Base. Rick's dad was in the Air Force. The military philosophy was prevalent in our area. The merchants made their living from the military, many of my peers were army brats, and the Pine Barrens is in many ways like the deep South when it comes to honor and country.

I tried to convince him that drugs were the last thing I wanted to be involved in.

Tom: Dad, I never touch drugs. I don't believe in them, they aren't natural. But I may be confused and maybe even directionless. Not for the same reasons most of my friends are, though. I'm disillusioned with our society, but not just because we are at war when we shouldn't be. We're missing something, Dad. We've gotten away from the land, the earth. Most people don't know what it's like to have birds eat out of their hand or the thrill of petting a deer and feeling its skin shiver. Most people never drink from a cold clear spring, bending down on bare knees in the mud and cupping the clear water with their hands after they brushed the leaves away. They don't know the joy of being alive, Dad.

Dad (with derision and disappointment): And you do, I suppose? My son the Indian.

This was a tone I seldom heard from my father. It could only come from a person who was threatened. Not wanting him to be hurt, I would try, desperately, to get my father to understand.

Tom: Dad, you sought a frontier, and you conquered it. You were like a pioneer. You came to this country from Scotland. A strange land, a different culture, a total adventure. You had your frontier, your adventure. All I'm asking is that you allow me to have mine. You challenged the world in your way. You struck out into the unknown, and you made it. Would you deny me the same opportunity?

Dad (compassionate, understanding, but not yet willing to yield his position: Son . . . the reason I took the chances I did was not to prove something to myself but to make a better life for my children than I had. I want you to benefit from my struggles.

Tom: I know, I know. But without the struggle, life hardly seems worth it. Okay, I understand that, I have benefited from your struggles. I've had a good home and never wanted for anything. I just don't think I can follow the way you and Mom have mapped out for me. It's alien to me. I want you to understand this. It's very important to me that you understand. I don't feel comfortable in buildings, with books, with lots of people around.

Dad: You don't try.

Tom: You know how I try, but I'm different, Dad. I know it, and they know it. Do you think it's fun, being so different? Wondering if what you believe is wrong because everyone you know disagrees with you? It would be easier to give in and do what everyone else does and get lost in the crowd. But that's a maze out there that leads nowhere. It's unnatural. I feel it. The woods are natural, they go somewhere, and I understand them.

I just don't think I'm ready to face the world as you know it. I'll stay in mine for a little while longer.

Dad: Tom, your mother is upset. I'm worried about her. She wants to see you make something of yourself, and so do I.

Tom: What do you want me to do?

My father would do something then that was unusual for him. He'd put his arm around my shoulders and speak very softly, almost apologetically.

Dad: Why don't you get a job or go to the community college? I'll pay the first semester.

I wouldn't answer him. I'd sit and listen to the wind blow.

I heard about a job at college that appealed to me. It wouldn't be permanent. It was in the Zoology Department and required a B.S. degree. I always enjoyed a challenge. I applied in person, ready to meet all objections.

The job was to be an assistant to a professor on a field trip to Wyoming. He was going to study badgers for ten days. To me this was silly. We cannot know an animal in ten days. We must live with it through all the seasons and observe its changes and habits. To know a badger you must almost become a badger, you must play with an animal before you know it.

When Professor Michael Ice looked at my application, he might have been surprised, but he didn't show it. What seemed to come across was admiration.

"All you have here is your name and address."

"That's right, sir."

"I don't even know your age."

"Eighteen, sir."

"What's your educational background? Don't you know that this job requires a degree? You haven't even offered any references."

"I know, sir, but I'd like to explain if you'll give me a chance."

"Go right ahead, I've got all the time in the world to waste. After all, the head of a department doesn't have much to do."

I was bold but young, and I could sense the sarcasm in his voice. I didn't know if I should leave or go on.

"Get on with it," he looked at my application, "ah—Tom."

"This job that you want filled, I know I can do it. It doesn't require a college degree, but it will require a knowledge of nature and an ability to find animals. I have both."

"Oh, and how did you learn so much?"

"I've spent about sixty hours a week in the woods since I was eight, studying and observing."

"That's impressive. Although I don't see how you found the time or how good your study methods were."

"I was taught by an Apache Indian."

"Now, isn't that interesting? An Apache in New Jersey. Are you putting me on?"

"Listen, you have to give me a chance. You're going to study badgers, and I can find you as many badgers as you want."

"Oh?" He was still playing with me, letting the episode run to its foregone conclusion. He had the ending already written in his mind. He would prove me a fool, tell me to stop playing games when there was so much of serious consequence going on in the world, and would send me home properly scolded so that I would stop dreaming and get on with life. He was playing the same role my father had to get me here to apply for this job, and I wasn't going to let him win too. "How do you propose to do that?"

"Come outside, and I'll show you how."

"You're going to find badgers on a college campus in New Jersey?"

"No, they don't live east of the Ohio. They're a Western species. *Taxidea taxus,* an ally of the weasel family, the Mustelidae."

This impressed the professor, but he still didn't yield. "Okay, Tom, show me what you can do that will make me hire you over some graduate student."

We went onto the campus just outside the science building, which was surrounded by oaks and rhododendron and ivy. I began to scan the ground and read it to him.

"There are squirrel here. One sat in this spot an hour ago and made off toward that oak when a young girl walked toward it. She had on a backpack that caused her to walk leaning forward. She weighed about a hundred and three pounds with the pack. There's a family of chipmunks who live in the ivy by the door we just came out. They gather their food about the lawn and drink from the rain spout."

"How do you know all this?"

"It's written on the earth. All you have to do is read it."

"Show me more." He was beginning to weaken, and I was feeling more confident out of the office and in my familiar surroundings.

"Did you know that a red fox went through here last night?"

"Prove it to me, Tom."

I pointed to the tracks at the base of the oak. He looked very closely and said, "Why can't they be dog prints? After all, dogs are all around this campus, and they are known to frequent trees."

"You're right about the similarity, but there is one significant difference. When the fox walks, his hind foot registers in the front. He walks like a cat, while a dog's four prints will be separate." I began to walk at a moderate pace toward a parking lot that was bordered by small woods and some fields. I looked back and saw the professor leaning over the tracks looking at them very closely. "Come on," I yelled.

"Where are you going?"

"I'm going to find the fox."

He was excited now, but doubtful. "How can you do that?"

I pointed out the tracks between his legs and helped him see how they led from the tree to the parking lot.

"We'll follow his tracks."

"But won't you lose him in the lot?"

"I don't think so. The fox will most likely stay around the edge, and use the bushes like he would a hedgerow for concealment. Besides, there's no game in the middle of the asphalt. See, he's turning right and heading up the inside of these evergreen bushes."

We followed the fox's trail, and as we walked and sighted the small pads some eleven inches apart, we talked about the plants and animal life around us. When a fox trots, his imprints are about eleven inches apart; the toes are not readily visible, and the imprints are like little inkblots. The fox is fun to track, and we found ourselves really getting into it. We found where he had caught a mouse unawares and where he had taken it to devour. Just before noon, I spotted where the fox was bedding down for the day. "There's where he's sleeping, under that fallen tree."

"Why wouldn't he be in a burrow?"

"He might be if this were spring and there were young to protect, but in the fall, they usually find some sheltered spot and bed down for the day."

"Do you really think the fox is under that log?"

"His tracks lead there. Want to touch him?"

"You've got to be kidding! Touch a wild animal? Impossible!"

We walked as quietly as possible toward the log, but as we drew near, the professor snapped a branch under his foot, and we saw the fox bound out and head in the opposite direction. "He *was* in there, wasn't he?" The professor couldn't believe it.

"Dr. Ice, I can find animals. You are going on a field trip to study badger. What you need, essentially, is a porter to carry your equipment, but I can do something all your degree people can't. I can track animals." I don't know why I was so intent on talking this man into a job. It was all I could do to talk myself into looking for one, and here I was fighting for it. There must be a competitive spirit about.

We were walking back toward the school when I noticed the professor scratching at his ankle.

"What's the problem?"

"It's this damn poison ivy. I've tried everything, but it won't go away."

I looked quickly about and found some jewelweed, peeled off the skin and approached him. "Bet you haven't tried this."

"What is it?" He was a little uneasy, but not totally unreceptive.

"It's a weed whose juices relieve the itching of poison ivy and eventually clear it up. Want to try it?"

"Do you use it?"

"Yes."

"I think I've read about that, but I could never find the stuff. Are you sure that is what you say it is?"

"If it isn't, you'll probably die," I joked.

"That's what I like, a man who knows what he's talking about."

I applied the jewelweed to his ankle and calf. I left the skin of the plant on the worst infections. "There, by tomorrow you'll be a new man."

"You're pretty cocky, aren't you?" He asked this question without expecting an answer and went on to say, "I'll call you after I've interviewed the other candidates."

The phone rang about eleven the next morning. "Tom Brown?"

"Speaking."

"This is Mike Ice."

"Yes?" I was waiting for an "I'm sorry," but all he said was, "You're hired." I was speechless, and there was a long pause before he asked, "Aren't you curious as to why you were chosen over the applicants with college degrees?"

I was still stunned as I stuttered out, "I—ah—well—yes, I guess so."

He answered, "Because my poison ivy is clearing up, and I need you to find some more of that damned weed for me. You start tommorow. Come at eight and plan to work late. We have a lot to do before we leave for Wyoming."

I went immediately to my mother and told her that I had been hired. She was ecstatic, as was my father. I was turning out to be the man they always knew I would be. I received all sorts of advice on the proper conduct of a worker toward his employer, how I should dress and always be on time, etc. We had an extensive conversation at dinner, and I was happy just to see my parents proud of their son.

Later that evening, I stole out of the house and walked a way back into my beloved Barrens. A Barrens tree frog was making noises close to me. "Have I done the right thing? What will tomorrow hold? What will the sunrise bring? Will we ever be the same? You will be Barrens, unless man destroys you, but I'm changing, and I'm not sure that I'm comfortable with what's happening." This was an enormous step for me, though at the time I couldn't understand why I was so wary of my move. I felt as if I had betrayed something by taking a job. Something was out of place, and I could feel it, as a bird feels a storm coming, but I couldn't explain it.

We tripped to Wyoming. For a few of the half dozen students who went with us, that's exactly what it was—a "trip." We were no sooner on our way than one of the students, Boss, offered a joint.

"No thanks, I don't smoke." I thought I was being very polite and clear about my habits. But there is one thing I've learned about marijuana smokers: they won't take no for an answer.

"Ever tried it?" Boss continued as I knew he would. He was a muscular young man from Newark. He treated everyone as if they were day laborers. He wasn't necessarily offensive, just a bit crude, and so he was called Boss. To most people a name like that would be an insult, but to him it was a joke. He liked it.

"No," I answered—succinctly and, I thought, coldly. But Boss was a bit thick-skinned and wasn't easily put off.

"Well, there's no better time to start than now." He pushed one of his joints over to me and beckoned smilingly.

"I don't think so." I wasn't contemplating taking the thing, but it must have sounded that way, because Boss persisted almost seductively:

"Come on, get high."

I began to get annoyed and decided to give up my passive resistance approach. I barked at him, "Why?" Most of the other students were enjoying their smokes or looking out of the windows until I raised my voice. Then they all seemed to tense up and listen to our conversation. But Boss didn't tense up at all. He shot one of his famous broad, gleaming grins at me and lighted up the joint he had been trying to get me to accept. He took a deep breath, filling his lungs with the smoke, and exhaled ever so slowly. He knew I was waiting for an answer to my question, because I never took my eyes off him. He was playing with me, and the sounds that were beginning to come from the other students—sounds of approval of his little act—annoyed me. I wasn't going to let him get the best of me.

"Well?" I challenged.

"Well, what?" he smirked.

"Why should I get high? I really want to know, Boss, because that grin you have is telling me you think you have the answer. I want to hear it."

He was challenged, but he hid behind his good humor and looking out the window at the passing landscape mumbled, "You'll notice things more." Some of the other students smiled and nodded their agreement. I looked out and immediately caught sight of a red-tailed hawk circling high above a field, and as I watched, he twisted his tail at an angle to his body in order to turn.

"Like that red-tailed hawk working that far field?" I was wondering what Boss's joint was enabling him to notice more.

He answered, "Where?"

He hadn't seen it. The hawk was the only moving thing in the sky. What had he been looking at? Tail lights?

"Over there," I answered, pointing up to where the hawk had made his turn at about eighty-five feet. He was magnificent, and I longed to hear his quealing *kee-a-a-a-r-r-r* that sounded much like escaping steam.

All the students were craning their necks to see him, and Boss, catching sight of him, exclaimed gutturally, "Yeah, now I see it. Wow! Look at it soar, man."

I was excited by the bird's freedom and said, "Notice how it turns by using its tail feathers?"

"Yeah, man, that's wild. Far out. Say, where did you learn that about his tail?"

I couldn't take my eyes off the hawk even though he was now far behind the van. When I did look back at Boss, I had my answer, and I smiled as I said it. "I notice things more."

"But not like I do, man," Boss retorted. The smoker never gives up, but then neither do I.

"You're right, Boss, I don't see things like you do. I see things as they are, not distorted by some so-called mind-expanding weed. You think you see things more clearly, but the fact of the matter is, you miss almost everything. You were looking out of the window, watching the sun reflect off car bumpers, while one of the most magnificent birds nature has created soared over your head, and you were too high to look up. No, Boss, I don't want to smoke, because it doesn't make you notice more, it makes you see less."

With that, I let it go, and surprisingly so did Boss. That doesn't mean he or any of the other smokers stopped for the rest of the trip. They just didn't offer me any more joints. Also, I was allowed to sit by the window for the remainder of the trip so that I could "notice more."

We arrived in Wyoming and set up camp in the semiarid foothills of the Wind River Range. It is red, rugged, and honest country. It gives exactly what it takes. Life balances there more precariously than in more fertile well-watered areas, but it balances.

We worked hard setting camp and hunting and studying badgers. It was a concentrated time of study, and in the evenings we would unwind around the campfire. In the informality of the camp, where all chores are shared equally, we were all on a first-name basis. However, it did not mean we all agreed.

One evening in the middle of a conversation, Dr. Ice almost exploded.

"You're a damn fool, Tom. Life just isn't the way you think it is."

"You may be right, but I don't think so. Maybe it isn't the way I say it could be because people have lost sight of those things that should be of value—they're so busy trying to put things in order that they can't see the natural order all around them."

"It's no use. You—you're fighting a losing battle. People won't listen to you," replied Mike.

"I know. I've been called all sorts of names, ranging from crazy to crazy. No matter how they phrase it, it all means the same."

"Tom, I respect your abilities in the wild, but I just can't buy your rationale. You don't have to believe all that prattle about the sacredness of the earth in order to understand it. I understand the badger, but I certainly don't consider it sacred."

"Then you'll never be able to talk with it."

"What? Why in the hell would I ever want to talk to a badger?"

"How else will you be able to understand it?"

"Excuse me—ah—Mr. Badger—er—ah—may I call you Badge? Do thunderstorms scare you? That's asinine, Tom, and you know it."

"But they aren't afraid of thunder. Their frantic behavior during a thunderstorm is something else. A ploy to make their prey misjudge and run for cover heedless of the wary badger. Many rabbits have been caught thinking that it was safe for them to dash for cover. They look out at this frantic and even cowering badger and consider him helplessly afraid and, *wham*, they've been had."

"Tom, that can be seen and understood, but you don't have to worship the ground to understand that."

"I don't worship the ground. The earth is sacred, that's all. My life comes from it, so I cherish it."

"Sounds like worship to me."

"Your problem is that you can't accept anything being superior to man. Or man being dependent on anything. You can't accept subjection to anything. According to your definition, you worship science."

"You know better than that. Science is just a means to an end—knowledge."

"So's the earth. It can teach me all it knows, which is everything, if I'll respect her and listen to her. She's a history book and encyclopedia, a scientific journal lying here . . ." I was excited, and I picked up a handful of the Wyoming dirt and held it right under his nose. "Smell it."

"Are you crazy?"

"Smell it, dammit! And you'll be able to tell what it's made of."

Mike reluctantly sniffed at my grubby hand of dry sandy dirt and said with a superior air, "Smells like dirt to me, mingled with sweat."

"Now you're cooking. Did you know that the sandy soil around here will hold the smell of a man for only a few hours, but the muddy bank of a river could hold it an entire week. And look here, right beneath your feet."

Mike looked down and saw nothing but the marred dry earth covered with the flickering shadows cast by the campfire. He saw what most of us see when we look at the ground—dirt.

We don't listen to what it is saying to us. We don't take the time to read its story. The earth is like a giant jigsaw puzzle that will paint us a picture if we take the time to put it together, but we're too busy looking at our feet so we won't trip, and we never take the time to look at the earth beneath our feet.

"There by your left foot. A field mouse stopped there to eat a crumb this afternoon. See his markings and where he dragged his tail as he came up to the scrap of food? Here is where he squatted to eat." I was pointing with a stick and circling each mark. "Look, he jumped to here and ran off, his tail up now. Something must have scared him."

"You're pretty good, Tom. But you go overboard with your philosophy." Mike was taken aback for a moment, and I could see him studying the markings to figure out if I was telling the truth or just trying to hustle him. "Interesting, very interesting." That's what a scientist says when he's been proved wrong and needs time to think of a rebuttal. He'll back off a ways and regroup and then qualify his last statement, but he'll never admit that he might be wrong. "But all that proves is you can track. I could learn that if I took the time, and I wouldn't have to venerate Mother Earth to do it."

"Yes, you would, because if you didn't venerate it, as you say, you wouldn't take the time. The Indians called it listening to Mother. . . ."

"Tom, you are a real piece of work. The Indian quotations that come out of your mouth are hard to believe. I just can't see a group of intelligent people sitting around making up such trite phrases."

"It has to be complicated to be true, right?"

He took another sip of his pine-needle tea and said, "Not necessarily, but I resent simplifying some very complicated concepts. When you do that, you run the risk of superstition. What isn't explained is imagined by the ignorant."

"Blessed are the poor in spirit, for they shall inherit the kingdom of God."

"What did you say?"

"Nothing, just a little bit of my past surfacing to make a point."

"Most of the most profound truths are simplified for

teaching purposes. You're right there. But I think we're talking on two levels here. I'm trying to be rational and scientific, and you're trying to be emotional and philosophical. They just don't mesh."

"Listen to the owl," I said, "he's crying."

"He might be hungry."

"Or sad?" I answered.

"Sad?"

"Yes, he might have been listening to our conversation hoping I could persuade you to be a believer."

He ignored me, with a little laugh, threw the remainder of his tea behind his tent, and said good night. He entered his little cocoon of civilization, shaking his head. I soon heard the crackling of the portable radio emanating from the cocoon of bright iridescent orange. He was listening to the news before he retired.

I rolled up in my buffalo robe and listened to the night sounds: the wind over the dry earth, the owl's lament, the coyote playing in the moonlight. Thank you for the good news, Mother . . . and I fell asleep.

"Look at that!" I said to Mike, who was busy about his equipment the next morning. He was fixing a trap that he brought to catch badgers. He didn't look up but said, 'I saw it!" He hadn't seen the golden eagle, just as he had missed so much we had observed during the past week.

We had come to Wyoming to observe the habits of badgers. The way Dr. Ice was going to do this was to capture badgers, put them to sleep, attach a homing device, and follow them electronically to observe their habits. I told him that the best way to observe an animal is to track it, but he just said that's what he was going to do.

What he couldn't realize was how much could be learned about an animal along the way when you are following its trail. You can tell what it eats and how often, whether it hurries or meanders; you can examine its droppings and can figure how it plays, how it mates, and finally where it lives. The professor would trap it with bait and then let it go and follow it to its home and there observe it. He would miss everything in between—the stuff that gives the animal its personality. He will determine its habits by what it does at home, what food it brings, etc. I know we act differently at home from the way we do when we're abroad, and an animal at home is cautious where he might be playful on his way to and from. An animal protects his home through sleuthing or aggression so he is apt to have a different personality away from home. The good professor would miss that.

"*Aquila chrysaëtos.*"

"You know the name?"

"Yes. Want to stick around and watch it fly?"

"I've seen dozens of them in flight, and besides, that's not why I've come here."

"Do you want me with you today?"

"No, you were useful yesterday, why not just sit and watch the eagle fly? You'll enjoy that."

He didn't understand. He thought it was a waste of time to share the flight of an eagle through observation. He couldn't let himself go enough to imagine himself with the eagle in flight, searching the earth for food, and therefore he would never understand the eagle.

"I'll stay here, there's a badger den just up the arroyo gully. I think I'll wade up there and play with him."

He looked at me incredulously. He knew the meanness of the badger, and he was here to discover why it was so ferocious. "You've told me a lot of stories, Tom, and sometimes I'm almost convinced, but in order to play with a badger, you must first tame him, and that's impossible. Especially a mother badger. I wouldn't advise it, unless you want to feed it a couple of your fingers."

"We'll see," I said, "but first the eagle." The eagle was good medicine, and I hoped that this would be a special day for me and perhaps for the professor. We had talked long and hard around the campfire and were really quite close, despite our differing views. We had our differences in common, and we were growing to respect each other.

Mike went off to the north, and I sat and watched the eagle. He was mature, maybe as much as twenty years old. His color was bronze, and the ring had disappeared from his tail feathers.

Is it strange to talk to nature? It is natural to me. I've

caught myself talking to the wind or a tree and often to deer. "You're coming from the east today, what have you passed over and through?" And I would sniff, lift my head to scent the wind and hear its answer as it rustled the leaves and brought the scent of the flowering bushes in spring or the acrid odor of a road-killed rabbit. The wind always aroused me.

Which way are we headed today? I thought to the eagle. He cocked his head and took off. So did I.

I knew where I was going, and I knew what I was going to do. The eagle had inspired me. I headed toward a badger's den I had tried to get the doctor to use as a testing site. He looked at it, but didn't think that it could be active. The cover was too sparse for the small game and birds that would support a badger. What he said was true. The den was in an area that was quite open and rocky. It was unlike any other badger den we had found, but I argued for the professor to trust my judgment. The tracks to and from his hole were fresh. He pointed out that there were no remains of its kills around, and therefore this could not be its permanent home but just a resting place or an escape route. Perhaps it was another animal's den and the badger had entered to kill. Besides, he argued, there wasn't enough time to take a chance on my speculative thinking, and so we left the den and found others.

I stood on the open and rocky hill and searched my senses for the reason I felt that this was a badger's home. There were no signs of its kills anywhere about the opening that I took to be the primary entrance to his den. Why? My eyes scanned the area for some clue. There was none. At that moment a quail flew up over the rise at my back. I was curious and climbed the rocks to see where it had come from. To my surprise there was a deep gully behind those rocks that was filled with vegetation and wildlife. We hadn't seen it when we were scouting the area. It was like a tiny box canyon, and we had missed the opening on its western edge. So that's how the badger survived. He would climb these rocks and enter his hidden valley at night. There were no remains by his home, because he commuted to work.

I climbed back down the red rocks to his den opening. The sun was beginning to heat the land, and I could see the waves of heat rising from the dry land that surrounded me. A lizard slithered from rock to rock looking for shade.

I placed myself down beside the opening and just a little in front of it.

I sat just in front of the opening to the badger den. My shadow fell across the hole, so that he would know I was there. The wind was coming up over the rise behind the den and my scent was traveling away across the prairie. I didn't move or make a sound. I sat and listened and dreamed. The sun warmed me, and the breeze brought messages that triggered memories of other warm mornings. If I sit and remain peaceful, the badger will sense more than my presence, he will sense my spirit.

A harsh shrieking *jo-ree* caught my attention and drew it to a dead scrub pine not twenty yards away. There in its upper branches a northern shrike was perched and watching for prey. Every once in a while, it would pump its black tail and give a shriek. This bird isn't observed very often, and I felt a certain sense of pride on spying her. She was a good size, about ten inches, with a brown bill that let me know it was the female of the species.

I quickly scanned the horizon for prey. There, about a mile across the rolling prairie, was a small flock of sparrows. They were moving in our direction out of the sun. Had she seen them? She sat like some bandit with her mask and hooked beak waiting patiently for her prey. When she saw the sparrows, she suddenly stiffened and prepared for flight. Boldly, she took flight close to the ground, using the hills as cover, toward the sparrows. Her flight was undulating, but straight as a line drawn over this hilly landscape. She swept up on the sparrows as they came over a hill and caught her victim by its breast. She flew almost straight up, searching the land as she climbed with the sparrow struggling in her talons. I knew what she was looking for, but I had never seen it before. I was fascinated by her strength and grace as she abruptly turned in midflight and dived toward a thorn bush. She flew in straight and hard and impaled her victim on the thorns. Very efficient, I thought.

Wyoming was red in the morning sun, and the long shadows made the landscape look large and ominous. Small hills looked like mountains and narrow washes looked like giant valleys. The air was warming steadily as the sun rose, and not a cloud marred the bright blue of the sky. I felt at peace with my surroundings. It was then I sensed some movement in the den. It wasn't much, only a faint scratching, as if something was inching toward the entrance.

I turned slowly and smiled at the eyes shining at me. I made a soft kissing sound and called to the eyes, "Morning, quite a place you've got here. Nice view. Good hunting. Come on out, the sun's warm, and the sky is clear." The eyes continued to stare as I prattled on about the weather and the landscape. It seemed as though they never once blinked. The stare they gave me was one of caution, but I didn't receive a feeling of fear or anger. I was encouraged that the animal hadn't growled or grunted a warning, so I lay down in front of the entrance to the den and stretched my hand slowly toward the eyes that suddenly assumed a surprised look.

I lay there for a long time coaxing and making kissing sounds. I even gave an oral treatise on all I knew about the badger. I was trying to let it know that I was friendly and meant it no harm. "Catch any ground squirrels lately? What are the quail eggs like this time of year? I haven't seen any prairie dogs in the area, have you? What about the pocket gophers—get many this season? This is a good time of year to get honey, I'll bet, if you haven't cleaned out all the hives in the area already. How deep's your burrow, thirty feet? By the looks of it, it could have belonged to a marmot. Did it?" I went on and on like that till the sun was almost directly overhead.

"Listen," I said, "I don't know about you, but I'm thirsty." I sat up, poured some water from my canteen into my hand and sipped it as loudly as I dared. Then I poured some more in the palm of my hand and stretched it out toward the eyes. I beckoned, "Come on, don't be shy. Have a little drink." I tried not to move as the eyes for the first time blinked and began to move closer to the opening.

It's coming, I thought. Now what'll I do? Here I was coaxing a wild badger from its den to take a drink from my hand, and I really wasn't sure whether it would lick or bite. However, it was too late to worry about that, because the animal moved very swiftly and covered my palm with its tongue. I did it! It worked! The badger was out of its den in broad daylight licking water from my hand. I quickly refilled my palm and let the badger satisfy its thirst.

It was a beautiful animal, a full thirty inches long and as

many pounds. Its grayish yellow fur was beginning to thicken for the winter. Its feet were black and its front claws were enormous. No wonder they can outdig a man with a shovel.

I decided to see how far our friendship could develop, and how much this young male badger could trust me. For that matter, I was wondering how much I could trust him. I began by slowing stroking the side of his head with the back of the hand that he had just taken water from. To my surprise, he didn't move away but nuzzled closer to my hand as I stroked him.

What was the next step? I decided to throw all caution to the wind and treat him as I would a house cat or dog. I reached behind his ear and scratched. He moaned. My God, he likes it! I thought. I was ecstatic. I reached under his chin and scratched again, and he promptly rolled over on his back and grunted in long low tones as if to say, "Don't stop, I love it." I didn't.

Our play progressed to the point where we were play-fighting and rolling around together. My hand was in his mouth a number of times, and he never tightened his jaw to bite. In fact, after his first groan I never expected it, and I think he sensed that.

Why had he come out of his den at all? He could have stayed holed up there all day and ignored my presence. He must have sensed something about the way I felt. I feel that he sensed my spirit the same way I sensed his. The spirit that moves in all things spoke to us, and we listened. Most humans have lost their sense of oneness with the land and its animals. Most are sensed by animals as intruders, as aliens, and are avoided at all costs. If we could change our attitudes and appreciate the uniqueness of the life all about us and stop fighting it, perhaps its beauty would stop avoiding us. If the rabbits knew that every human who saw them would not throw a stone or try to run them down with the car, they might be more visible. Animals have a fear and hatred of man that has become instinctual and necessary to their survival. If we want to enjoy the land on which we depend for survival, and if we expect her to keep feeding us, then we had better learn how to be at peace with her and our brothers and sisters, her other sacred inhabitants.

I decided to name the badger after my old pet raccoon. "Ricky!" I called. "How do you like that name? Ricky was a raccoon I had in New Jersey, back by the big river. She taught me a lesson in survival, and you're teaching me one now. It's good for you to be named Ricky. At least for me."

We played the afternoon away. I was on my back with Ricky on my stomach, just sort of snoozing and talking to each other, when we heard the professor and one of the students coming down the gulch. Really, Ricky scented them first, and I sensed them because his body tightened and his head swung north. Then we both heard them plodding down the trail, banging and clanking and talking.

They stopped short when they saw me lying with a badger on my chest. They must have thought I had been attacked, because Boss called out, "Are you okay?" Ricky's hair was standing straight up on his back, and he was beginning to hiss. I petted him and told him they were friends, but that wouldn't calm him. He simply sensed danger. I motioned Doc and Boss to go back and around. They did, but hesitantly. I could tell that they didn't believe their eyes. Ricky followed them with his nose as they made their way to camp behind the hills to the east. He didn't let his guard down for a moment, until they were long gone.

"You don't trust most of us do you?" I asked Ricky. "Well, some of us just haven't learned yet not to be afraid." I played with Ricky for a while longer and then watched him back into his den. He would have to get some sleep if he wanted to catch his supper tonight.

I was anxious to get back to camp and see what my skeptical friends would have to say. It really didn't matter at this point. Things were beginning to fall into place in my mind. My encounter with Ricky had opened my mind to many of the answers to the questions that had driven me here, and I knew that, before I left this beautiful arid wilderness, I would know where I was going, and why.

That evening about the campfire the usual banter and joshing were absent. In fact, there was silence for the first time, and everyone seemed to be listening to the night sounds and waiting. I didn't realize what they were waiting for until Boss asked me a question.

"What was that noise?"

I thought he was talking to one of the other students because his tone was civil, so I didn't answer him.

"Tom?" He directed his gaze at me, and I noticed his leering grin was gone. "Do you recognize that noise?"

"Sure, Boss, that's a screech owl."

"What's he saying?"

I couldn't believe my ears. Boss was asking questions like a schoolchild who had just discovered his teacher didn't bite.

"He's calling to his mate, that's all. Letting her know where he's hunting and that he's all right."

"But doesn't that warn his prey?"

"Yes."

"So?" Boss waited for me to go on.

"So what?" I answered.

"So how can he catch anything if everything knows he's around?" Boss wanted to know.

I answered with Stalking Wolf's favorite phrase: "Go ask the mice."

"Come on, Tom, tell me and shut off the Indian talk!"

"Okay, Boss. He's already caught something, eaten it and is telling his mate. He'll move on after a while to another location."

"Sort of like 'I've made it, woman. How's it going with you?'"

"Sort of, Boss, sort of. But not quite. Animals don't brag like humans. They don't know pride the way we do. The owl's cry was a matter-of-fact reporting of an occurrence. That's all—just part of the whole and not the reason for it."

"Part of the whole?"

"Humans want to be on top of the world. Animals just want to be a part of it, Boss. We've got to discover how to be a part of it and see our part in it if we ever expect to know what life's all about."

That's how the evening went, and this same good medicine extended through the rest of our time in Wyoming. It was a different kind of expedition from that time on. We spent our time observing and sharing our discoveries. It was like a school, and I was teaching. We made bow-and-drill fires, tomahawks out of rocks, rabbit sticks, and went tracking. We took down the tents and slept in the open, and there was more silence.

Silence is not bad. We need silence in order to listen. Most would say, "Well, what is there to hear if everyone is quiet?"

My answer to that is the sounds of the earth. The cricket's chirps, the coyote's bark, the owl's call, the wind's song, the heart's beat, the sounds of breathing. All of these speak to us and minister to us and calm us if we but listen. You would think that more silence among a group of students was a sign of tension. But it wasn't so in this case. We grew closer because we were less tense, were taking time to listen and were respecting each other's individuality.

If one of us wanted to spend an hour alone with the sunset, that was okay. If Boss wanted to stalk a prairie dog or whittle a paiute trap, that was okay. We didn't need to be talking in order to communicate, because we were using everything about us to convey our feelings to each other.

Boss was telling us all how relaxed he was when he sat on the ridge and watched the sun disappear. For once, Boss was "high" without having to use marijuana or anything artificial. All he had to do was let himself go and notice everything about him. This isn't a fairy tale that claims the observance of nature will cure a habit, but in this case it replaced a penchant for smoking grass with the joy of noticing the myriad forms of life that live in it. Boss didn't smoke grass for the remainder of the expedition, because he didn't have to. It's as simple as that. If he wanted to get high, he'd go to the mountain!

Badgers were the reason we came west. We studied them now in a new way. The students were no longer afraid of the vicious badger, which could outdig a man with a spade and should never be cornered. They began to understand the purpose of its ferocity and how it fit into the greater plan of nature. The badger was not isolated in order to be studied, but studied according to its relation to everything around its environment. When understanding replaces fear, learning can take place.

The final days of our expedition went quickly. It was time to return to New Jersey, and we regretted our leaving. We had grown close there in the rugged Wyoming country, and we had discovered something about nature and ourselves, and we were a different group now. You might say we were satisfied.

I walked back up the dry gulch to Ricky's den after we had packed the van. I wanted to say good-bye. I knew by his tracks that he had just come back to his den. I knelt beside the opening and made a sound like a chipmunk. Soon his nose appeared. He sniffed the air, caught my scent, and, reassured that it was me, came out directly to where I knelt and curled up in my lap.

The sun was low in the eastern sky and red streaks warned of a coming storm. The birds were busy about the area, gathering seeds and stuffing their gullets. The wind came softly out of the hills to the northwest and stroked us with a damp warning of what the afternoon would hold.

"Thank you, Ricky," I said softly as I scratched behind his ears. I wonder if he knew what he had done for me. I had come searching for answers to some very disturbing questions. Ricky had reaffirmed my faith in my basic belief that my questions were not going to be answered by me but by nature. My part was not a waste, my ideas not insane, my ways not empty, my reality valid. Everyone comes to crossroads and diverging paths in their lives when they must decide to go one way or the other. This was one of those times in my life, and my way was directed by a badger. The feeling of fulfillment I had at that moment was enough to change my life and cause me to travel the path that has led to where I am today.

I picked him from my lap and held him close to my face. His fur was coarse and his odor strong. I turned his face to mine and looked deep into his dark eyes with a thankfulness. I feel he understood.

"Good-bye" was all I had to say. When I turned to look, he was backing into his den for the day. That's it, I thought, back to the wall and facing the world head on. It's the only way to be.

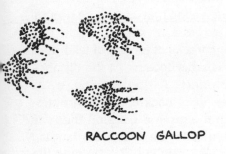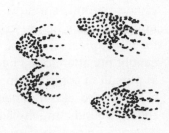

RACCOON GALLOP

2/Raccoon Encounter

"The spirit that moves in all things" is a reality to those who have experienced it. It is not some mysterious, overpowering force that would demand from its believers total subjection and an emotional response, although there have been times when I have knelt and wept tears of joy and gratitude because I have realized the beauty of the spirit in nature. My belief in this spirit is no substitute for religion; it is simply a reassuring reality that I feel exists and that enables me to understand my relationship to the world.

When I first began to understand the essence of this "spirit" the things of the "wild" ceased being "wild" because I realized that my spirit was one with theirs. Our life force was the same.

One of the most profound moments of my childhood was the moment in which I discovered the truth behind something Stalking Wolf said.

Early in the spring of my fifteenth year I came upon an orphaned raccoon. It was tiny and helpless, crouching in its den and unable, because of near-starvation, to resist my advances.

How I had come upon the particular den is interesting because I feel it was a kind of minor miracle—if any miracle is minor. I was meandering through the woods about two miles from my house, drinking in the sounds of the birds and appreciating the new spring growth. I was wandering gently, heading nowhere, quite happy to be alive, a feeling that used to be normal for fifteen-year-old boys. I came across a number of tracks that caught my attention. They were the tracks of a pack of wild dogs in pursuit of some victim. I could tell this because of the distance between the closely spaced paw prints. A dog running at full speed bounds much like a deer with back-arching, ground-covering leaps. The forefeet touch the ground first and then the powerful hindquarters come down with the back feet landing ahead of the spot where the front feet touched. By the time the hind feet have touched the ground, the body has already bunched itself and is uncoiling like a released spring. These leaps, depending on the size of the dog, can cover from six to twelve feet.

I counted at least seven dogs, and I wondered if they had been successful in their chase. It was at the edge of a clearing, where the quaking aspen and pine thin to form a tiny meadow.

I was in an area that had always intrigued me. Some years before, a forest fire had ravaged this part of the Barrens, and there was a definite line where the fire had stopped. Stalking Wolf said the wind must have changed suddenly and the fire burned itself out. It was almost as if someone had drawn a straight line through the forest and denied "fire" the right to cross it.

I often wandered in this part of the Barrens and dreamed of the good-medicine spirit that held back the flames and caused them to fight among themselves and burn themselves out. I could lie there for hours and re-create the imaginary battle in my young mind and see the animals cowering behind the good spirit as he turned the flames upon themselves by persuading the west wind to come to his side.

The burned-out area was recovering from the fire—new trees were reaching out of the undergrowth that was flourishing in the ashes. It was interesting to watch the forest, like a line of infantry, march methodically back across the burned area, reclaiming it for its own. It was a slow process, and in the meantime the area burned became a no-man's-land for animals who were the normal prey for the wild-dog packs that roamed the Barrens.

Many small animals, lured by the rich new succulent grasses and plants growing there, were caught by these dogs and lost their lives away from the relative safety of the thick woods the fire hadn't touched. It had happened again, and I wondered what poor animal had fed these hungry dogs last night. I hoped romantically that whatever had been chased had been able to get away, but I knew the relentless ability of the dog packs, and I knew how little protective cover there was in the burned-out area, especially this early in spring before the undergrowth thickened.

Without making a deliberate decision but rather following my feeling, I began to track the markings left by the pack. The scene from the previous night began to unfold sadly before my eyes.

There by the edge of the forest and not five paces into the burned-out area were the prints of a fully grown raccoon. On closer examination I could see how it had turned quickly, kicking up the leaves, when it discovered it had been cut off. It began to run parallel to the woods toward a hanging branch that almost touched the ground. If the raccoon could reach that branch, it could climb into the tree and wait for the pack to move on. I headed for the tree at a dead run, glancing at the ground to reassure myself that my theory was correct and that the dog tracks were headed in this direction. They were, but my theory was not fully realized.

Just before the branch the ground was torn and blood-stained, the earth moist and the leaves scattered. The raccoon had been caught, torn apart, and devoured by the dogs. I fell to my knees and beat the earth, and tears welled up. Just hours before this spot had witnessed a bloody battle and death. Why? Why did this raccoon have to die so violently? I was sad and angry and filled with frustration.

Had I been there, I might have saved the raccoon and beaten off the dogs. Where was the Good Spirit, which had held back the flames and should have protected this raccoon from the savage dogs? What lured this animal out of the safety of the forest anyway? Why had it been so stupid? Why? Why? Why?

I am hard pressed to explain what caused me to act the way I did. Perhaps it was the area. When I was there, good and evil seemed so real. There was a definite line—good on one side, green and protective, and evil, barren and charred, on the other side. There I could dream and control these opposing forces. As I watched the forest slowly regaining ground, I was reassured that good would eventually overcome evil. This death broke into that dream-ordered world with a harsh reality. The struggle for supremacy was real and violent, and good did not always win.

My spring had been destroyed—here, in the midst of a forest coming to life, was a death that I wasn't ready to accept. I walked straight home that morning and spent the rest of the weekend in silence. I would talk to no one. I sulked.

In church, where I used to come alive when they read the psalms glorifying nature, I sat sadly, head bowed, unable to respond. Why had that raccoon died? What good was this life if the innocent died needlessly?

On my way home from school Monday afternoon, I stopped at Stalking Wolf's. "Hello, Tom," he called as he saw me coming up the path. "What did you learn today?"

He always communicated with questions that I call real. He did not know the meaning of small talk. I never heard him greet someone with "Hi, how are you doing?" the way we do, not expecting a real answer. He did not believe in wasting time with idle chatter. He either taught or he learned; he never just passed time.

My answer was a sullen and hardly audible "Nothing!"

"That can't be, Tom. We always learn something whatever we do!"

I just couldn't take his patience that day. I almost screamed back at him: "Everything means something to you, doesn't it?"

"Yes," he said.

I said, "All things?"

Stalking Wolf looked grave, but not worried or hurried. He answered me in a soft voice, forcing me to strain in order to hear, "Yes, all things connect. We are all part of the whole. Each has its part. Each comes and goes in its own time."

I didn't want to hear his philosophy. I didn't want to cope with his calmness. I was angry—at him for having lied to me about the beauty of nature and the peace it brings. I screamed at him, "You have all the answers! It's all so simple to you!"

A cardinal called from high up in an aspen. He stopped to listen, cocking his head ever so slightly to pick up the full shrill of its whistle. He looked up at the sky and noticed the thick cumulus clouds moving at an alarming rate, and said, "No, everything is not simple. Nor is everything easily understood. Many things must just be accepted."

I rejected this idea: "Grandfather, you're wrong. I will never accept all things. They don't make sense."

I saw a change in his face at that moment. There was no longer any graveness as if he had an insight that took it from him. He was like no ordinary man when it came to understanding life, and he seemed to know me better than anyone else. I felt that he knew what was troubling me.

"Did you see something that hurt you?"

I don't know where they came from, the tears that welled up and found their way out of the corners of my eyes. But they were there. This was the anger and the frustration that I had been feeling for two days, since I had knelt in the ashes where the wild dogs had taken the raccoon and cried. "Saturday morning, I found where a raccoon had been run down and torn apart by dogs. One lone raccoon against a wild and savage pack. Why? Why would they have to do this? Why does one animal have to eat another? Tell me," I raged. "Grandfather, what—what—is the meaning of this?"

The sun had broken through those high clouds. The birds were reflecting the sunlight in their song. Yet, there was no joy in my heart, no hope in my young mind that afternoon—only anger and frustration as I stood before my mentor and defied him to answer my question.

His answer is one I will never forget, and one that led me at an early age to an understanding of death.

"Sometimes you must go back in order to discover what happens beyond the end of a trail," was all Stalking Wolf offered.

I knew better than to say what I next said, but I couldn't help it. "That's bull, Grandfather. It means nothing. It's only words . . . words. There is no answer, is there?" Answering my own question, I screamed, *"There is no answer!"* I turned and walked down the path, tears flowing from my eyes.

I didn't eat dinner that night, but went straight to my room. I guess you could say I sort of fell asleep. I awoke in the middle of the night. I walked to my window, troubled and seeking solace. The pines, my mother, and my father always hid me and protected me and reassured me. The woods were still, but high above the clouds played tag with the moon, now high and bright. A storm was on its way, and would be here by the afternoon of the following day at the latest. That fact just heightened my sadness. Stalking Wolf's statement that had infuriated me earlier came to me then: "You must go back in order to discover what happens beyond the end of a trail." What did that mean? Whatever it was, I knew this—that if I were to find some release from my sorrow, I would have to go back to that spot.

What I thought he was telling me was that I must go back to the place where I had found the remains of the raccoon, and somehow in that place I must come to terms with death. Knowing nothing else, I dressed and stole silently from the house and into my back yard, the Pine Barrens. I made my way by daybreak to the burned out section and sat cross-legged by the fallen branch. I thought again of Stalking Wolf's words as the Barrens began to awaken around me: "Sometimes you must go back in order to discover what happens beyond the end of the trail." When he told me, was he telling me to follow the pack? To see where it led? No, that would be to go on. This was the end of the trail for the raccoon. That's what saddened me. What did he mean?

I returned to the place where the raccoon had been killed. The words, "Go back!" echoing in my mind.

I was still angry. I took my knife from my sheath and finding a charred stick, began to whittle away at the charcoal. My whittling worked into an intense hacking. My breathing became labored as I vented my frustration. Words without meaning raced through my troubled mind: "Why? How? It isn't fair! Why . . .why . . . why?"

I screamed at the wind, "Go back, hell!"

I began to cry and fell forward on my face in the ashes and sobbed. My knife was still in my hand. In my anger I began to stab at the ashes. "Go back," I said and I cut at the black ash. "Go back! Go back!" And with each thought, I cut more deeply into the black ash until I was slashing like some mad animal, trying to hurt the earth. Or kill it.

Instead, my slashing uncovered the shoots of plant life that had not yet broken through the ash. There it was—life growing out of death.

Go back? I decided that I hadn't gone back far enough and decided to backtrack the raccoon. Its tracks, faint now at best and very difficult to follow, led directly into the forest and up a knoll through dense thicket. The sky had darkened, and I knew I must hurry or lose the tracks to the rain. Fortunately, I didn't have far to go before I discovered the raccoon's den, because it started raining. There on the other side of the knoll was a hole dug under a clump of reeds. There were no fresh tracks of any animals about the opening, and I assumed it was empty. Nevertheless, I approached it cautiously on my belly and peered into it, listening intently and straining my eyes to see if there was anything alive there.

I thought I heard a faint, high-pitched sound much like a kitten's mew, but I couldn't be sure. It was raining rather hard, and the wind was blowing. Anything could be in there, I thought, from a rabbit to a snake. But I had a strong suspicion that it was neither of those, but rather a baby raccoon or two. If that was the case, I would probably get a nasty bite if I stuck my hand in there.

I reached for a stick and poked it gently into the hole. The stick was not attacked, but it did nudge against something soft. There was some kind of animal in there, but its lack of movement made me think that it might very possibly be dead.

I waited for some time, debating how I would get whatever it was in there out, and finally decided to grit my teeth and reach for it. I reached in and grabbed a handful of fur and pulled it out. There in my hand was a baby raccoon, dead. I was shocked and thought I'd cry again until I remembered that raccoons give birth to more than one baby. I reached again and again, and each time I pulled out a dead baby raccoon. This was all I could take, but I was too drained to cry. I just rested my head in my arms and listened to the rain fall angrily.

I felt hollow. Yet somewhere deep within me, there was

a sound—a wordless sound—echoing, searching for a way out, to be released. I couldn't hear it, but I sensed its presence. A high-pitched whimpering. A weak, monosyllabic sound like the mew of the kitten.

I lifted my head and listened intently against the wind and the rain. I heard it again and forced my arm and hand to move toward the hole that had offered up nothing but death. I plunged my arm in and grabbed wildly at a little ball of fur, knowing that it would not be alive. But it was—it was weak and almost dead from hunger, but it was breathing.

Thank God, I thought and held it close to my chest, sheltering it from the rain. "You're alive," I said. "Alive! Alive!" And I screamed into the wind, *"It's alive!"*

I hurriedly pushed the dead baby raccoons back into the den and shoved some mud and rocks into the den to cover them. Then I made my way home to nurse the baby back to health.

Some weeks later, I took my healthy pet to Stalking Wolf's to show her off.

I had kept my adventure and little orphan a secret from my friend and teacher Stalking Wolf, because I didn't feel as though I had yet discovered the full meaning of his advice. I do know that as I nursed the baby raccoon, the hurt and emptiness slowly subsided.

Finally I was ready to share my discovery and on a fall afternoon, I picked up Little Orphan Annie, as I had come to call her, and walked over to Stalking Wolf's.

"What do you call her?" he asked, playing with her. She liked to roll on her back and have her belly rubbed.

"Little Orphan Annie!" I said without thinking.

He looked at me and down at Annie and again at me, reading my mind, I thought, and said, "I see. There is a word that I use to celebrate life. It is 'Alive.' I will call Annie 'Alive,' because she is no orphan, and because she seems so happy to be alive."

I didn't quite understand what Stalking Wolf meant and I asked, "What do you mean she is no orphan?"

"You are her father," he said. "And the earth is her mother."

"She is full of life, isn't she?" I remarked. "'Alive.' That's a good name." And I said it again, "Alive."

"She is about old enough to release," Stalking Wolf added as I was leaving. I didn't comment on it, but I knew it was true. Alive was a wild animal and deserved the freedom of the wild. However, I was not yet willing to give her up. I kept thinking of her mother and the horrible death she must have experienced, and I vowed to protect Alive forever, if need be.

As the weeks wore on toward winter, Stalking Wolf's words preyed on my mind. I had taught her to hunt in the streams and springs of the Barrens that summer. Showed her how to turn stones for crayfish and rotten logs for grubs. Taught her how to climb trees and never to go into a clearing without a way to escape. We hunted and fished and played all summer. In the fall, I taught her to climb the cornstalks for the ears of corn. I laughed when she tumbled from the stalks too narrow to hold her weight.

Alive was a good hunter and fisher and scavenger, and I knew she could fend for herself, but I wasn't convinced she could stay alive with the dog packs that roamed the Barrens.

It was a difficult decision to make to release her to the wild, but I finally decided to take her out to the place she had been born and release her.

It was a difficult parting. I left her by a spring, hunting. There was no long talk or backward glances. No questioning looks from my little animal friend. She was hunting, and I walked away.

It is not difficult to figure where I walked or what I thought about on the way. I remember talking about it to Stalking Wolf and sharing my fears that she would not be able to survive the winter and the dogs.

He warned me that I must not go back to where I had left her. That I must trust her and the spirit that moves in all things to work its will.

I was not totally convinced that the spirit did move in all things. I still questioned the ferocity of the dog packs, but I followed Stalking Wolf's advice and stayed out of Alive's part of the forest all winter.

It was not as difficult as you might imagine—there were so many things for a fifteen-year-old to do and experience. The winter came and went and soon rolled into summer.

I wasn't aware that I had wandered into Alive's territory.

I was just meandering again, dreaming of another time, when I settled myself down on a sunny rock beside a lazy stream and lay back for a nap.

It was cool there, and the mosquitoes hadn't gotten too bad yet. I closed my eyes and fell fast asleep. I woke with the realization that something *alive* was breathing on my neck. My first thought was wild dogs, and I almost bounded for the middle of the stream, but I caught myself and rolled very slowly toward the cold nose that was sniffing the base of my neck. As I turned, the animal, seemingly more curious than aggressive, put a paw on my shoulder, and poked its nose in my ear.

With that, I bolted upright and rolled off the stone into the stream. When I came to the surface, a masked face was peering over the edge of the rock into mine.

"Alive!" I screamed and laughed and splashed her. She was all over me, pawing and nudging and rolling on her back so I could rub her belly.

"Let's hunt," I said, and we searched the shallows for crayfish. I was proud of the way her hunting had improved. She discovered more than I.

I bent under a ledge, turned a stone, and found a large, succulent crayfish. I stood and yelled, "I found one!" but discovered that I was talking to myself. Alive had done to me what I had done to her the previous fall. She had left me hunting. Oh, well, I thought, what could I expect? She is wild and independent—no longer a pet but a free animal. Nevertheless, I felt rejected and lay back down on the rock to gather my thoughts.

Cirrus clouds dotted the bright blue sky and foretold the coming of heavier weather in a day or so. Showers tomorrow, I thought. Good. It'll keep it cooler. I wondered if I should follow Alive's tracks to her den so that I could find her when I wanted to but decided against it. If she wanted that, she would have stayed with me. It wouldn't be right to intrude on her privacy. Again I felt rejected. She was alive and didn't seem to require my protection. If only she could talk. There were so many questions I would ask her. How did she make it through the cold winter? It was cold, I knew. Did she still have trouble finding food? Had she met any other raccoons? Has she been treed by dogs? Did she miss me?

My mind raced over these questions until I realized that it was silly to try to relate to a raccoon as if she were a person. I had better be going, I thought; it was getting late, and I had to make my way home before sunset. I was lifting myself from the rock when Alive reappeared on the bank beside me. She walked right up to me, never hesitating, and lay down beside me and rolled over on her back, beckoning me to rub her belly. It was then that I discovered that she wasn't alone. Eyes and noses began to appear over the bank, and I found myself surrounded by tiny raccoons.

Alive had brought her family to meet me—all five of them. They swarmed over me. I was enveloped in live raccoons. They chewed at my ears, pulled and nudged and sniffed.

I was elated. We played until sunset. I was astounded that these little animals displayed no fear toward me at all. They related to me as their mother had. We were brothers—all raccoons or all people. There was something that connected us. The spirit that moves in all things was the connector that removed the fear and allowed this special moment. This time, when I left, I looked back.

Alive was teaching her children to hunt much as I had taught her. Five children. One to replace each of her brothers and sisters who had died and one for her mother. The Great Spirit had brought life out of death and had balanced it.

"Sometimes we must go back in order to discover what happens beyond the end of the trail." Life doesn't end, I thought, where the trail ends; it goes on. Death is not final, it only interrupts.

Alive's mother died but her life was renewed through Alive and her children. Someday, they too will die, but that is only part of it. To understand, we must know the whole story. Backtrack along the entire trail and see what that animal left behind as its contribution to the natural order. I realized then that to think of Alive's mother's death as meaningless was to think of life in the same terms. It didn't matter how or even where that mother raccoon died. What mattered most was what she did when she was alive.

I was renewed by the experience because I saw my part in it as being natural. I was part of the natural order of life in the

Barrens. I had witnessed the death and nurtured life, and I had learned a great lesson. The spirit does move in all things, and I am a part of the whole.

This story began with tears and ends with laughter. It began with death and ends with life. It began with a question and ends with an answer.

If we are to understand what lies beyond the end of the trail, we must go back.

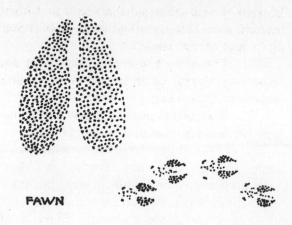

FAWN

3/Fawn Encounter

I love to watch fawns dance through the spring undergrowth. They are like children learning ballet. They are both graceful and clumsy. They are innocence dancing over fallen branches now, then marching to some inner Sousa, high stepping through the late spring grasses. I could watch them endlessly. I could watch them till their spots disappeared, until they become yearlings, and then I could watch some more, because they are more playful than before. However, they are more difficult to approach now, not because they are more cautious but because now, able to run and leap like their parents, they are more likely to rely on flight for escape than on camouflage.

If you have the eyes, you can see them when they are very young. Deer, when first born, are spotted. When they lie motionless in the leaves and grasses that abound in early summer, they are all but invisible. They lie about this way for most of three weeks until their legs are strong enough to allow them to avoid predators. Until that time, they lie and hide and wait for their mothers, who are never very far away, to come back and nurse them. I have observed one fawn being nursed five times in the course of the day.

Let me tell you about one of my encounters with a fawn, one of nature's most innocent creatures.

The leaves drip, heavy with moisture. Bead and drip onto the dark, damp soil. The sun is hiding behind a curtain of mist and clouds, and daylight struggles for existence against the element of water. Fire and water are in a battle for possession of the day. Water today is winning. She is in control, dripping with victory from every leaf or blade of grass capable of catching her sweet elusive soul. For it is water, the soul of nature, that enables all things to grow. She was being very generous today, caressing all her creation with a cool enlivening mist. She whispered through the forest on a gentle breeze, hardly noticeable, and brought to life a dry, parched woodlands.

She changed the forest's melody, softening the usual sharp sounds of twigs snapping and birds crying to a soft, almost mellow music of drip-drop and birdsong as if it were being filtered through a painted screen: oriental mountains and trees and birds perched on a branch above a beautiful lady who symbolized man in love and loved by nature. . . . *Drip-drop, tereu*—the forest sang a hushed song, celebrating a life sustained by water. Soft sounds were barely audible.

The mist brought out the deepest colors in all the leaves and woods she caressed, they reacting much like a young boy who blushes at the touch of a beautiful lady. The greens were deep like the ocean's deepest waters, and the browns were almost black; ominous and strong, the tiniest twig gave the appearance of forged steel. The quite birdsongs carry little distance in the wetness, and I walked into and out of continuous concerts, celebrations, and callings. The birds fly little during these misty days; instead they sit and sing and talk, each species gracing you with its unique celebration of life.

I was carried by this natural beauty into the womb of my existence, and I began to flow with it. I was a part of it and it of me; we were one. There was no friction between myself and the wet earth. My body did not shrink from the wet leaves or fight against the rain. I stretched out to witness and be a part of my surroundings. To receive along with the grasses and trees the life-renewing forces from the rain.

Wetness to me is just another state of being. It is no discomfort unless my mind fights it and demands dryness. That happens when I'm not at peace or when I'm not involved with the world around me. It happens when I'm not observing as a participant and when I'm preoccupied with my physical comfort or appearance.

This day, in the rain, I felt like a single drop of water falling endlessly through the forest. Flowing from leaf to leaf, renewing and being renewed, cleansing and being cleansed. My heartbeat was the drip-drop sound as my body moved from place to place—from a leaf to a blade of grass. My body seemed to shrink as I found myself growing closer and closer to the damp dark earth.

> *I was a spider.*
> *I was a mosquito.*
> *I was a ladybug, a gnat, an ant,*
> *a grasshopper, a beetle.*

As my eyes and mind moved in closer to the earth and the leaves, the nature from which man should never try to separate himself, I became small and could move from level to level and experience what each insect must feel in its own world. I was a daddy-long-legs clinging to the bottom of a birch leaf, seeking respite from the rain. I was the beetle scurrying from rock to rock, trying to find an uninhabited nest where I might feed on the moss. I was the gnat beating my wings three hundred times a minute in order to move from one leaf to another, all the while avoiding the spider's fine invisible web. I was nosing down and slithering along the landscape.

All that could be seen from above would be a rustle or slight movement of the grass or bush beneath which I was passing, but that would be mistaken for the wind, because I made no noise. I had practiced for hours, weeks, and months on end to learn to move silently through the woods. There was a time I remember well.

Stalking Wolf told Rick and me to follow him into the woods. We did, following him by about two paces. At one point he disappeared behind a pine, for no more than two seconds, but when we turned the corner, he was gone. We stood perfectly still and held our breath in order to hear his movement, but we could not. We strained our eyes on the path and the bushes before, beside, and behind us, but we could not see any movement. We stood perfectly still for five minutes and could see or hear nothing but the occasional song of a bird or the buzz of an insect.

When suddenly a hand rested on my shoulder, I assumed it was Rick's, except for the squeal which came from his lip when he was touched at the same time.

It was Stalking Wolf. He had come up on us silently. We asked him a dozen questions: "Where were you, where did you come from, how long have you been here, why couldn't we see or hear you?" We must have sounded like two machine-guns firing off questions at Stalking Wolf.

He smiled and answered, "Follow the snake, listen to the birds." With those words he crouched and literally slid off the path into the brush. Laurel leaves closed behind him, and he disappeared. He couldn't have been two feet from us, but we couldn't see him or hear him.

I looked at Rick and began to walk in the direction Stalking Wolf had gone—and almost fell on top of him. Rick and I lay in the brush beside him and followed his every move. We moved when he moved, picked carefully where we would place our hands, and looked all about us for obstacles or avenues of movement that would receive our bodies without revealing to anyone standing that we were below the surface. We moved like snakes or fish in the water, twisting our bodies around branches and under plants that most people would crush.

We noticed that Stalking Wolf moved only when there was some other sound in the woods. A bird calling or an insect buzzing or the wind blowing through the leaves were sounds he would pick up and move with. Most people talk of the peace and quiet of the woods. In reality it is full of sounds that all but drown the sounds of movement if you're careful. We also noticed that he moved rhythmically and tried not to break the rhythm, like a raindrop flowing over leaves.

Rick and I moved like two baby elephants through the bushes that day. But we were so excited about the possibility of gaining the ability to move silently and invisibly through the landscape that we vowed to practice until we could sneak up on Stalking Wolf.

That summer passed quickly because we were always on our bellies crawling. Our parents thought we had given up cleanliness. When asked if we crawled around in the mud all day and the answer was "yes," we'd get queer looks.

It was during this summer that I began to notice the levels of life that existed close to the ground. How certain bugs stayed at certain levels and how there were paths that the bugs followed in the dirt and also in the leaves. There were little highways from place to place, like interconnected freeway systems at each level, and only a few of the insects would move from level to level. Most stayed where they could obtain food.

Flying insects had the greatest freedom, but also the greatest risk. In moving from level to level they were vulnerable to spider webs and larger insects and even birds. I discovered that movement was what attracted danger. Most insects find safety only in camouflage. The greater numbers of living things in this world are not predators, but prey, and must defend themselves by making themselves invisible. Man, the greatest predator, has lost his ability to be invisible or silent.

When I walk through the woods, I can tell if there are other people near me, even if it is only one other person, by the noise created by their movement. Most people don't step over or around, they step through. It's our pride, I guess. We say to the plants, "Don't get in my way, or I'll bowl you over." We have no need to be quiet, because everything is afraid of us. What we don't realize is that we miss most life in the woods or along the trail because we warn everything we are coming. If we want to see more, we must learn how to walk silently and how to be seen less.

Rick and I found that this crawling on our bellies like reptiles, moving only when some other animal made a sound and developing a rhythm, opened a whole new world to us, a world most people miss and never experience. Most of us are afraid of bugs and don't want to get dirty or wet.

But we found that there was nothing to be afraid of. We

learned to be aware of spiders and not afraid of them. (We are bitten by bugs when we disturb them or threaten them. Don't threaten them, and there is no danger of being bitten.) We were enchanted by the miniature world that we had so often walked over. It was like shrinking and becoming a part of it.

Through the years I learned that looking in enabled me to have a larger view of the world. To view the food chain at its smallest visible denominator is awesome; it allows one to see the interdependency of all things on this blessed earth.

When most of us are taught to look at nature, we are taught to observe it from a certain perspective. We view it for its beauty or its oddness. We look at it through microscopes or field glasses or single-lens reflex cameras. I was taught to flow with my surroundings and discover the purpose of something through being as close to that object or animal as the spirit would allow.

I was a part of the mist being blown through the forest on a gentle breeze. I touched everything with my spirit and tasted its sweetness as I flowed in and through the undergrowth. When I made the discovery, I could hardly contain myself. I had happened on a birthing site where a fawn had been born not more than twenty hours before. The doe and fawn were gone, because a doe wishes to leave the area of birth before a predator is attracted to the spot.

I studied the area and reassured myself that only one fawn had been born. It made quite a few interesting marks, trying to learn to stand and walk. A fawn can stand within ten minutes of birth, but it usually takes it an hour or more to learn to walk. Its attempts are comical, but no more so than those of a human baby taking its first steps.

I followed the trail made by the mother and her stumbling child. The fawn must have fallen a dozen times in as many yards. But the trail was circuitous, a valiant attempt on the part of the doe to conceal her baby. Once she had it safely some distance from the birthing site, its camouflage would keep it relatively safe, and predators couldn't find it by scent. Nature provided that a fawn would give no scent at all for three or four days until it developed the ability to run from a predator.

I was anxious to see the little fawn and perhaps observe it nurse. I knew that I was close to its hiding spot. If I was asked how I knew, I would probably answer that I heard its mother feeding and knew that a doe was always within earshot of its young. However, that wouldn't be the whole truth. The whole truth is that I sensed that I was getting close. The doe's prints were getting closer together, as if she were slowing and searching for a place to conceal her fawn. The underbrush was getting thicker and would lend better cover for a newborn. All the signs told me that the fawn was near, but most of all, I felt its presence.

I was determined to stalk as close as possible to the fawn without alarming it. I felt confident that I could move almost next to it soundlessly because of the way I felt that day. I moved ahead with the wind and the birdsong and the insect sounds into a clump of bayberry bushes. I parted the bush with the bridge of my nose, and there on the forest floor, not eighteen inches from my face, lay the day-old fawn.

When I first came upon the fawn, I was startled by its beauty. It was hardly twenty hours old. Yet I was not startled the way I might be if I heard a sudden noise while tracking a grizzly. It was the startling of a philosopher enlivened by the discovery of a new thought. When astronomers were searching for the planet Pluto, all they had to go on were signs, mathematical formulas and gravitational equations, but they knew that it must be there. They searched for twenty-five years until they discovered it. I knew that the fawn was near me. It had to be. Everything I knew about tracking told me it was there—the prints in the damp earth, the bent foliage, and most of all my sixth sense, all told me the fawn was near. And yet, the discovery startled me.

I felt many things at that moment of discovery that I want to share with you. There was a deep feeling of pride that comes with the accomplishment of a task made up of all my skills. There was also gratitude. I was blessed by being at this spot on the earth at this time, witnessing the life of this fawn. Finally, I felt a sense of reverence. There was a holy quality about the innocent helpless-ness of the tiny fawn that cannot be ignored by any person capable of feelings and thought.

I observed the tiny fawn for some time. It was curled up, almost a ball of mottled, spotted fur, in amongst the bayberry bushes, nestled in among twigs and leaves fallen from the oak that towered above the undergrowth. When it laid its head on the ground and its outsized ears back flat against its neck, it was all but invisible, blended with the ground cover.

I began to count the spots that I could see on its exposed back and rump. The spots on its back were in rows, bright white against different shades of brown. The spots on its rump were larger and splattered as if some artist had decided to clean his brush and flicked white paint about its rear quarters. The impression—or misimpression—this gave was of sunlight through the sparse spring growth on the forest floor. Quite ingenious.

Periodically it would raise its head and sniff the gentle breeze for signs of danger and look about his hiding place for some sweet new growth within easy reach, and lick any moisture from his coat that might have found its way through the oak and bayberry. He was, all in all, very cozy and contented.

The fawn was breathing not eighteen inches from my nose. Its warm breath tickled my nose so that I wanted to reach out and touch it. I could see its hide ripple when a raindrop struck a nerve. I could hear its sighs and breathing and soft grunts as it snuffled about in the leaves. They blended with the sounds of insects buzzing, frogs croaking, and moisture dripping from leaf to leaf. There was a rhythm, hardly detectable, that went from the animal to the earth and back. It was as if they were breathing together.

Then it saw me. I must have blinked, because the pupils of its eyes dilated, then narrowed, as if it had sensed some movement, and its ears stood and turned toward me. I didn't move but remained motionless. I held my breath and stared without blinking.

Call it to you, a voice within me whispered. I knew this voice. It was a voice out of my past and out of my feelings that I trusted more than logic. *Call it to you*, it whispered, *but not out loud, with your spirit*. I reached out to it with my spirit.

The fawn studied me for some moments. A cricket chirped. It was enough time for me to breathe. It cocked its head as if it was trying to figure out what was different about the bayberry bush where my nose broke the symmetry of the leaves.

It stood, wobbled on its new legs, and stumbled two short steps toward me. I knew that it wasn't afraid as soon as it stood. A fawn, if it were frightened, would instinctively lie still. We were nose to nose, and it seemed to be in no hurry to finish its examination of the strange bush that blinked. It sniffed profusely about my nose, mouth, and eyes. All the while I moved not a muscle, nor did I breathe a breath.

I was curious as to what it would eventually do to my face. Would it try to munch at my nose? Would it suddenly become startled and bound off, as best it could, bleating for its mother? It sniffed some more, opened its mouth, and licked my nose! It must have liked the salt taste, because it continued to lick and seemed not to notice as I slowly raised my hand and began to stroke and pet its neck and flank.

I laughed inside. I was happy to have this playmate and reaffirmed in my belief that I was at one with my surroundings. The fawn laughed with me. I felt its hide quiver beneath my touch. After some very precious moments, my spotted playmate knelt as if in prayer, curled up at my knees, and went back to sleep.

I silently stole away through the dripping forest, flowing with nature's rhythm, listening to the sounds of insects, birds, and water dripping. I stole away satisfied.

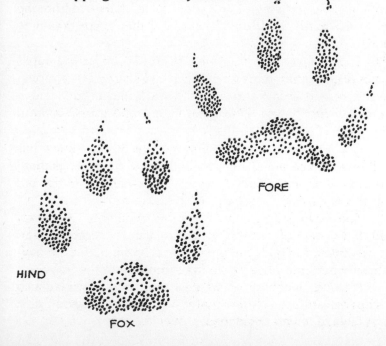

FORE

HIND

FOX

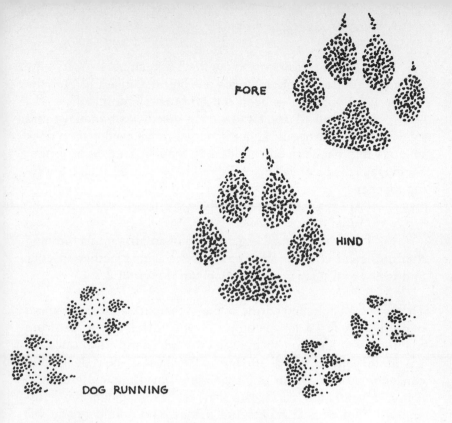

FORE

HIND

DOG RUNNING

4/Witch Encounter

"*Do you believe in Satan?*" *Aaron asked.*

The young boy was serious, and I was curious as to why he would ask me such a question when he was learning how to track. But young boys' minds can think of almost anything at almost any time, and I've learned to answer their questions point-blank rather than avoid them, so I answered, "I don't know, Aaron. I suppose there is some force that we have come to call the devil. I don't really think about it much. Why do you ask?"

He hesitated a moment, shrugged his shoulders as eight-year-olds do when they don't know exactly what to say, and tried to change the subject. "Uh—how old is this track?" He was pointing to a fresh deer track that was perhaps an hour old.

I was beginning to get upset. Aaron had been acting strangely all morning, and I suppose my impatience got the best of me because

I snapped at him, "Now you know that's a fresh track. You know the rules. You try to determine the age before you ask. What's the matter with you? You've been out of touch all morning!"

"I'm—ah—I don't know." His voice was trembling, and he was looking all about like a frightened rabbit waiting for a pack of dogs that had him surrounded to leap in and destroy him. Surely my little bit of yelling could not have caused such a terrifying reaction.

"Are you afraid of something, Aaron?"

"What?"

"You heard me!" I said. "You're so jumpy this morning that you can't concentrate. Now tell me what's bothering you, and we'll see if there's anything we can do about it."

That was the beginning of one of the most harrowing experiences of my life, my first witch encounter. I believe that fear comes from not understanding, so I always seek to understand. Ever since my encounter with my imaginary Jersey Devil years ago, I decided to challenge every noise or uneasy feeling I ever encountered with action. I feel that if I can face a fear, real or imagined, it will disappear. That doesn't mean that a thousand-pound grizzly will fade away into the wilderness if I face it, but I will be able to meet the threat with some positive action rather than paralyzed fear.

Most people perish in the wilderness because they panic. They are killed not by the elements but by their fear of them. Through this witch encounter I learned that fear can be very real indeed and can be generated by the most feared animal in the world—man. But I also learned that fear can be overcome and panic abated by simple trust in oneself and one's knowledge.

I have been on manhunts where hunters have been found starved to death next to their loaded guns in forests alive with game, and I have discovered adult males frozen to death in an open field when there was plenty of protective cover available near at hand. The problem was that their fear overtook them, they lost their ability to reason, and they panicked. They were literally destroyed by their fear.

Perhaps it was my preoccupation with fear, its causes and effects, that led me on my own personal witch hunt in the Pine Barrens of New Jersey. I wanted to understand the causes of the deep fear that had possessed my little friend Aaron.

Aaron, while meandering through the Barrens, came upon a young couple making some markings in the sand and arranging some rocks. He had often seen the markings left by boys and girls in the forest—initials and hearts carved into fallen logs or painted on rocks—and he was curious as to why they would leave these signs behind. I had taught Aaron that a good woodsman was like the Indian and left a campsite as if no one had been there but the wind. He was going to pass on that knowledge to this couple as well as some advice about disposing of the litter they had spread about the area when he began to sense something wrong. He told me he felt bad medicine as soon as the couple turned to respond to his cheery good morning.

Their faces were like masks and almost gray. They never once blinked that he could recall, and though they smiled almost continually, he felt instinctively afraid. He didn't feel that their smiles were genuine. He said, "They looked like kids who had been caught in the act of doing something wrong and were trying to deny it with their smiles."

Aaron said that they began to speak to him and move toward him. He doesn't remember exactly what they said, but the way they spoke stuck fast in his mind: "It was like they were singing on one note." I took that for a chant, and they were probably trying to charm him much like a cat does to a bird before it pounces for the kill.

The couple chanted to him and moved closer, watching for anyone else who might be with him. It was at this point that Aaron noticed the markings. Before, they had been hidden behind the two people as they knelt. They weren't scrapings at all as he expected to see; there were no hearts or initials. Instead, there were pictures drawn in red in the sand. I had told Aaron about the Indian art of sand painting, and how they used it not only to tell stories but to heal their sick. He wondered if they were using colored sand or if they were artists. He was curious but afraid, and so instinctively took a step back from the advancing couple.

There was a snap as his right foot caught in a fallen pine bough, and he tumbled onto his back. He was thrown to his side so that his vision was directed not up at the boy and girl approaching him, but along the ground between their legs. I had been teaching him to observe, so anything unusual or out of the ordinary would naturally catch his eye. It was at this point that he saw the dead cat. Its throat had been cut, and it was draped over some rocks so that its blood could drain into a paper cup. He knew then that the red in the drawing was not sand.

"What are you doing?" he cried. "Why did you kill the cat?"

They never answered his questions, but continued to move toward him, uttering their chants and smiling. Aaron finally decided it was time to get out of there and away from those gray, smiling, masked chanters who could kill so coldly and draw pictures with blood. He picked himself up and ran like a fox toward the thickest part of the woods. He dived into the thicket and crawled and ran, never minding the thorns or branches that whipped at his thin body as he plunged blindly on.

He stopped once; he came to a main trail, thinking that he hadn't been followed, when one of them appeared on the path in front of him. He hadn't been seen, because most of what happens in the woods goes unnoticed by humans, and so he moved silently into the bushes by the side of the trail. It was good that he did, because immediately the girl came down the path behind him. After some discussion, they gave up their chase and went back up the trail toward their camp. They made some mention of Satan, and it stuck in the very frightened eight-year-old mind of my little friend.

Aaron was scared so much that he couldn't move for quite some time. When he could, he ran straight home and went to his room. The following day he was with me and told me this story. I had no reason to doubt him, because so many strange things had happened to me. Yet what impressed me more than anything else was the deep sense of fear that pervaded the story. Aaron's voice cracked, and he was continuously fighting back tears. He was genuinely afraid and couldn't shake the fear. It was like he was under its power and couldn't be himself.

"You afraid, Aaron?" I asked.

"No," he answered. He looked around, up at the sky, down at his feet, and finally at my face and whispered, "Yes."

"You think they were going to kill you, don't you?"

"Yes." Aaron's voice was trembly and he asked, "Were they?"

"You just stay out of that area for a while, Aaron, and don't be afraid. They can't find you now."

"I'm not afraid of them, Tom. I'm afraid of him."

"Him?"

"Satan," he mumbled, fighting with his emotions to get the word out.

"Aaron, Satan has no power if you're not afraid of him. He becomes real through man's fear and superstition. The bear is a large and ferocious animal, but he won't attack a badger. Do you know why?"

Aaron answered, "Because the badger is not afraid of him?"

"That's right, and the badger also stays out of the bear's way."

Aaron looked directly at me with his dark brown eyes and burst into tears. I grabbed him and hugged him close. For a long while we didn't speak, and I didn't try to comfort him with words. There were only the sounds of his muffled sobs and the scream of a jay to break the silence. The badger had almost been devoured by the bear.

"That's a bad-medicine camp, isn't it, Tom?" he asked when his sobbing had subsided.

"Yes," I answered, "bad medicine," and I felt a shiver go up my back. I said it again, "Bad medicine," just to hear it and make sure I believed it. When the shiver came a second time, I knew it was true. I asked him to tell me exactly where it had happened and vowed to go there and find out what I could. Aaron wanted to come with me, but I thought it would be wiser to leave him off at his home. I did this and continued to the place Aaron had described.

It was a beautiful walk from the road to the camp of the young couple. It had been an unusually mild October in South Jersey, and the leaves were slow to turn. It was like a late summer afternoon, and many of the songbirds, who might have been silent this time of year, entertained me with their music as I moved through our woods. I wondered how any place so peaceful and beautiful could harbor the fear and death Aaron had described.

I have often heard the squeal of a mouse as it is swept up

in the talons of an owl to become the evening meal for the barred owl's young. Yes, there is death in this beautiful place, and there is fear. But it is a natural death and a natural fear that grows out of a desire to live. The owl kills to feed, and not to make, with the blood of its kill, some senseless scratchings to an evil force. The fear of the mouse comes from its desire to live, not from its desire to appease an unknown quantity. What animal would make a sacrifice to an unknown god? What animal would kill except to eat? What animal fears anything other than what he knows might harm him? The answer to all these questions is man.

We are the only animal that has moved outside its natural state and kills for pleasure, passion, or power. We are the only animal that can destroy the very earth that has mothered us. It is during pensive moments such as the one I experienced walking toward Aaron's bad-medicine camp that I feel a deep sense of shame at being a human. Yet, I have learned not to be discouraged by such feelings, but rather to be strengthened in my resolve to change man's nature and bring it back in communion with the earth.

I was at the spot Aaron had described, and began my search for signs that would prove what Aaron had told me was the truth and not some child's fantasy. I began with a walk around the perimeter of the campsite and was immediately struck with the fact that someone had tried to brush out the prints that led in and out of the camp. There, at the edge of the site were the broken branches of the bushes that Aaron had run through in his effort to escape, but the footprints that should have led up to them were gone. I crawled into the thicket and found the scuffle marks of Aaron's boots and even a bit of his hair stuck on a thorn. He had been through this thicket, and he had been in a hurry. But would the rest of his story prove true?

I followed his frenetic path through the thickets to the main path, where his trail stopped. I went down on my stomach and surveyed the path. There they were for anyone to read—the footprints of two other people. One had been wearing a deck shoe and was quite a bit lighter than the other, who had been wearing a heavy hiking boot. The one wearing the hiking boot had apparently run down the trail, stopped, and walked back. I could tell this because his stride was much greater going out, a bit deeper, and showed more weight in the toe area than the stride coming back. Another thing I noticed that I would not soon forget was the way he dragged his right foot, so that there was a very slight line in the dust caused by the toe of his right boot as he walked. He must have some injury to his right hip, I thought.

I was where they had faced each other and talked, and I followed their prints back to the camp. So far so good. But where were the blood drawings and the cat's carcass and the bloody stones Aaron had seen? Again I circled the camp looking for signs and discovered some footprints the couple had not been able to erase. Why were they so deep? Perhaps they were made by the grinding motion of a body throwing a heavy object?

How far could a man with a bad hip throw a heavy rock? I calculated the approximate distance and covered the area. I found it! It hadn't been too difficult, because it had bounced off an aspen and left quite a gouge in its back right at eye level. It was quite a large stone and must have weighed fifteen pounds. The young man must have been strong. The rock had blood on it. I began to feel more and more uneasy about everything that had happened.

Even if this couple had sacrificed a cat, why were they trying so hard to hide the fact? Why had they chased Aaron? I was driven now to find the final piece of evidence, the cat's body.

The couple's trail led toward an old fire road. It was easy to follow once they were some distance from their camp and felt safe. The man's limp was more pronounced now, as if he were carrying a heavy load. They stopped only once, and again I recognized the grinding motion in the man's prints. This is where they got rid of the cat's body! How convenient for their path to pass by a pit used for years as a dumping ground by the local residents. There, by an old refrigerator on a rotting mattress, were the remains of the poor cat. The rats were still fighting over its bones.

I felt a deep sense of remorse at this final discovery. It had all been true. It seemed so alien. Why? Why? My mind searched for an explanation I could use to excuse this senseless act and continue to feel some pride in being human. These were my brothers who had killed. What could have driven them to such a senseless act? How had we humans wandered so far from our purpose? I felt remorse and shame.

The next thing I remember is beating at the rats with a rusty iron bar and screaming, "Get away, get away! It's wrong,

wrong!" I grabbed what remained of the cat, climbed out of the garbage heap, and scratched a shallow grave beneath a tiny oak where I laid the cat's remains. When I finished, I wiped tears from my eyes and continued the track. I didn't look back.

The young man and woman walked to some sort of vehicle with bald tires and drove off toward the main road. I stood there, looking down the road and wondering if our paths would ever cross again, and if they did, what I would do. For the moment, it was over, and I was relieved. I followed the car tracks for some time and then cut off toward where I had parked my jeep. It was getting late, and besides, I wanted to leave the area. It would be some time before I would feel comfortable in this area of the Barrens again. Aaron was right when he named it bad-medicine camp.

It was sometime in November that I was reminded of that unsavory track I had followed more than a month before. I was enjoying the challenge of full-moon stalking in a remote area of the Barrens. I had been following the erratic path of a raccoon since moonrise. His meanderings were a joy to behold. He would wander from rock to rock as if he were chasing the sounds of a cricket. Once, twice, he thought he had it and turned the stones. I wondered if he found anything and lay very still and held my breath and listened intently.

The sounds of crickets filled the air around me. I followed the sound of one and reached slowly for a rock just inches from my nose. I flipped and grabbed. I had it. It was a good sign, and I held it to my ear to listen to its unique chirp. "Did the raccoon get your brother?" I asked. "No? I'm glad." I placed my hands gently on the ground and opened them to the moonlight. His black form stood out clearly against my white flesh, and he hesitated to move. Fear, I thought and I whispered, "Go, and join your brother who escaped the mighty claws of the raccoon. Go and tell him how you escaped an even greater enemy." He jumped from my hands in the midst of my poem and disappeared in the bushes.

I was moving again, silently as I had been taught and practiced for so many years. I was a part of the forest and in touch with its heartbeat. When there was silence, I would freeze and hold my breath. When there was movement of air or animal, I would move. I was like a shadow caused by a cloud crossing the moon as I moved toward the stream where I knew I would catch the raccoon hunting. I wondered how close I could come to him in the moonlight undetected.

Crossing a trail I noticed something that spoke not to my conscious mind but to what I call my sixth sense. There was a boot print that couldn't have been three hours old. I had started moving on toward the stream, following the raccoon's trail, when suddenly I realized where I had seen that boot print before. I turned back and looked hard at the trail. There, heading north, were a number of pairs of footprints. But this one pair stood out because the person who made it dragged his right foot ever so lightly, so that there was a shallow furrow in the sand between his steps. I turned north on the trail.

As I headed north, I began to feel uneasy. It could have been caused by my anticipation of what I would do or say to the man who had made these prints and scared my little friend Aaron. But as I look back on it, I can honestly say that it was probably a glow about the area that made me feel different. There was a faraway glow from numerous campfires that my subconscious picked up, but was so minute that it didn't register in my conscious mind. However, I don't shrug off feelings as silly or unfounded. I trust them. So my method of tracking changed almost imperceptibly to a silent stalk.

I found myself lifting my knee high and placing my feet carefully one before the other. I moved with the wind, amidst the sound of crickets and hunting owls. I moved swiftly and silently toward that yet indiscernible glow. The outer edge of the pad or ball of my foot would kiss the ground before any weight was placed on it. That way, any stones or twigs could be discerned through the thin soles of my moccasins before any weight shift. Then I would roll my weight forward over my foot and place my weight on the edge of the ball of my foot and slowly roll toward the arch. In this way I could compensate with a mere shift of foot position or weight for any obstruction and thereby take a step forward that was all but silent.

First I heard them, making one-note sing-song talk. It was definitely a chant, but I was yet too far away to hear their words. I fell on my stomach and began to crawl off the path toward the sound, but not before my nostrils twitched in reaction to an uncommon odor. What was that odor? I thought as I approached the chanters. It was vaguely familiar. I had smelled it before, but where?

I was moving. I was observing. I was aware of every noise, smell, and movement about me, and yet my mind raced through my past, searching for the source of that odor. It stopped in the middle of a scorched pine forest where I was kneeling beside the charred remains of a rabbit. The odor was from burned flesh. The hairs stood up on my neck, and I began to sweat profusely. Was it animal or human flesh I had smelled?

There, in a small clearing, were two dozen people in a circle beneath a black oak. Its leaves had turned a brilliant red, and the reflection from the fire at its base gave the impression that the entire tree was aflame.

On a rock before the fire was a cup of blood. The leader of the coven was dipping into it and pouring it on the earth while chanting obscene incantations. In the fire a small body was burning and filling the clearing with the fetid odor of burning flesh. All I could feel was revulsion. Aliens were in the forest desecrating its life and its sacred earth.

The anger that I had been carrying for over a month welled up in me. There was no containing it. They had already killed some small animal and were about to kill a dog that was tied to the tree. The leader, after dripping blood on the ground around the frightened animal, drew his knife and raised it high above his head. His knife was flashing in the firelight while his voice chanted hideous prayers to the devil. I could not allow them to continue to desecrate life in this way. I dived through the bushes into the clearing screaming at the top of my lungs, *"Nooooo!"*

I must have looked like a spirit from the underworld, racing across the clearing in nothing but my breechcloth and moccasins. My eyes darted from side to side, watching for any movement from the circle of worshippers, as I ran headlong toward their leader like some mad demon. I hadn't taken the time to consider what would happen when I reached him and had to face his knife. But that didn't seem to matter. I was incensed that anyone would think so little of life that they would sacrifice it. To kill in order to live is understandable, but to kill for blood is wrong and should not be allowed.

I need not have worried about the leader with the knife because when he turned and saw me coming, he was so startled that he fell over backward. I ran right over him and ripped the rope that held the dog from the tree. I threw the mutt over my shoulder and dived into the underbrush. I ran on for about a hundred yards before I stopped to listen.

They were coming after me. All of them were in the woods behind me. I thought they would thrash about in the dark for a while, then give up and go back to their games. But they didn't give up. They spread out and kept coming. As I looked back, I could see the flash of moonlight on their knife blades thrashing at the bushes. I realized then that they wanted to do more than just get their dog back for sacrifice. They wanted to have my life too.

I had never been hunted before. It was frightening hiding there in the dark, figuring against time and the odds what to do next. I was outnumbered and had the disadvantge of a tied and frightened dog to carry, who wouldn't stop crying and would surely give my position away. I decided to release the dog and let it make its own escape. Then I heard someone call out, "Here, Joe! Com'ere boy!" He was someone's pet. If I released him, he would go to his owner and end up on that unholy fire, a sacrifice to a savage god. "You'll stay with me, Joe. You'll be safe, but stay calm." I looked up and saw the progress of my pursuers had slowed but hadn't stopped. If I wanted to get to my jeep, I would have to sneak right through the middle of them, go back through the clearing and make a run for it. It was possible if the dog remained silent.

"Listen, Joe," I whispered as I stroked his neck and belly, "we'll make it out of here, and I'll find you a good home, but you've got to be quiet." I tried to communicate a feeling of confidence and friendship. Gradually the muscles on the back of his neck relaxed, and he became quiet. "Good boy, now just stay calm till we get out of here." I picked him up around the belly and stalked silently in a duck-waddle crouch back toward the clearing. Complete silence on my part was not necessary since the Satan worshippers were still beating and stabbing at the underbrush and cursing me wildly. However, they were very near, and I had to remain out of their sight. I couldn't figure why they hadn't moved on by me. It was as if they sensed I was somewhere close.

I waddled toward the clearing and had covered almost fifty yards when my thighs began to burn. The muscles were tightening, and I felt that if I didn't stand and stretch, my legs would burn up. I looked for some place to stand, but there wasn't any. If I stood now I'd surely be discovered. My only hope was to make it to the clearing and pray that my legs wouldn't cramp.

I wanted to stop. The pain became intense, and I wanted just to lie down and give up. In order to overcome the pain, I focused on the firelight from the clearing and refused to recognize the pain. I had seen deer do this when hunters were near. They could actually crawl along on their bellies through the underbrush till they were clear and could make a run for safety. If I could make it to the clearing, no one could catch me.

Just before I broke into the clearing, I sensed a presence. A shadow played across the bushes before me. There was someone there to give the alarm if I tried to circle back. I had run over one man tonight, maybe it would work a second time. I peered through and saw immediately that it wouldn't. The man standing there was huge. I would have to avoid him. But how?

I felt as a fox must feel when the dogs are closing on him and he has to decide whether to run or hide. The other members of the coven had suddenly turned around and were coming back toward the clearing. I was caught in between.

As so often happens in my life, circumstances directed me. The burning in my legs cried out for relief, and in answer I lunged through the underbrush and into the clearing to begin my run for freedom and fell flat on my face. "Damn!" I cursed as the dog went flying and the huge sentry turned toward me. "A cramp!"

The man had drawn a knife and was holding it low, as if he knew how to use it and was going to—on me. He moved quickly enough, but there was something about his walk. A limp. He walked with a limp, dragging his right foot so that it left a furrow in the sand. For the first time, I looked at his face. He was smiling, the way he had smiled at Aaron, I suppose. I wanted to get out of there and to safety, but more than that, I wanted to bring that big bear of a man down. I shifted my weight to my arms and waited for him to step on his right leg. When he did, I threw my legs out and caught him just below the knee with my shins and swept him off his feet. He fell hard, and I only had to hit him once on the temple to keep him down.

The others were breaking into the clearing as I grabbed the dog and ran for the path. It would be a footrace now, and I was confident that I could outdistance them. One of them threw a knife at me, but only its handle hit me, glancing off my shoulder. I was into the woods and away from the light of the fire and as I heard them running after me, I hoped that there were no long-distance runners among them.

Their footfalls and curses began to diminish, and soon there was only the sound of my labored breathing. I ran on for another mile before I would allow myself to slow to a fast walk. In the silence that is all but imperceptible to the untrained ear, between my steps, I listened intently for any sound which might be a pursuer. There were none.

I stopped only for a brief moment when I jumped into my jeep and found the ignition with the key. The moon was high. Somewhere a frog croaked and a cool breeze promising frost played across my bare shoulders. The night was still new, but enough had happened to make it old for me. I had never felt the need to leave my beloved Barrens before this night. But now I did. There were aliens in the Barrens, and the feeling of revulsion made me want to drive as far from this place as possible. I looked down at the dog, Joe, and for the first time since I had stroked his neck, took time to notice the fear that was in his eyes. He was afraid of me.

"Take it easy, boy. It's all over now. There's a better place for you. Don't worry, we'll find it, and if we can't, we'll make it." The jeep took us to the road that led to my home.

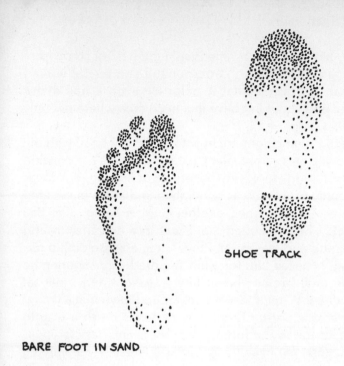

SHOE TRACK

BARE FOOT IN SAND

5/Caribe Island

In August, the Barrens are almost impossible. The heat is intense, and the mosquitoes swarm. If a person did not know how to cool off or protect himself from the bugs, he could very easily be driven from the Barrens. There have been cases of severe injury from excessive insect bites among people who have become lost in the Barrens. Children who have been lost must be found within forty-eight hours, not because they'll die of thirst but because they'll succumb to insect bites.

I have learned how to survive in the Barrens in the sultry heat and amidst the swarming mosquitoes. I know where to find the cool spring streams in which to bathe, and I have learned to cover my body with mud to protect it from insects. Many years ago, the Indians used bear grease as a protection against insects. It was very effective, but its odor was offensive. I got hold of some from a mountain man with whom I corresponded and tried it when I was fifteen, but discovered that its odor left such a trail that it attracted dogs, and I couldn't have that in an area where my only enemy was wild dogs.

Stalking Wolf taught me how to smear my body with the thick black muck that is so prevalent in the Barrens as a protection against insects. It didn't look very becoming or inviting, but it was effective. My only problem was remembering that I was covered with mud when I approached another human being. The first time I did that, I had forgotten that I was in a breechcloth and covered with mud and leaves, and the young boy took off in terror, screaming. I chased him for a few hundred yards figuring he was in trouble until I remembered how I looked, and I just sat down and laughed. When the word got around town that a young boy had sighted the Jersey Devil, I knew I was on to a way to have some great fun in the future. But that is another story.

In August, the fawns, although still nursing, are varying their diet by eating plants. They usually nibble experimentally at plantains and orchard grass when about one week old and continue to eat larger amounts as they get older. They grow from five pounds to about thirty through the summer on their diet of rich doe milk and plants. I had been observing the fawn who had licked my face throughout the summer. I felt very close to the little buck and wanted to learn more of the deer's habits when it came to raising the young and especially in the weaning stages. It had been a fascinating summer from that viewpoint. I had tracked my fawn in its area almost every day since the beginning of June, taking care not to reveal myself to it or its mother. That wasn't easy, and more than once they discovered my presence and bounded off through the Barrens, and I would be in for a day of tracking in order to discover where to begin my observation the next day.

It was an especially hot August. I had been out since dawn, covered myself with mud against the mosquitoes, and was lying under a pine at the edge of a small clearing, watching the deer at their last feeding before bedding for the hot day. There was my little buck, playing at the edge of the herd, hardly taking time to eat. Watching him jump and romp made my heart soar.

I wanted to leap with him and run through the field and feel as free as he. I was wondering how he would get through the day with so little food in his stomach, when he wandered over to his mother to nurse. Deer usually wean their fawns by September, although I've seen fawns that had lost the spotted coat of the young deer try to nurse in November. Now most fawns wean themselves, but my little friend, who would rather romp than browse, seemed to want to stay on his mother until his horns got in the way. However, his mother was not one to baby her fawn as some mothers do, allowing them to nurse for a much longer period than is usual. It was amusing to watch the mother in the process of weaning her fawn in order to make him self-reliant.

As the sun began to rise, burning the haze from the moisture-ridden air, the fawn approached his mother from the side. She just refused to stand still. At first she turned her body in the opposite direction, then she walked away. He tried to stick his head between her legs from the rear, and again she walked off. I could hardly control myself. It was sad, but amusing. Finally the fawn overcame his mother's movements and found her udder. She's given in, I thought. Then she raised her leg over the fawn's head and pushed the young one away as she brought her rear leg down. The fawn began to bleat like a sheep, and all I could think of was a spoiled child having a tantrum. The mother ignored its pleadings and continued to graze. My fawn looked about for some sympathy and, finding none, began to munch busily on the grass about its feet. I knew now that it only had a short time before the herd would move back into the thick undergrowth to sleep through the hottest hours of the day.

I was happy. This summer had gone quickly. Daily I would stalk and observe the deer whom I first encountered in that wet thicket in June. It was almost like raising him myself. I was happy, having spent almost the entire summer on my stomach close to the ground hiding. Most of the time I was observing in the late evening or the very early morning hours. These are times most people miss. They are quiet times. I became very peaceful. My outlook, which this past year had been somewhat frenetic because of the strain of trying to decide what to do with my life, had gradually become tranquil. The sound of the birds and the insects was a kind of music as beautiful as a Beethoven sonata. I would lie and listen to the bats at night catching mosquitoes. Their high shrills were in no way scary, but were instead reassuring. Everything had its place in this natural system. I would find mine. The bats were to feed on the insects and keep that population balanced. I? I didn't know, but I was reassured that I would some-day discover my ultimate purpose. I was at peace.

I was closer to the Great Spirit than I had been in a long time. Not from any exciting near-death experience but from the fact that I was so close to the earth for such an extended period of time. I was covered most of the time in mud. I was lying in the leaves and pine needles and dirt and sand. I could smell the earth, and more than once I tasted it as I licked my lips in thirst, only to have my tongue covered with mud.

This day, though, I felt restless. I would not spend the day sleeping near where my fawn bedded. I had learned to follow my feelings, and I would go home. Today I took one last look at my fawn and backed, crawling, out from the pine I was under and headed toward the cool stream I called Jordan. There I bathed and dressed. I wore only a loincloth in the summer. It was not difficult to do that since so few people venture through the heat and insects in August. I wouldn't shock too many tourists.

When I arrived home, my mother greeted me with a message to call overseas operator, number 23.

"Hello! This is Tom Brown, Jr."

"Would you hold while I connect you?"

"Certainly." Where was I calling?

"Hello, I have your call from Tom Brown, Jr."

"Thank you, put him through, please." The voice I heard talking to the operator was a man's and very precise. The words seemed almost like a woodpecker would sound if it could speak. Each word was clipped.

"Hello, Tom Brown?"

"Yes?"

"I'm Inspector Barrett of the Caribe Island police depart-ment. I have been requested by Mrs. Robertson to call you. Her husband has been missing for five days, and we have reason to believe he has been kidnapped, but she insisted we call you before we call off our search of the grounds of her estate."

"What makes you think he was kidnapped?"

"We have been searching this island for five days with our men and dogs, and have found no trace of this man. He must have been abducted. He is a very wealthy executive, and there are those who would take him for money. We are pretty sure he is a victim."

"Have you had any ransom notes?"

"No."

"Then you can't be sure."

"No."

"What does Mrs. Robertson want from me?"

"She wants to fly you down here to track her husband. I tried to tell her that, if our dogs couldn't find him, no human could, but she is terribly upset and wouldn't listen to reason. I called you, hoping you could persuade her to listen to reason."

"Has it rained since he turned missing?"

"No."

"Okay."

"Okay what?"

"Okay, I'll come as soon as possible."

"But, Mr. Brown," he answered, "I was hoping—"

"I know what you were hoping, but I won't tell Mrs. Robertson anything until I've had a try. Tell her to call the airline and reserve me a seat on the next plane out of Philadelphia."

Hours later I was on a plane, flying over the Atlantic to one of the most beautiful and unusual islands in the Caribbean. It is near the American Virgin Islands, but it is different from St. John or St. Thomas because it has a European flavor.

I was met at the airport by the same inspector who had spoken to me on the phone. He was a very tall, strong-looking black man. He had closely cropped hair and a high forehead. His suit was clean and creased and dazzling white. He offered me a very firm handshake and directed me curtly to the police car that was waiting.

"Have any baggage?" he asked as he looked at my faded jeans, moccasins, and T-shirt with rather obvious disdain.

"Only my loincloth," and I patted my back pocket.

"Yes," he mumbled as we headed for the car.

The inspector was busy informing me as to the impossibility of my task, but I wasn't paying very much attention. This was my first time on a Caribbean island, and I was drinking in the scenery and animal life.

"Mr. Brown, are you listening?"

"Oh, excuse me," I said, slightly startled and embarrassed. "I was just admiring your island."

"Yes, it is quite beautiful, but very hot at this time of the year. We have very few tourists here now. But the trade winds make it bearable in the evening."

"It's hot in New Jersey now, only it's very humid and has very few breezes."

"Oh? How do you keep cool there?" he asked, expecting me to answer "Air conditioning." Instead, I said, "Mud."

"Oh?"

"Yes, smeared all over, much like elephants do in Africa. It's also a very effective protection against mosquitoes." I noticed him glance up and catch the eye of the driver, who was staring into the rear-view mirror. He couldn't believe what he was hearing. I didn't feel like explaining, so I asked a question:

"Do you have many mosquitoes here?"

"Oh, some, but not so many. We don't use screens as you can see. We do have insects here called by the locals no-see-ums, because they are tiny and hard to see against the black skin in the dark. They can be very annoying."

I was again looking at the countryside as we sped across the island. The land was dry and sandy and full of cactus and scrub. It reminded me of the desert in our Southwest, except that it was greener. There was a goat grazing on the almost perpendicular hillside.

The silence must have been bothering the inspector. He challenged me, "What makes you think you can find this man when our police and dog men have had no success?"

"I'm not sure, but I can track, and I'm going to try. I've been reading tracks, human and animal, most of my life. I can read them and understand them like you can read a manual on a Smith and Wesson and know its capabilities."

"How did you learn this?"

"I spent my childhood in the woods observing and being taught by an Apache Indian. He was a very thorough teacher, and the Great Spirit was kind to me and granted me patience."

"The Great Spirit?"

"It's my name for God."

"Oh," he answered with absolutely no expression in his voice.

"I would sit for hours and watch the wind or rain wear at a track until it had all but disappeared. I memorized each stage of deterioration and knew the effects of each climatic change on the track. If this man has only been missing five days, there is a good chance that there will still be traces of his tracks left, if indeed there were any tracks in the first place. Are you sure it hasn't rained since his disappearance?"

"Positive!"

"Where was he last seen?"

"About a hundred yards from his home."

"By whom? Someone who can definitely identify him?"

"By his wife." His voice had begun to soften. He liked the questions I was asking, although he was not yet convinced that I could do what I claimed.

I was taken to a hotel where I spent the night. When I woke before dawn, I decided to get an early start.

The inspector and I went straight to the villa. It sat high on a hill overlooking the ocean. There were sheer cliffs that fell away through the desert brush straight to the ocean. It was a very beautiful setting, but I was surprised to see how the land resembled the desert. The soil was hard and rocky, and the predominant vegetation was cactus. There were stunted trees and bushes. Tracking would be difficult at best. I knelt and scraped the sandy soil and immediately realized that beneath most of the shallow soil was shale. A track couldn't hold more than a couple of days on ground like this.

The inspector's voice broke my concentration. "It will be difficult, won't it, Mr. Brown?"

I nodded. "But not impossible." I am instructed by everything I see and hear—even challenged—but never discouraged. We had walked from the car to the patio and left very faint marks in the path. I pointed to them and said, "See, we made tracks."

"Smudges, scrapings. You can't tell if they were made

by us or a servant earlier today. Come on, Mr. Brown, we both know it is hopeless, and I don't want to see Mrs. Robertson hurt any more than she has been already."

"You pulled a muscle in your right leg, and it isn't fully healed. You weigh exactly one hundred and eighty-two pounds and are left-handed. Also you carry a revolver under your right shoulder."

"What are you getting at, Mr. Brown?"

"Did you?"

"Did I what?"

"Pull a muscle in your right leg?"

"Yes, but I don't see what bearing that would have on whether or not you will be able to track Mr. Robertson on our hard dry ground."

"I learned everything that I told you by looking at those smudges you made. You favor your left leg just enough to point your right toe slightly in. See?" I pointed to his marks.

"That proves nothing. You just watched me walk. You are very observant, but I warn you, I will not be hustled or taken in."

"Okay, I don't want to get you angry, just tried to show you that I might be able to track in this soil." I looked around and waited for the inspector to ring the bell. "Bet you she's got a dog that's about eighteen inches long, weighs twelve pounds, and has long black hair."

The maid answered the door, and a nosy little Cairn stuck its nose between her legs and growled at us. The inspector frowned.

"His prints are all over the yard," I said.

"Mrs. Robertson is expecting us. I'm Inspector Barrett, and this is Mr. Tom Brown." We were shown to a large open room overlooking the green-blue ocean. A sugar bird, as the natives call them, sat on the windowsill waiting for a handout.

Mrs. Robertson was a sophisticated, graying woman in her early sixties. She held herself very erect, but I could tell by the redness of her eyes that she had been under a tremendous strain. She smoked long filtered cigarettes, the ashtrays were full of them half-smoked. Her hands held each other almost constantly. Her voice shook with emotion. I knew now why the inspector was so protective.

"Do you have any recent pictures of Mr. Robertson? Could I see a pair of his shoes? Preferably a pair much like the ones he was wearing when he disappeared. Also, could you tell me his weight, which hand he favored, or if there was anything unusual about his walk. Did he limp? Was he pigeon-toed?"

"Can you find my husband, Mr. Brown?" she cried. "I don't know what I'll do without him! He was everything to me. We had no children."

"I'll try, Mrs. Robertson." I wasn't at all sure that, if I found her husband, he would be alive. It had been a full five days since he was reported missing, and there had been some unrest among a radical group on the island. A tourist had been murdered some weeks before. It could well be that he had been murdered or kidnapped. However, no ransom note had appeared.

The maid brought me sneakers, a picture, and a cold lemonade. I noticed he wore his sneakers out from the inside of the heel, and there were holes by the big toes and little toes of both feet.

"He liked comfortable shoes, didn't he?"

"Yes, and he would wear them everywhere. Didn't care what people thought. He'd even wear them with a suit. He dressed very casually."

"Looks like he never cut his toenails, Mrs. Robertson."

"Only when he had to. I don't know what made them grow so. His fingernails were long too. Never bit them. Not a bit nervous. I would cut them for him, and tell him, I should have nails like yours. Levis and deck shoes and button-down shirts. The button-down cowboy, I called him."

"If you'll point out where you last saw your husband, I'll get started."

She walked to the window and gave the sugar bird a cube of sugar. It pecked at it, picked it up in its beak, and flew off over the cliff. "Right up there, Mr. Brown." She pointed to a spot higher on the hill about a hundred yards from the house.

"What was he doing up there, walking the dog?"

"No, the dog is mine. He never walked it. He was taking pictures. Said the light was just right and wanted to get the house at sunset. We have beautiful sunsets here."

"He never came back?"

"No."

"And the camera?"

The inspector interrupted, "We've been over all this more times than Mrs. Robertson cares to remember. No camera was found. No trace of anything was found, Mr. Brown. Nothing!"

The early morning was still. I walked in darkness along the narrow road that led to the Robertson's villa. I could hear my footfalls and the sounds of lizards skittering out of my way.

If I am to find any trace of this man, I must be resolved to suffer, I thought. The news said rain was expected the next day. If it rained, the land would be wiped clean. How do you read a blank page in a book? How do you track on smooth rock?

A lizard leaped into the bushes. It must have been one of those tiny green reptiles I had seen on Mrs. Robertson's patio. Perhaps it jumped into a poinsettia tree. They grew profusely about the island. I had never seen them so large. I was startled. I shouldn't have been, but my mind was a thousand miles away, in the desert of the Southwest.

I was seeking Stalking Wolf, following the trail he had deliberately left for me. Sometimes it was difficult, sometimes simple, and sometimes he would leave a message for me. Once when I lost his trail, I started running in ever-widening circles from where I had lost it. I ran at top speed searching the hard ground for a sign. He had taught me this years before. It usually worked but was very difficult. The chances of missing a vital sign are very great. However, it worked. I ran till I found a junco feather, gray, lying neatly between two rocks. It pointed the direction Stalking Wolf had taken. I recognized it as a sign and a message, because there are no juncos in that part of the United States and the junco was my favorite bird as a child.

My feet felt the sharp stones of the Robertson's driveway as the first rays of light broke over the Atlantic. A sugar bird called. Soon the gulls would be diving among the rocks for breakfast. There was a light in the kitchen.

"You're early." The maid was surprised to see me. She frowned at my bare feet on her clean floor.

"Sorry to bother you. Thought I'd get an early start. Is there a room I could change in?"

She pointed to a hall with a bathroom at the end. She looked puzzled because I had no other clothes with me. When I walked back into the kitchen, she turned to hand me a cup of coffee.

"Ooooooooooooh-eeee!" she screamed and spilled half the cup on my bare feet. I hopped back as she began to apologize.

"I'm sorry, Mr. Brown, but I just wasn't expecting— I mean, there ain't nothing wrong. But I just—I'm sorry. Did I burn you?"

"I'm fine." I had taken the towel she was using and was wiping my feet. "Nothing to worry about." I had to laugh. People just aren't used to grown men in loincloths.

"What's going on out there, Ginny?" Mrs. Robertson called from the bedroom.

"Nothing, Mrs. Robertson. Just spilled some coffee is all. Mr. Brown is here."

"Already? I didn't hear a car." She came walking into the room tying her robe. She looked as if she hadn't slept in a week. "What in the world?"

"I walked."

"Like that?"

"No. I—ah—changed when I got here." I was beginning to feel embarrassed. I backed toward the door to leave, muttering something about getting started and rain coming.

"Don't go yet, Mr. Brown." Mrs. Robertson poured herself a cup of coffee. Took a long swallow, black. "Is there any hope, really?"

"There's always hope," I offered.

"Oh, hell. That's not what I mean. If you find him, will he be alive?"

"I can't answer that, Mrs. Robertson. It wouldn't be right."

"I didn't think so," she cried.

"I'm going to get started. It's going to get hot, and—" I backed out of the door.

"Mr. Brown?" Mrs. Robertson called after me. I stopped to look back. "Good luck." I smiled.

At the spot Mr. Robertson was last seen, I stopped. The sun had broken full over the ocean. Gulls were crying in the surf. "How will I work this? Which way would he have gone?" I turned around and around, remembering that he was a photographer and that he had disappeared at sunset. Where would he go to get a better picture of the house. I looked up the mountain and decided to climb.

At first I walked in an ever-widening arc from the cliff to the road and back. It got hotter. There was no breeze. No-see-ums nibbled at my flesh. Back and forth I walked reading the ground, trying to pick up a clue, a feeling. Anything that might direct me. Nothing.

That's what Inspector Barrett had said. "Nothing." The sun was high. Half the day gone, and I hadn't gotten anywhere. I was still close to the house. I began to jog, looking down at my feet, forgetting the thorn bushes and stunted trees that grew on the hillside. I would run into them for sure, but there was so little time. I had to move. Fast.

With each step, it seemed, my pace picked up, until I was loping at a full gait back and forth across the hillside.

The birds perched. The lizards clung to the undersides of leaves. The heat was intense. The rock was hot on my feet. But there was no time.

I approached the road and noticed an unfamiliar marking. Made by a pointed shoe. Not a police boot. No sneaker made it. Then there was another and another of a different size. They led from the road. I stopped. Not visible from the house. I followed the prints back to the road. A car had stopped. Its tire marks were on the shoulder. There was a sign that the car had taken off in a hurry. Sand and stones were thrown up from its back wheel. I fell to my belly and searched the ground for any sign of a sneaker print or a struggle. Nothing. The prints were made by two men in a hurry, and that's all. They could have stopped to go to the bathroom. How old were the tracks? Five, six days.

I followed them back up the hillside, but they stopped on a piece of hard ground. I lost them. "Run!" And I did.

The sun was exhausting. I hadn't had anything to eat or drink since morning. I was getting dizzy. "Water." I marked where I had stopped and walked back to the house.

"Find anything?" Ginny asked, not expecting an answer. I looked whipped and discouraged. My body was a mass of bruises and scratches, and I was covered with dirt.

"Water, please," I said, as I shook my head, no.

Ginny gave me water and fixed a sandwich. We didn't speak. The sun was low in the sky. "I've got to go." I was determined to find something before dark.

"Run," Stalking Wolf would yell after us as we were trying to follow a trail made by a cottontail. "Run!" A spider hung suspended from a web and began to sway in the evening breeze. Night! I thought. Darkness. "Nothing!"

I ran. The light was fading fast, when I came across an overturned stone. So what? Beside it was a scuff mark with an indentation. Could have been made by a sharp object. A toenail? Down.

I crawled. Strained my eyes against the fading light and saw the imprint of a sneakered foot. The little ridges, sparse from a worn sneaker, protected from the wind by a ledge. The light was gone. I curled up by the print, exhausted, and fell asleep.

A lizard crawling across my arm woke me. I opened one eye and followed his progress up my arm to my shoulder. He looked me right in the eye and flicked his tongue. He was green, with yellow eyes.

"Time to get up?" I asked. My voice startled him. He leaped to a thorn bush and scurried off on its branches. The sun rose Indian red, turning the sky deep shades of scarlet. It looked like a poppy growing in a sea of blood. "Red sky at morning." I'd better get started.

My body was stiff and sunburned. I thought I had been tanned, but all those days covered with mud had protected my skin from the sun. Each branch my body touched stung. I reeled back when the first thorn touched my tender skin. "Damn!" The shrill screams of the gulls diving for their food turned my attention toward the sky. "If it rains, it's all over." I ran. Forget the pain, just follow the track.

I was back in the Barrens, racing with Rick. He was a step ahead and branches were flying back at me. They whipped at my face and legs. "I'm going to win," he shouted when I slowed to avoid the pain of the slashing branches. "The hell you will!" I dived forward, blindly forgetting the pain, and broke into the clearing beside my friend and beat him by a half step. "I knew that'd get you!" Rick wheezed and laughed as he lay on the ground, gasping for breath. I stood with my head between my knees sucking wind. "Why, you sneaky little weasel!" I leaped on him and beat at his arms and stomach. It only made him laugh harder.

There it was again. At the crest of the hill there was another sneaker mark. It was made by a stumbling motion. Was he clumsy? Twice he had tripped. Was he ill? Or was someone chasing him? No other footprints were in the area. He must have gone down the other side of the hill. Strange. Wasn't he taking pictures of the house? The sky turned gray. Insects, spiders, and lizards moved quickly to avoid my running feet.

I was on his trail now. I felt it. There were no dog prints or boot prints. They hadn't checked this area. Why? I was in a ravine that led to the cliffs. What little there was of his trail led down this narrow crevice in the rock toward the sea. Each mark had been made by a man in a hurry. Rocks knocked from the sides of the ravine. Branches broken and bushes partially torn from the ground. These were his prints. I was assured of that when I found a clear print in a sandy area caused by erosion. He came this way.

The ground became more and more rocky as I approached the edge of the cliffs that fell for hundreds of feet to the sea. Volcanoes rising from the ocean floor had formed this island millions of years ago. The waves beat against the rocks at the base of the cliffs. There was no beach there, and it would be a very difficult climb if anyone wanted to attempt it. Would Mr. Robertson have tried that at night? I searched the rock for some sign of what might have happened. Nothing. Except at shoulder height on the face of a rock was a mark that looked as if it were made by a hard object striking the rock with great force. Another rock? Mr. Robertson's camera? Had he lost his balance and swung his arms for something to hold onto? Had his camera flown up and struck the rock? Anything was possible. It must have been dark when he was in this place. That could account for his clumsiness. He might have come to the edge of the cliff without realizing it and slipped. . . .

A wind blew dust over the ravine. It filtered down on my shoulders. Rain! I thought. I'd better get back to the house and call the police so my story can be substantiated.

I climbed up the side of the ravine and was about to run to the house, which was well out of sight by now, when something caught my eye. A footprint made by a pointed shoe. A man 5 feet 10, 180 pounds had stood here, six, seven days ago. At the same time Mr. Robertson was down in the ravine, or at least the same day, someone had stood here looking into it. It was the only print in the area. I couldn't understand it. The first raindrops hit my back as I leaned over the print. "Run!"

We stood in the rain at the edge of the cliff. The dogs had led us there from the place I thought Mr. Robertson had entered. He had definitely come to this spot. What had happened after that is still a mystery. The rain made any further tracking impossible. Perhaps he climbed down and just ran away. Perhaps he fell. We couldn't tell.

"What do you make of this mark?" I asked the inspector.

"A simple mark. Why? Was it made recently?"

"I'd say about the time Mr. Robertson disappeared."

"Could have been made by anything. Even a ricocheted bullet."

"Do any of your men wear pointed shoes? Any of the dog handlers wear a pointed boot?"

"Of course not. We wear a standard army shoe or boot, and the dog handlers also. Why do you ask?"

"I found some prints. One at the top of the ravine here. The others down by the road. There were tire marks on the shoulder. All made about the same time Mr. Robertson disappeared."

"What are you getting at?"

"Just a feeling—nothing." It wasn't enough, I know. It was a hunch and a horrible one at that. It would be too painful to pursue. It would probably lead nowhere. "Let's go." I turned and walked back up the ravine. A green lizard with yellow eyes watched.

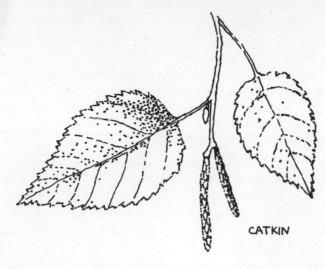

CATKIN

PAPER BIRCH

6/Stab Death

Prologue to a very sad story:
He was just eleven. He weighed about a hundred pounds. Had a
broad smile and sandy hair. Stood about five foot three or four.
Came from a broken home. Had a free spirit.

Sounds like half the kids in the country. He wasn't a bad
kid, nor was he good. He hadn't quite arrived yet. He was de-
veloping, like most of us. And probably, like most of us, against
the odds, would have made it.

He died suddenly and tragically one spring afternoon
while skipping school. He was stabbed and hacked by a yet un-
known assailant. He died alone. The coroner said he bled to death.

I found him.

I had not been called through official channels. A friend of mine
on the police force telephoned one afternoon and told me that a

young boy was missing and they were dragging a pond near his home for his body. He thought it would be nice if I could just happen to drive by in my jeep and offer an observation or two. I did.

The search was taking place less than a hundred yards from a busy highway. I could see the police and volunteers on and around the pond. It was a repulsive sight. I wanted to ignore it and drive by. I turned onto a sandy truck road and found my friend.

He gave me a general description of the boy. I searched the area for prints that might be the boy's. I found them. They did go into the pond. My heart sank. Maybe he had drowned. I continued to scan the area and found another set of prints that came out of the pond. On close examination, I perceived the second set of prints to be the more recent. The boy had been in the water for perhaps a half an hour.

These prints led away from the pond. Unless they wound their way back again, I was convinced the boy was not still in the pond.

I followed his trail to a stand of willowy birches by the pond. He had come out of these same trees with his bicycle. But there was something different about the trees. Two—no, three of them looked more bent than they should have been. No ice or heavy snow had bent these trees. I remembered when I had been a swinger of birches. . . .

"Rick!" I yelled from the top of a young birch. "Watch!" I kicked straight out into space, screaming, with all my weight. A full thirty feet from the forest floor. I clung with a young boy's tenacity to the thin upper trunk of the tree and watched the branches of pine and aspen fly by. The tree bent. Like an old man bending to pick a flower, it stretched slowly toward the earth, and when I felt it about to groan or snap, I would release my grip and free-fall the last few feet to the ground. "Whoooweeee! Neeetoooo!" And off I'd go to climb another birch. The forest's parachute.

Billy had taken time to climb these trees and swing to earth. There were the scrapings on the gray white bark, the broken twigs, and the scuffs where he had fallen. Took quite a plunge from one. Looked as if he fell heels first and rolled over backward into a young bayberry. Didn't seem to have hurt him. He stood and ran to the next tree.

"You have found the young boy's bow." Stalking Wolf smiled as he watched us swing with delight. One time Rick misjudged and was left hanging ten feet from the ground. "Jump, Rick!" I called and laughed.

"No. Too far!" he screamed.

Stalking Wolf looked amused, but motioned me to climb the tree and help with my weight. I climbed farther on the trunk than I should have, and it broke. We both landed with a thud. I sprained my wrist. Rick hurt his pride. We laughed.

"You must always judge how far to go. Now you have ruined the birch."

We were hurt because Stalking Wolf seemed unconcerned for Rick and me. He was busy surveying the damage to the tree. We used its bark for crafts and its wood for fire. We used the fall as a lesson. There are limits which we must respect, personal and natural. My life would be a series of tests of those limits, but not without a healthy respect for what could happen if those limits were ignored.

He swung one more time. It was a small tree. He was bored or tired or both. From this swing he sauntered to his bike, and walked it out of the grove. I followed, but felt compelled to look back. Someone passing this place would think those trees were bent by ice or snow as they cut across the lines made by the straighter pine and oak. I would know differently.

A flock of starlings flew into the grove, and it was as if he were still there swinging and kicking and laughing. I closed my eyes hard and listened to the birds light on branches like so much rain falling from the sky. For a moment I heard his laughter, but realized it was only a memory of happy days, long gone.

I told the police that they were wasting their time looking for the missing boy in the pond. It was obvious to me that he had taken his bike and ridden up the road toward the highway. I showed them the tire marks in the sand and backtracked them through some pretty dense undergrowth to where the boy had concealed his bike. His prints, those of a young boy about his weight and only hours old, shuffled around and finally walked the bike out to the truck road. I was very careful to show them where the boy had jumped on his bike and began to ride. It was very easy to see. The footprints stopped, and the tire tracks were deeper.

"How do you know that they belong to the missing boy?"

"You say he weighs a hundred pounds?"

"Right."

"This boy weighs that much."

"Sure."

"Do I have to prove it to you?"

"Yes."

"How much do you weigh?"

"What does that have to do with it?"

"Come here." I motioned him toward an area of the road that was covered with footprints. I pointed to them and asked him to pick out his own prints.

"I can't do that."

"Try, please."

He pointed to a print that was three sizes too large and about a hundred pounds too deep.

"Wrong. They belong to that man there." I directed his eyes to a policeman 6 feet 3, 260 pounds. "These are yours. Come here and put your foot in the print you claim is yours."

He did, and it surrounded his boot on all sides.

"Now put your foot in the one I pointed out." He did again, and it fit.

"You're having a little back problem, aren't you?"

"How'd you know?"

"You favor your right leg and put most of your weight on the outside of the foot. You made this print about two hours ago, and these were made twenty minutes ago, and these are my prints."

"How?" He was astounded at my ability to read prints. But I was not here to impress him, just to convince him, so he would listen and follow my advice.

I was kneeling, and I beckoned him to get down close to the earth with me. I broke off some dry rye grass and measured the depth of the tracks with it so that his eye could perceive the difference in depth of a print made by weight.

He was convinced that I knew how to read tracks.

"How'd you learn that?"

"Patience."

"Oh." He thought for a while, pondering the footprints. I had him, I thought, until he smiled and turned away toward the men dragging the pond. They looked clumsy throwing their weighted ropes about and dragging the bottom of the pond.

"But how do you know they were this particular boy's prints?"

"There's only one way to find that out."

"I know."

"Follow them."

"What am I supposed to do with all these men dragging the pond and searching the woods? Tell them to forget it and follow you off down the road? We don't even know if they are his prints or if it was his bike. There just is not enough proof in what you say to cause me to follow you up that road. I'm sorry."

"So am I."

"Now don't get smart with me."

"Smart? I think you're wasting valuable time here. Call up the mother and find out what kind of sneakers he was wearing and ask her to check the garage to see if his bike is missing. Ask her if he ever skips school!"

"What do you mean?"

"His tracks were made this morning around nine-thirty."

"That's impossible."

"Why?"

"He would have been in school."

"Did he go to school?"

"His mother said."

"All she said was he didn't come home from school. Did you talk to any of his friends and find out if he went to school?"

"No."

"Well, why don't you?"

"We will."

"So you think he stopped off for a swim and drowned?"

"We hope not."

"He was playing hooky. He did take a swim. But when he was through, he came out of the water and rode off down this road to the highway. That's all I'm saying."

"Why don't you follow your trail, Tom—Mr. Brown, and let us know if you find anything. I'll take your advice and ask the mother your questions when we're done here."

"You already are. You won't find anything."

"Well, I hope you're right."

"I am." I pondered as I started down the road toward the highway. The sound of the anchors splashing into the muddy water was muffled by the roar of trucks and cars speeding on their way.

I really shouldn't be disappointed, I told myself. I know that they don't understand or trust—they can't. They're too set in their ways. They are educated to think the way they do. Don't take it personally. It's their problem, not yours. They can only think and see and do one thing at a time. Stalking Wolf's method of splatter-vision is unknown to them. They can't hear when they're speaking or see more than one object at a time or realize what someone else is doing on the other side of the room by the movement or voice tone of the person to whom they are speaking. They are boxed in, limited, and they like it that way.

The details of the track were not very exciting. It was not too difficult to follow the tire tracks of his bicycle up the side of the highway. They would wander off and on the asphalt according to the density of the traffic. Any boy would rather coast on the smooth surface of a highway than struggle pumping through the rocky, sandy soil that was the shoulder.

He stopped three times. Once to hide behind a bush and relieve his kidneys—the ride was bumpy. Once to play with a stray dog. He got off his bike and sat in the grass by the side of the road and played with the dog. There he rolled with it. A small dog, about twenty pounds. Someone must have called him, for he ran off across the road into a housing development.

The third time the boy stopped was to talk with someone. There were another set of prints beside his bike. They stood and shuffled about, kicking stones and passing the time. The other set was large. They were made by a right-handed man of 180 pounds. I think he had a backpack, because his weight was shifted to the ball of his feet, and there was a place beside the road where something had depressed the grass and his prints led to and from it. I studied them for quite a while, trying to figure out what it was he did when he walked off the road. I lay down on my stomach and studied the sand and grass and measured the prints with my eyes. He took three long strides to where the bundle had lain. He lifted it. His tracks got perceptibly deeper. He moved to his right and swung the load to his back, where it remained. His turn back to the road left a much deeper depression than his turn from the road, and his stride was shortened and more labored. As I said before, his weight shifted to the balls of his feet, as if he was constantly trying to keep his balance.

There was one more peculiarity that was in his step both before and after he assumed his burden. His right heel dragged ever so lightly as he stepped down. What could have caused that?

There was a time when I was young, when Rick and I were loaded like pack mules, and ready for our first campout with the boy scouts. My pack weighed as much as I did. Rick carried not only a pack, but an official boy scout hatchet and knife, which hung from their own special belt on his right hip. Five miles was a long way for young boys to walk carrying all that weight, but we made it. I remember following Rick most of the way over those sandy barren paths and noticing how he dragged his right heel ever so slightly so that it made a light drag mark as he stepped down. When we got to camp, I talked to him about it. I was very familiar with Rick's footprints. If I went to heaven, I could find Rick by following his tracks through the clouds. I asked him why he was dragging his right heel. He said he hadn't noticed anything different. His leg didn't hurt and his pack was packed evenly. We couldn't figure it out until one of the other scouts asked to borrow his hatchet. "That's it!" I cried. The other boy thought I was nuts and jumped back, but Rick knew exactly what I meant. He jumped up and walked around the camp once. He took the hatchet off, gave it to the boy who wanted to borrow it, and walked around again exactly beside his previous tracks. We both jumped for joy when we saw the difference. We had just solved a mystery and were elated. His first set of tracks showed the heel drag. The second didn't. The hatchet banging against his hip caused the drag.

The man who had made these prints had something hanging on

his right hip. A hatchet, perhaps, although I've seen the footprints of soldiers at Fort Dix similar to these. Their heel drag was made by a bayonet banging against their hips. A cold chill ran up my back. I had a bad-medicine feeling, and quickly stood from where I knelt, anxious to get on with my search.

The boy was walking his bike now, and the man walked on beside him. Then the boy got on his bike and rode off. The man's prints disappeared onto the asphalt and never reappeared. He must have hitched a ride. The boy's tire tracks continued on down the road and into a development. I lost him there. All the roads were paved and they were curbed, without shoulders. It was impossible to follow him any longer.

I decided to go home and call the police and have them check the development. He might have been going to a friend's house there. My call was very productive. The police had checked with the boy's mother, and his bike was missing. He had been wearing sneakers, and they had decided to call off the dragging of the pond. They were very cooperative and were interested in what I had discovered. I told them that I could continue my search in the morning, but they begged me to come out with two of their men while there was still some light; the police had decided to call off the more intensive search until morning.

I had a feeling that we had to find the boy soon, if we wanted to find him alive. I had absolutely no evidence to point to foul play, but I had strong feelings ever since I saw the backpacker's prints.

We met at the development. I told the two men what to look for, showed them a tire track made by the boy's bike, and sent them north on either side of the road with instructions to yell out if they saw anything that resembled the track. I took the west side of the road and headed south toward where the boy lived. The sun was going down. The starlings, which are so plentiful, were beginning their pilgrimage to their evening roost. A column of thousands blackened the sky and stretched for as far as the eye could see. I knew where they were nesting. Down the road about two miles was a grove of oak, aspen, and beech where thousands of them came each night in the spring. Why they picked that grove is a mystery. It was right beside the road. With all the barren isolated land in this part of the state, I couldn't figure why they would want to nest by a noisy highway.

I had seen this sight hundreds of times, but it never became boring. Black birds against a graying sky flying in various formations, sometimes twenty abreast in a line literally miles long. They would pass over for the better part of an hour. They had just begun, and I knew that I had less than an hour's light left and must hurry.

I broke into a jog and had run about a half mile when I saw the tire mark. It was a partial mark, but it was his. I turned and yelled at the two policemen who were walking north. I had a following breeze, and there was no traffic, so they heard me. One of them turned and waved, and I motioned them to come. When I was sure they were on their way, I turned back to my track. I was jogging again, and following the tire tracks. There were other bike tracks, of course, but they were decidedly different. I had been following his the entire afternoon and was familiar with the tread and depth. These were undoubtedly his tracks.

I was drawing nearer the hosting grounds of the starlings, and their cries filled the air. His tracks left the road at this point and headed into the grove. He had stopped and dismounted. Had stood by his bike as if talking to someone. He made an attempt to remount his bike. One foot left the ground and swung over the bike, and he rested his weight on the seat, but didn't move very far. He pushed himself with his left toe about ten feet. He stopped, dismounted, and walked the bike into the grove.

By this time the policemen were beside me, asking what I had found. I answered that I thought the boy had entered the grove. They looked up and saw the thousands of birds flying in to roost and almost had to yell to be heard over their evening calls.

"What makes you think he went in there? I wouldn't go in there."

"His prints lead in there. I also think someone called him."

"Why do you think that?"

"Because he hesitated before he went in. I can't be sure, but his actions as I read them from his prints are those of a boy trying to make up his mind. From what I have learned from this boy's tracks, he was not one to hesitate when he wanted to do something. The way he skipped school. His skinny dip. The birch swing. His free ride up the highway in plain view so anyone could see him and report him. If he hesitated before going into this grove—well . . . that's all I know."

"We're going in there?" One of the officers asked incredulously. He couldn't see going into a woods filled with swarming starlings. It guess he had seen the picture, *The Birds*, and was frightened.

"Come on," I motioned as I started following the tracks into the grove. "They won't hurt you."

A small hill rose in the center of the grove. It had a depression in it so that someone standing in the depression could not be seen from the road. The bike was just inside the grove, and the boy's prints led up the hill.

"Why don't you try up there." I motioned to the hill as I yelled above the din of the starlings. "I'm going to check the road for other prints." I had that feeling again. I looked closely at the trail for any indication of other prints, but found none, even though I expected to see the boot prints of the boy's roadside companion.

"Here. Up here!" One of the policemen was yelling, and the other was running down the hillside vomiting.

What I saw on that hilltop sent me into convulsions. The starlings took wing from their perches like a giant black cloud rising. Then they settled. But I didn't. I beat the ground and ripped at the underbrush in a rage. The slight boy's body lay grotesquely half covered with leaves and debris under a bayberry bush. It had been slashed and hacked with a large sharp instrument. He had been dead for a day.

What would have possessed anyone to do this to another human being, or to anything alive, is beyond my comprehension. The person who performed this wanton act was more dead than alive.

The light had almost gone. Our eyes were accustomed to the darkness, and the sky was clear and promised moonlight. I searched the ground around the body for any footprints, other than those made by the policemen and the boy. Strange. There were none. They had been deliberately wiped out. The murderer had taken a branch and wiped out his prints, and even the sign of struggle, which there must have been. I followed the smooth marks made by the swishing branch out of the grove to the road.

I was sure the killer, however clever, would make a mistake and leave at least one print.

He was very careful. No signs came in sight. However, the smooth ground path led to the asphalt and some sand was left there, carried by the assailant's feet. I looked and found the branch he had used to strike out his prints, but there was no sign of a print anywhere. How was he smart enough to wipe out his prints? Had he been trained to do it?

I stood by the roadside as trucks and cars sped by and wept. A trucker leaned on his horn as he passed within inches of where I stood weeping. Cinders flew up to sting my face. I instinctively raised my hands to protest. "No!" I lashed out with my fists toward the truck, now hundreds of feet down the road. "You did it. You killed him."

He hadn't of course, but I had to direct my frustration somewhere. The boy was dead. Wasted. While trucks plied their trade noisily up and down the highway. They seemed to disturb no one but me. Not even the birds were alarmed. They seemed affected neither by the traffic nor the boy's death. What was happening to me? Was I the only thing that felt such a sense of revulsion? Of course not. The mother would be hurt more deeply than I could ever imagine. The policeman had to escape the grotesque scene. I was feeling sorry for myself. I couldn't accept failure. I had found the boy, but he was not alive. I blamed everyone else to keep from blaming myself.

The truth is, we were all to blame. Everyone who ever touched the boy or the environment he grew in. I was disgusted with myself and the world in which I lived, and I was ashamed to be a human. All I wanted to do was run. Flee into the wilderness and live off the land and never associate with another human being for the rest of my life. I wanted to disclaim any responsibility for society. I wanted to hide from societal reality and sink into nature's womb and hibernate till man destroyed himself and the animals took over again.

"There you are, Tom. We need you for our report." The sergeant was yelling at me as he walked down the highway. I looked up and saw a dozen police cars lining the road. How long had they been there? We walked back into the grove toward the body. The birds had gone to sleep. Only the sounds of racing

trucks and automobiles competed with the muffled whispering of
the men working busily about the boy's body. Why do we whisper
in the presence of death?

Epilogue
*I will never see a birch that I won't envision a sandy-haired boy
climbing and swinging for joy. Launching his body . . . willowy
strong, from its uppermost trunk, kicking joyously to the ground.*

*There is hope for me in those birches. They are for
me a reminder of what pain exists midst the joy when we run
amok—when we forget the birches and the joy of being one with
our earth.*

*I will try to change this land and her people. I will teach
what I have learned and trust that someday we might all be
"swingers of birches. . . ."*

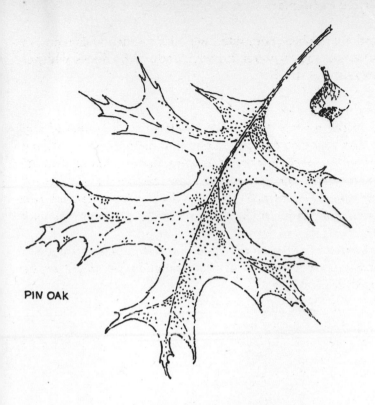

PIN OAK

part two

PARK RANGER

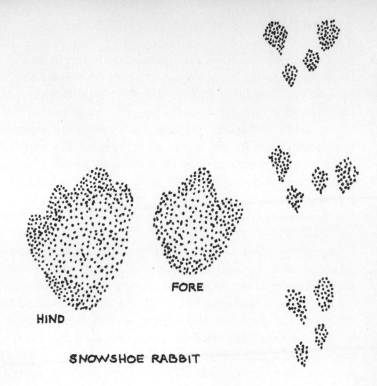

FORE

HIND

SNOWSHOE RABBIT

7/Park Ranger

Have you ever been in the wilderness? Have you ever been in a place that is so isolated that it would take you days, even if you knew the way, to walk out and find another human being? Have you ever been completely alone in the wilderness, away from all other people and all the sounds of civilization? When you have been able to sit for hours and listen to the natural sounds about you blend with your breathing and heartbeat?

If you have, then you know that the rhythm of nature is different from that of man. It is slower and very steady. If you stop your car by the roadside and try to listen to the sounds, other than those of the noisy highway, and take your heartbeat, you will realize how out of sync, out of rhythm you are, because of the tension you experience on the road. Your heartbeat will be much too fast. But get away from the hustle of the highway and relax in the Great Spirit's wilderness, and see your part in it, and you will begin to sense the slow, steady rhythm of eternity that exists all around you. And the chances are very good that your heartbeat will slow to keep pace with the world around you.

We live much too fast. Faster than we were meant to live, and it takes its toll. If you sit in a forest and think about the stock market, you'll be out of place and never experience the relaxation and greater sense of peace that is available if you listen to the cricket and watch the sun fall through the leaves or smell the rich natural odor of rotting leaves.

I have been where man seldom goes and have experienced a oneness with my surroundings that brings with it the greatest sense of peace that anyone can imagine outside of church.

There was a period in my life when I traveled the country, living off the land and visiting our National Parks. I spent weeks at a time deep within our natural wilderness areas, enjoying the beauty and variety of life that it has been set aside for. All I took on this journey was a blanket roll and my favorite knife. Because I was hitchhiking, it was a folding buck and not one of my handmade sheath knives. I would never pick up a hitchhiker who was wearing a sheath, although they are quite popular and many truckers are wearing them today. I was trekking to enjoy and didn't feel as if I wanted to encounter any resistance because of my appearance. I have a rule that I have tried to live by. When I am in the woods, I will wear what is the least alien to that environment. Hence, I'll often wear buskskins or a loincloth, but most often just a wool shirt and jeans. The shirt will be a plaid for camouflage purposes. A deer can discern solid colors, but the plaid will break you up enough to stand undetected, if you remain perfectly still, in the middle of a field.

When I traveled across the country, I dressed just that way. I didn't try to draw attention to myself or make a statement through my trappings. That's the way of the white man. The Indian would wear fancy dress only during a ceremony, when it meant something. He didn't run naked because he thought it would shock someone or offend someone with whom he disagreed. I could have wandered about the country in my buckskins and have everyone think that I was some sort of an eccentric, but that wasn't the purpose of my wanderings. I traveled to observe, not to be observed, and I was as interested in all the people I met as I was in the wilderness I explored, but that, as they say, is another story.

There was one wilderness area in which I spent quite a good deal of time and impressed me enough to write about it. There are two reasons I remember it so vividly. The first reason is that I experienced a great storm there and had a great truth revealed to me through it. The second reason is that I discovered why the wilderness, and nature itself, is so difficult for most people to understand. I hope you'll be able to discover with me through this portrayal the truths that so impressed me. I'm calling this part "Park Ranger."

"You're going backpacking into this wilderness area with no backpack, no sleeping bag, no food, and no weapon?"

"That's right." I smiled at the ranger who had been questioning me for an hour.

"I don't suppose you have a hunting license?" He was looking for some excuse to keep me out of this wilderness area. He couldn't believe what he was hearing.

I answered politely, "No, because I don't expect to kill anything."

"Excuse me for asking, but what are you going to eat?"

"In this specific wilderness area, there are over a thousand edible plants," I began my canned lecture. "Of course that number is greatly reduced because of the time of the year, but there's still plenty."

"You a vegetarian?" He reached for a cigarette.

"No, but at times I feel that I shouldn't take life. This is one of those times." I added, "I might even fast a day or two."

"Are you some kind of religious freak?" His match burned blue white, and a tiny sliver of smoke curled away from it and disappeared.

"Not really, though my beliefs are somewhat Indian in nature."

He shook his head and took a long hard drag on his cigarette. "I've never met anyone like you. Lots of kids want to hike back in this area and aren't prepared, but after I tell them what they can expect, they are usually discouraged."

"Sir, I don't discourage easily. Besides, I know exactly

what to expect. That's why I'm not taking a weapon and am not going to eat any meat."

"How's that?" He was curious.

"It's hunting season!" I answered as if everyone would realize the truth of what I was going to say. "I want to see animals. They'll be avoiding any man with a weapon. If I don't have a weapon, the animals will know that I come in peace and mean them no harm, and won't hide from me."

"You talk as if the animals were human." He avoided my eyes.

"They're not human, but they are our brothers." I reinforced my point with a finger directed at the park ranger.

"Listen, kid, if you come across a grizzly who's mean and hungry, don't try any of that brother stuff on him, or you'll end up in your brother's stomach." He coughed on some smoke.

"I don't think so, but if I did, that would be all right. It's better than rotting in the ground somewhere doing no one any good."

He finished his cigarette and crushed it under the heel of his boot. "I know that you are determined to go into this area, but I feel it's my duty to forbid you entrance. I know these mountains and the weather here. It's a time of storms. The sun can be shining one minute, and you'll be in the middle of a blizzard the next. You could die in these mountains. If that ever happened, I'd never be able to forgive myself."

"You let the hunters go," I argued.

"Only with experienced guides and with horses, kid."

I knew I had lost. He wouldn't let me into the area, but I offered one last plea. "I don't know what I can say to convince you that I'm capable of surviving up there in any weather and with any animals."

"Nothing. Just do us both a favor and drop it. You're a nice kid, but you're no Indian. You'd die in there."

I shrugged. "Okay."

"That's better." He smiled and reached for another cigarette, offered one to me. I declined.

That night I left a note on his door that explained the way I would be going into the Wilderness Area and the way I would be coming out. I told him that I did not know exactly how long I would stay or where I could wander, but would probably come out soon after the first big snowfall. I also told him that I could bring him a gift from our brother.

I knew that he would try to find me the first day, so I found a very thick briar patch, climbed into it, and waited. He was soon riding up the trail I had followed. I could hear him for minutes before I saw him. He was making so much noise that a rabbit jumped into the briars to hide with me. He wouldn't see the rabbit either, I thought. His horse stopped on the trail just a few feet from where I lay. He looked all about him, across the fields and ahead into the mountains. He never looked down into the briars. Most people don't. They look for what they want to see, but fail to see most of what is all around them.

I had been in hiding from rangers before. I had lived for weeks right under their noses, and they never knew that I was there. Why? Because they see only what they want to see. The tragedy is they are well-educated. They can name the scientific Latin names of the plant life, they know many of the habits of the animals. They even love the wilderness. They revere nature and fight to preserve it, but most of them don't understand its soul. They don't relate to nature personally, but scientifically.

This ranger couldn't see any sign of me. I hadn't walked, like most campers, leaving a stream of messages of my presence. I didn't break branches or carry a walking stick and hack at the weeds. I didn't drop cigarettes on the trail or gum wrappers. I didn't kick at big rocks or shuffle through piles of leaves, disturbing the grubs. He would have expected to overtake me on the trail because most hikers would get tired and sit for a rest. But I didn't do any of these things, and I think he felt that my note had been a bluff. He turned his horse and rode back toward the entrance of the park. I wondered if he would be waiting for me at the place I told him I would be coming out?

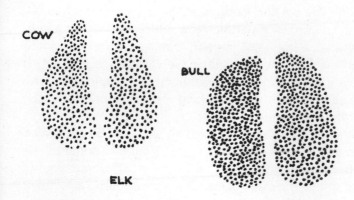

COW

BULL

ELK

8/Cathedral

I had been wandering for four days through the Wilderness Area in Montana. The weather was turning colder. The foliage had turned, and much of it had fallen. When I walked, I left my prints on nature's Oriental rug. I had been following a ridge line on the main trail and stopped where a smaller trail led down into a tiny valley.

The first set of prints I saw heading down the trail made me realize that I would be descending into the valley before long. A bobcat had walked down the trail the night before. *Lynx rufus*, I thought. I'm going to follow you to your den if I have to track you twenty-five miles. I was excited to have found the tracks of this rare cat. At first, I didn't believe my eyes. I thought someone's cat had gone wild, but I'd never seen a cat print this big. They were two inches long, and registered thirteen inches apart, and were made by an animal that weighed at least twenty-five pounds.

It was not an easy track. The ground was covered with leaves and was very rocky. However, I was able to deduce where the cat would go and so would go to that spot, search, and usually find at least a partial print to go by.

By the time I had arrived on the floor of the valley, it was late afternoon. The cat had stopped at the stream that ran down the center of this gorge for a drink. Now which way would a bobcat go? I looked across the stream, but saw no sign on the opposite bank where the cat might have climbed or jumped. It probably stayed on the rocks along the stream, hoping to come on some small animal fishing or taking a drink. But which way would this cat have wandered?

"When you can't see, feel." The words of Stalking Wolf came to me as I knelt beside the stream. I cupped some of the cold water in my hand and drank. "If I were a cat, where would I go?" I sniffed the air for some clues. The air was damp and full of the smell of pine and rotting leaves. I listened hard against the sounds of the forest and stream. The grosbeak and siskin spoke to me. The red squirrel scolded. A trout jumped. Somewhere far upstream a sound came through. It was a sound of water falling.

At that moment I felt like heading upstream. I did. I walked into the most dazzling experience I could ever imagine. What I saw made me forget the bobcat. I had wandered into a natural cathedral.

I fell to my knees and cried. They were tears of joy and awe, respect and gratitude. The sunlight angled down through the tall pines and diffused into a pattern of shadow and light on the rocks and water pools that would shame any man-made mosaic. The birdsongs of redpoll, goldfinch, siskin, junco, grosbeak, and tanager filled the air with a cacophony of music. My spirit soared.

A rainbow formed in the mist thrown up by the waterfall. The giant pines created a canopy a hundred feet from the valley floor and supported the blue-green sky.

There is a creation story told by the Kato Indians that begins, "He stood up pines along his way. He placed yellow pines. Far away he placed them." These words came to my mind as I knelt on hard rock and watched the sun set softly through the tall pines, yellow like candlelight. No cathedral constructed by man's hands could ever be this perfect. I worshipped, fasted, and meditated there for three days. I will never forget the experience.

In the morning, early, before the first light, elk would come to drink from the pools. I would watch them come single file to the water's edge and drink while one kept watch. They had already begun to turn grayish-brown, and their manes were growing longer for the winter. One of the calves still had light spots. It must have been born late. They were such a proud animal that I couldn't imagine how man could have exterminated them in the eastern states.

I would go next to the pool. I would lie down on a flat rock near the falls and douse my head full in the water. I would drink my fill and then roll onto my back to watch the sun rise in the cathedral. The first light was ushered in by a pine grosbeak's sweet warble. As the gray turned slowly golden, a thousand bird-songs would herald the sun. Each dawn was more magnificent than the previous had been. I was each time overwhelmed by its beauty. I would lie there, arms outstretched, and welcome the new day. The second day I filled my hands with seeds and fed the choir of birds who were supplying the cathedral's music. Many birds came that day, but when I spread seeds about the rock the next day, hundreds came. I was surrounded by them. A red crossbill nibbled pine seeds from my hand and thanked me with its *Too-tee* song. Every bird whose song I had heard came to partake of the grain offerings.

Later in the morning the red squirrel would sally forth, and his friend the least chipmunk would join him. Sometimes a muskrat would poke its head above the water's surface to listen to the squirrels' chatter. I would lie concealed by the flat rock and watch them eat and drink of the cool water.

The red fox came silently to the stream from above the falls. But he was not looking for game. He did not sniff at the ground or follow the scent of the squirrel or the snowshoe or the chipmunk. He stopped for a brief instant on the flat rock beside me and looked up at the sunlight. Golden rays made his red coat shine with an ethereal brilliance. He turned and went out the way he had entered. It was as if he had come here to give thanks.

The sunset brought a weasel, a skunk, and a red-backed mouse. I lay breathless every evening to see if the weasel would cross the stream and take the mouse. He didn't. There was something about this place that made killing in it impossible. It was a good-medicine place, but more than that, it was holy ground, and every living thing that entered this place sensed its difference and respected it.

I had discovered a natural cathedral, where peace was a way of life. I felt good there. Too good. I could spend the rest of my life there, enveloped in awesome peacefulness. There, the concept that the earth and all it produced and nurtured was holy, was real. I felt it. I was it. I heard it. It was true. What could draw me away from this place?

Hunger.

I fasted three days. Although I was completely relaxed and content, I was beginning to feel a little weak. What was I to do? I had no desire to kill any of the other worshippers in this sacred place, but I knew that I had to eat. I could forage, but again I had no desire to disturb the perfect harmony that surrounded me. I decided to leave in the morning.

The screech and great horned, both, roosted high in the pines and called the forest to prayer at night. These territorial birds shared this place. I had shared it also and must move on. Perhaps that is the way it was meant to be. Perhaps no man could spend his entire life in such a place. The spirit, after all, is at home in the body, and the body needs sustenance. I answered the owls' call and thanked the Great Spirit for my good fortune. Three days of perfect peace. It was more than some experience in a lifetime.

I rose before the grosbeak called, before the elk descended to the stream. I wanted to take my leave in silence and alone. I moved toward the stream and was startled by a shadowy form standing on the rock where I had spent the last three days. Its eyes met mine and seemed to recognize me. Yes, that was the feeling I received from its gaze—recognition. Then it turned and bounded off toward the falls. "*Lynx rufus*," I whispered, "you led me here."

I followed the bobcat up and out of the tiny valley into the gray morning just as the grosbeak sang. The golden light came earlier this morning as I climbed through fir, pine, spruce, and larch. It would be a good day.

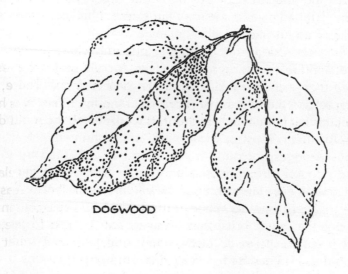

DOGWOOD

9/The Soul of a Tree

My fire was small, like the Indians used. Stalking Wolf said, "The white man builds a big fire and sits far away. The Indian builds a small fire and sits close." I had my blanket wrapped about my shoulders and almost around the fire. As it died down, I would encompass it with the blanket and let the heat of the coals warm me as I slept squatting. I had done this before, but only when it was very cold. The first time I tried it, I slumped to one side in my sleep, and my blanket smoldered. Stalking Wolf stamped on it before it became a flame. This time he didn't laugh. "Don't try it until you can sleep the whole night in squat without falling." Then and there I decided not to use this method to keep warm unless it was an emergency and unless there was someone awake on watch.

I was alone, and there was no emergency. I just wanted to warm myself before I crawled into my leaf hut for the night. This had been a peaceful time for me, and I was reminiscing about my childhood and the many evenings I spent with Rick and Stalking Wolf around the campfire at our good-medicine cabin. This helped me remember.

It had been a cool day but sunny. I had come across the tracks of about fifteen pack horses and their riders. They were heading north along a ridge I had explored two days earlier. They were hunters searching for elk. They would find none up the valley they were headed toward. The elk had pastured there a week before, but had moved west over the mountain to a tender aspen grove. I doubt if these hunters would climb the mountain to look for them. Most of these pack-animal hunters just scan the opposite ridges, looking for browsing elk, and then try to stalk close enough through some very rugged terrain to get a shot. Theirs is no easy task, because the elk have excellent senses, and most of these hunters make a devil of a racket climbing down through thick underbrush and up over rocks in order to get a clear shot. I can't say I'm unhappy about that, and as I studied the hoofprints, I wondered if they had enough provisions to keep them going until they found some elk. I hoped not, and I think I was right, because I didn't hear any shots that day, and that night the storm struck.

In the middle of my dream I became aware of the absence of sound. It is unusual to have no sound in the woods. The screech owl that worked this part of the mountain was silent. The mice weren't scurrying with the chipmunks, and the wind wasn't soughing through the dried leaves. It was quiet and warm. There was little moon, and the weather had been generally cloudy, and so the blackness of the night wasn't unusual, but the stillness and the warmth were. "It's a storm." I knew it instinctively before I said it aloud to myself.

There was a giant oak beside my leaf hut. The reason I had constructed the hut at its base was because the Indians had always considered the oak a sacred tree and often had tribal ceremonies beneath it. To me the oak with its deep root system, reaching far into Mother Earth, and its hardness was good medicine. It gave me a sense of security to be near it and a sense of timelessness. This night it seemed to beckon me into its outspread branches.

I climbed high into its branches and secured my right arm to the trunk with my belt. I was going to ride the oak through the storm and hopefully discover its soul in the process. What happened to me that night was a miracle of no less proportions than Constantine's vision of the cross in the sky.

The storm that hit the mountains that night had winds of hurricane force, and the rain at times was driven parallel to the mountain. In the blue light of almost constant bursts of lightning, I saw trees pulled up by the roots and blown across the ravine. One small tree broken in half by the wind was driven into a pine like some spear thrown by a giant. The lightning struck all around me, and the wind howled like a pack of wolves and went on through the night till just before dawn.

All during the storm I clung to the tree with all my strength and felt it twist and sway in my grip. It spoke as it fought against the swirling winds and held on tight to its mother with its miles of roots. "I have met you before, mighty wind. When I was a sapling, you raced over this mountain and tore at my father's trunk and almost toppled him. His mighty weight shielded me. Again when I was young, you came without warning when my branches were heavy with leaves and green fruit and the squirrels were playing at my feet; and then you took a limb from me and with it my youth. You returned many times and broke my branches and gave me a gnarled look, but you have never taken me from my mother or stopped my groping for the sky by taking my upper body. I have been bent and twisted but never broken or uprooted, and I won't give in this time either." The tree creaked and groaned and lost a limb, but it never gave in.

Grasping the trunk with my face pressed into the gray bark, I could see the water as it ran in rushing rivers down the tree's side, following the contours of the bark. The texture changed as did the color when the tree was wet. The gray became an almost determined black, and it softened to the touch and became more pliable. It didn't bruise as easily when hit by flying debris. Instead it would dent.

Its leaves, brown and ready to fall, took flight that night, and filled the air around me like a swarm of gnats. The wind seemed to swirl around the tree as if it had a personal vendetta against this oak, causing the leaves to be whipped about like a small tornado. They lashed at my body and head and cut at my arms and ankles. In the morning, when the winds had died down and there was enough light to see, the oak stood naked save for one trembling leaf in jeans and plaid wool clinging to its upper trunk.

When I looked down, what I saw brought gooseflesh alive up and down my back. The large branch that had been broken from the oak had fallen butt end, straight through the leaf hut I had slept in the past two nights. If I had stayed there, I would surely have been killed.

The Indians tell a story about a great battle between the Good Spirit and the Evil Spirit. The Good Spirit wins, but the Evil Spirit, who must live in a cave and never see the sun, continues to send demons to the surface of the earth to harm man and disrupt nature. This wind seemed to be attacking this very oak to which I clung, and there was a moment, when the rain was driving hard into my face and the lightning was striking close, that I felt as if it were attacking me. But the oak twisted and spoke to me at that moment, and I smiled in the knowledge that this oak that was sacred to the Indian was also my friend.

That night in the tree made me understand the oak more than any book. I didn't know her exact age, but I knew she was old. I learned the sounds she makes when a wind of over a hundred knots whips at her branches. I know what her wood sounds like when it is broken green from her ancient body. I know the color she turns as she soaks the rain into her thick skin, and the odor she emits from her wet bark. I know her fully clothed, changing, and naked, and I have seen her bleed. That night in the tree I realized how our ancestors could worship her in their anthropomorphic way, because that night I discovered that she had a soul.

The soul of a tree is not like the soul of a human being. It is its personality. The willow has a soul that cries for man. The ash has a soul that laughs. The birch has a pure soul, the pine is gentle, the dogwood innocent, the aspen fickle, the sweet gum sultry, the beech enchanting, the redwood majestic.

The oak has a sacred soul. It is strong and protective. The oak is a friend to man. The gallant way it stands against the elements is an inspiration, and I honestly feel that she spoke to me that night and beckoned me to come into her branches for protection against the forces. I believe she saved my life. Call it instinct if you care to, or call it intuition, or a sixth sense that registered in my subconscious the fact that there was a weak limb fifty feet over my hut, or call it luck. I call it a miracle.

The night of the storm, I learned all about a tree. The following day I learned about myself.

I asked myself a lot of questions that were not easy to answer. Why had I climbed the tree? Why wasn't I killed? What am I supposed to do now—now that I have realized I had been spared? Would this experience change my life? What was there left for me to do or experience for which I had been saved? To me there is no coincidence in this life. Everything has a purpose, and therefore every action or lack of it has a purpose. Most people would squash a tiny insect without realizing that it is a vital link in the food chain that allows them to live. We are learning more and more the interdependency of all life. We see how an insecticide in the fields of Iowa affect the fish in the Gulf of Mexico. We are all related, and nothing is complete without the other. We are all essentially one huge organism like the cells of a large body, each doing our job to keep the whole alive and well.

I climbed down out of the tree and pulled what remained of the leaf hut apart in order to get my blanket. The limb of the oak had pierced it through. Again I thanked the Great Spirit for my safety, for my escape. Again I was reassured that my life-style of following instinct, my sixth sense, was valid.

The trail north was the one I followed that day. I was curious as to what might have happened to the pack train. I didn't try to follow their trail. It would have been difficult at best after the storm of the previous night, but not impossible. Instead I figured that they would have traveled straight up the valley to a pass that ran between the giant mountains to the east and out of the park. After that storm, I was sure that they would be anxious to get out of these mountains.

It was a clear cool day with a breeze out of the west that came down from the mountain carrying my scent before it into the valley. The trail was littered with leaves and branches, but every so often I spotted a print of an animal that had been caught away from its burrow by the storm and was hurrying home before it was discovered—like some husband who lost track of the time at a poker game and is trying to sneak in before his wife discovers what time it is.

The prints of a striped skunk were headed north with me along this trail. He would stop momentarily to look around and sniff the air, but he was quite intent on getting to his hole. I guessed it would be down the mountain toward the stream. Once he stopped to dig by the trail for some insects. I suppose he didn't have much time last night to hunt. I was right. When he left the trail, he headed on an elk run down into the valley and, I hope, safety. A skunk abroad during the day is easy prey for fox, cougar, or even a hungry bear.

Suddenly there was a sound similar to an explosive alarm clock coming from the pines above me. It was a red squirrel. Something must be coming. I looked up the elk run and saw a group of cows being led by an antlered bull down the mountain to graze in some of the lowland pasture. If only the hunting party had been here, they would have had a chance at a kill. I wonder how anyone could kill such a magnificent animal. This male was at least 700 pounds and proud with his dark maned neck stretching to catch the scent and lead his herd to a safe feeding ground. He looked back up the mountain for a moment, and at that instant I moved back. First out of his line of vision, and then to a spot where I might conceal myself and watch them pass closely. I knew that as soon as they got downwind, my scent would alert them and send them in a mad dash into the valley.

The spot I chose was right on the run and concealed by some boulders and small pine trees. I flattened out behind the rocks and listened as their hooves scraped the rocks in their descent. They passed me on the run, not ten inches from where I lay. They are huge animals, especially if you're looking up at them, so I remained very still and careful not to spook them. One kick from their sharp hoofs could disable a cougar and, I'm sure, crush my skull. Three females passed me with their young bull. About ten yards down the run, one of them caught my scent, gave the alarm, and the race was on.

I was tempted to jump up and run after them down the mountain, but knew that their great speed would make me look completely ridiculous. Instead, I looked up to the pine where the red squirrel was chewing on a cone and nodded in gratitude.

The trail was a treasure-trove of tracks. Every animal on the mountain must be out repairing or exploring what damage had been caused by the storm. It was exciting to see the prints of porcupine and fox and deer mice crossing each other. I laughed, thinking of the Keystone Kops running in and out of hotel doors, chasing themselves and some criminal. The fox was like that, crisscrossing the trail numerous times in pursuit of some prey— a mouse or red squirrel. I don't believe he was very successful.

At one point on the trail, I saw the prints of a black bear. It must have been five feet long and, judging by the depth of his paw prints, 320 pounds. He was the only animal heading up the mountain. Must have passed the storm in the valley and was heading over the mountain where it might be safer. Why didn't he stay where he was? There was plenty of food here.

I had almost forgotten. The hunting party! They must have gone off the trail and into the valley to camp. I decided to backtrack the bear and see if my assumption was correct.

What I found was interesting indeed. The bear and the hunters had spent the night not twenty yards from each other. I'm glad that most hunters are inept at finding game. It gives the animals better-than-average chance in the woods. On the plains, or in an open area, it is another story. There, all a hunter needs is a good pair of field glasses and a steady hand. The rifles that are used today can fell an elk at five hundred yards. That's almost too far for the animal to be able to scent.

This bear woke up early and headed in the opposite way the hunters were moving. He followed their trail up the mountain. I wished I had been here to see the show. Hunters rustling around, trying to clean up their camp from the storm, not noticing a 300-pound bear sneaking off up the mountain. One thing did impress me. They were making good time. Too good to notice the raccoon who had sat on a rock and watched them ride by. Too good to notice the owl at the base of a pine or the screech owl which sat high up in the branches and slept the day away. Too good to stop and watch the trout feed or notice the way the red squirrel placed mushrooms on tree branches to dry for its winter feasts.

These hunters were good woodsmen. They were clean and careful, but because they had come to kill, they were alien.

They missed the essential beauty of this great wilderness area. I'm sure they noticed the mountains and valleys, and could experience the sunsets the same as anyone, but they missed the majority of the abundant animal life that surrounded them constantly.

I came to this wilderness to experience all that it had to offer. I wanted to observe its wildlife and taste its wild grasses. I wanted to sleep under her stars and feel her rain and snow on my face. I wanted to track her game and watch her birds of prey hunt the mountainsides. I came to this wilderness to learn, not to kill. All I would take from her was the knowledge of her heartbeat not the rack of a mature bull elk.

I know that in years to come, I will have no trophies hanging on my den wall. No visual remembrance of my trip to this wilderness. What I will have, instead, is the knowledge of what makes this wilderness different from all the others. That is what I'll be able to relate to my children. I won't be able to tell them how I sighted through the scope of my 357 magnum Winchester and felled a mighty elk with one shot at four hundred yards. I can only tell them that a herd passed ten inches from my nose, and they smelled wet and sour. I can only tell of the grunts they made to each other as they made their way down the mountain, like the grunts of acknowledgement I make when my son points out something interesting to me.

Life in this wilderness area was abundant beyond belief. I have never seen such a variety of life and so much of it. There were raccoons, woodchuck, red bats, and white-tailed rabbit. My time there was meaningful. Up to this time I had discovered a natural cathedral and experienced the soul of an oak. I had come so close to an elk that I could have touched it and had avoided death by choosing a night of danger in a tree. It was, you might say, satisfying.

The group of hunters traveled on. I gave up my pursuit. The area was too interesting to let it pass without a more thorough investigation. I stayed in this area by the stream for three days until the first snowfall, before I decided it was time to be heading on.

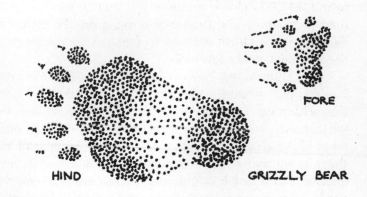

FORE

HIND   GRIZZLY BEAR

10/My Brother the Grizzly

*I woke one morning, crawled out of my leaf hut into six inches of
snow. It had fallen softly the night before and blanketed the area
white and sparkling in the morning sun. Tracks of chipmunk, rabbit, squirrel, and raccoon crisscrossed the clearing in front of my
hut. Seeing all those tracks and not an animal in sight made me
realize just how late I was getting up. A gray jay in a nearby pine
scolded me for sleeping so late.*

More snow than I had expected fell that night. There was well
over a foot of new snow accumulated, and it was still falling.
However, its quiet beauty more than made up for the difficulty of
travel its depth might impose. Snow falls lightly for me, even in a
blizzard. It comforts my spirit as it covers me and my Mother Earth
with its feathery comforter. Snow does not chill me. It does not

make me cold. Rather it is an insulation, like so many down feathers. Snow falls and flows through me, filling me with a sense of pureness. All things are equal under the snow. All are one— one color, one brilliance in the sun. All covered, protected as if the Great Spirit tossed a giant quilt over His creation to protect it from the icy northern winds.

Snow is an excellent insulation. Ask any Eskimo. If the snow kept coming, I would make a shelter from it. Though taken by the snow's hypnotic dance on the light air that was getting ever stronger, I knew that I must be moving on. To insure an easier passage, I cut some saplings and began to construct a pair of crude but effective snowshoes.

I cut the saplings which were about an inch round into four two-and-a-half-foot lengths. These would be the side bars for the snowshoes. I always carried lengths of leather about my waist for just such emergencies. I cut some and tied the ends of the saplings, after a little carving, to form the outline of my snow-shoes. I cut some shorter pieces to use as crossbars and lashed them securely to the side pieces. I was careful to use the longer and sturdier pieces where the greatest weight of the foot would be placed. It looked much like a conventional snowshoe when I was finished. The pair I left in New Jersey had leather stretched and sewn over it to give it yet more strength, but I didn't have any leather. Instead, I used pine boughs and wove them tightly between the crossbars. They would help support my weight in the deep snow, even if they did slow me down. I was happy with my craft and allowed myself a compliment as I used the last of my leather strips to lash the snowshoes to my feet and legs. By the time I finished, the snow had almost stopped falling.

I decided to cut over the mountain instead of following the main trail. It was the way the bear had gone, avoiding well-worn paths in order to avoid the hunters. I would do well to follow the bear, I thought. Off I climbed, though I couldn't have climbed any higher than I felt. The past couple of weeks had been enriching. I had experienced a spiritual reawakening. I had been reaffirmed dozens of times. I had grown. The time spent in these mountains had been good. I was high.

At the edge of the tree line, before a meadow that stretched over the summit of the mountain, I spied a fallen tree. It had been blown over, perhaps a year before in a storm long forgotten except for this giant fir tree, which points an accusing finger in the direction the storm had taken and gone. Its root system was immense. It looked like the ruins of some ancient castle leaning there brown and white against the gray sky. Somewhere a jay called.

I wondered what kind of a cave that forgotten storm had created under its roots when it toppled that giant fir. If it was as large as I figured, it would be an excellent hibernation spot for a sleepy bear. A grizzly, perhaps. I wondered if I should stop and say hello to my brother. My mind wandered longer than my legs. I headed straight for the tree.

When I was twenty yards from it, I quietly removed my snowshoes and began a very cautious crawl toward the opening left by the torn-up roots of the fir. If there was a grizzly in there, and if I ever woke him, I would be my brother's final meal before his winter nap.

Bears sleep very soundly in hibernation. Small animals have been known to curl up to them for warmth. The females do awaken enough to bear their cubs during this time, and some bears have been known to wander about when they should be sleeping, but on the whole, they sleep long and hard. I was counting on this, but was being cautious just in case I should happen on a light sleeper. All I thought of was the bear-slapping story Stalking Wolf had told me, which ended in the tragic death of his boyhood friend.

A deep, heavy breathing coming from under the roots alerted me. I was so happy I could shout. What kind of a bear would it be? I bellied over the trunk of the tree and hung my body over the opening like some fat snake looking for an afternoon meal. There by the opening was the rump of a grizzly. I remembered my promise to the park ranger to bring him a present from my brother.

I reached for my knife and wrapped my legs around a giant root and hung suspended over the opening so that I could touch the grizzly. With my knife I cut a swatch of hair from his rump. "Hope you don't catch cold, my brother," I whispered.

The next thing I was doing was tumbling down the opposite side of the mountain. I took great strides on my snowshoes and leaped high into the air, flipped over, and landed flat on my back. I did this over and over and laughed till my lungs burned. I was happy.

That evening I fashioned a necklace of the grizzly hair. It was shaped around an acorn to symbolize the night I spent in the oak. A necklace from my brother the grizzly and the oak for my brother the park ranger. The wind increased and blew drifts against the trees. I lay warm in my snow hut and dreamed.

It snowed again that night. The branches of the fir and pine groaned under the weight of the snow. The sun was bright, however, and the trees would soon be relieved of their winter burdens. In the snow along the way I spotted the tracks of a weasel. He was a long-tailed weasel and must have been active just before dawn. What a mess he'd made of the snow where he was hunting. His trail showed swift changes of direction, odd loopings, backtracking. He was a curious little creature. Where his prints were clear, they were twin with four toes and a pad that formed a triangle. These pairs were anywhere from ten to eighteen inches apart. This animal used alternately long and short leaps, and often its hind feet would register on its foreprints.

I followed this little critter's prints till the sun was very high. Every so often his tail would register in the snow. How I wished I had been here the night before to watch this efficient hunter white against the snow, leap about like a coiled spring in search of food. He couldn't have been ten inches long or more than an inch in diameter. Stalking Wolf said they look like a piece of rope.

I followed his erratic path into a grove of fir and discovered where he had dived into the snow, tunneled for some twenty feet, and reemerged to go on about his hunting. He was looking for a rabbit hole he remembered being around here someplace, because he did this same thing three times in the same area. I don't believe he found the hole, however, because there were no rabbit remains in the vicinity. Some people will have you believe that weasels sometimes kill for the sheer enjoyment of it, but I have never found that to be true.

The weasel loped off deeper into the woods, but I didn't follow. By the signs of his trail I knew that they had been made at about the time of first light, and he would be heading for his den. I didn't want to disturb his sleep. He had had a difficult night and had been unsuccessful in his hunt. I turned and headed down the mountain toward the park ranger's cabin. A rough-legged hawk soared overhead with its wing tips flared. I shaded my eyes against the late afternoon sun and watched it spiral upward on an invisible thermal escalator of rushing air.

Buteo logopus hunts at dawn and at dusk, I thought. I'd better hurry if I want to reach the cabin before sunset. I wanted to stay and get a glimpse of the hawk's feathered legs as it lowered its talons to swoop on a mouse or a lemming, but decided against it. My days in this wilderness were almost numbered. It was time to go. I continued my descent. A shrill squeal that I knew immediately to be the death cry of a deer mouse turned my attention back toward the hawk. The mouse was silent in death, but the heavy flapping of the hawk's wings directed my eyes. I saw the feathers on his legs and below them the limp body of his evening meal.

The sun was at my back, and I cast a long shadow as I came over the last rise that led across a broad meadow to the ranger's cabin. I was excited as most people are when they are nearing the end of a journey. The birds were flying in great flocks overhead to their evening roosts. I felt elated, like a soldier coming home from the wars, marching to the music made by a thousand bird voices. I stepped high and lengthened my stride. Snow was flying everywhere. With my antics and giant shadow, I must have looked like Big Foot loping down the hill.

The ranger was out with his Irish setter and saw me. I waved and did a flip in the snow and continued down the hill as if I were a living snowball. I tumbled over and over. I could hear the dog barking and the ranger laughing. The bark was friendly.

As I approached the ranger, he said, "I didn't expect to see you coming out of the woods. I thought you had gone on your way weeks ago."

"Didn't you believe what I wrote to you?"

"At first I did, but when I rode up the trail and couldn't find you, I figured you had left the note as a practical joke."

"I saw you when you came after me. I hid beside the trail, just before the large meadow that runs down to the stream and halfway up the mountain. You looked for me in that meadow and turned back."

"How do you know that?"

"I told you. I watched you."

"If you had been there, I would have seen you."

"I was there. Had you turned your horse to the left, you would have trampled me. I was under a very small bush."

"I would have seen you!" He was like most people. He couldn't believe that he had missed something that should have been obvious to him.

"Did you know that a great horned owl hunted here last night?"

"There's a great horned in the forest across the road, so I guess that it's possible. But how would I know if it had hunted here? I sleep at night."

"Come here." I led him about five steps toward the meadow I had come across and pointed to a depression in the snow.

He looked down at it and said, "So?"

I knelt and outlined the tail and wing marks of the owl and then pointed to the talon marks at the center of the picture. "The owl swooped down on a mouse here last night, after the snow had stopped falling. He missed the mouse. See the mouse's frantic steps? He ran under that bush. The owl's body just brushed the snow here as his wings beat against the wind to break its fall. Lucky little mouse."

The ranger was convinced. "I walked right by that ten minutes ago and didn't notice it."

"I know. Here are the tracks you made then. See how the wind has worn at the edges ever so lightly? Look at this. The mouse has been back since you passed here and is in that tree." The Irish setter was at the base of the tree sniffing wildly.

"You really know your way around, don't you? I doubted you at first, but you seem to know what you're talking about."

I reached inside my shift and pulled out the necklace I had made and handed it to him.

"What's this?"

"It's the gift I promised you from my brother."

"This is grizzly hair?" He felt it and smelled it. "It is! Where did you get this, in a tree where he had rubbed?"

"No, I cut it from his rump as he was sleeping."

He was about to say something, but changed his mind and just smiled. He was through doubting what I said. He accepted it, but stood there shaking his head anyway. "There's an acorn in the middle of this."

"It's a symbol of good life and good health. My brother the oak wanted you to have it."

"Now the oak is your brother. You're related to everything, aren't you?

"We all are. Well, I'm going to be on my way." I turned and headed for the road that led to the main highway. "I'll be seeing you. Take good care of the park for us. You've got a big responsibility."

"Where are you going to stay tonight? It's cold!"

"Is it? I hadn't noticed."

"You noticed," he yelled after me. "You notice everything. You just don't care. Take care." He hesitated a moment and added, "Brother."

I turned and waved. My brother.

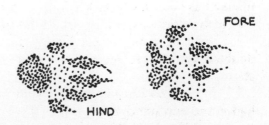

WOODCHUCK, ALSO KNOWN AS GROUNDHOG

BLACKBERRY

part three

THE SEARCH

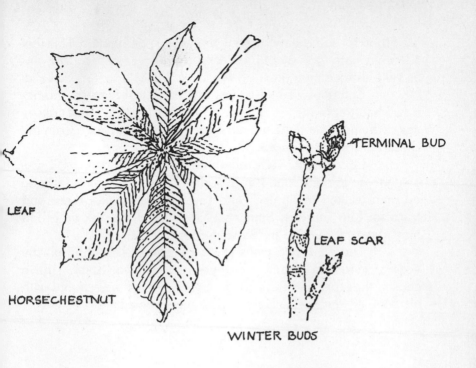

LEAF

HORSECHESTNUT

TERMINAL BUD

LEAF SCAR

WINTER BUDS

11/One Year of Survival

After Stalking Wolf had left for the reservation, and before I began a period of travel that took me throughout the United States, I spent a year in the Pine Barrens of New Jersey, completely isolated from all other people. I had tried different jobs and even tried college, but found that I was not suited for them. I knew instinctively that I belonged in the woods, but I didn't know what that meant.

Most of the stimuli I was receiving from the people around me was negative. They thought it silly, immature, or just plain irresponsible to spend so much time wandering through the woods. I should have a job and contribute to society. They couldn't see living in the woods as a contribution. I figured that if I ate wild roots that would not be eaten by anyone else and leave more civilized food for some starving soul, that was a contribution. I felt that if I could learn the way of the deer through observation, that was as valid as reading a book on the subject. No, it was more valid!

Somehow, I had to test my instinctual feelings. Somehow I had to put myself in a position to learn more. I was college age. Why not attend the university of the pines and learn from the Creator through His creation?

I decided to try living an entire year off the land. I was going to go into the Pine Barrens, deep, where no roads ran and no man walked or hunted, and I was going to exist there and learn for four seasons. Stalking Wolf called it the Twelve Moon hunt; I called it a year in the wilderness.

There are two ways to look at the world—through the eyes of man and through the eyes of the Great Spirit. I have chosen the latter and have made my peace with myself and with my Mother, the Earth. Here is how it happened.

Summer: Gentle Wanderings

I walked toward the trees across an isolated meadow. The sun was at my back, warming me and helping me gently on my way. My shirt caught on a thorn. I took it off and placed it at the foot of the bush. I spoke to the bush.

"Take my shirt, blackberry bush. You give me pleasure when I take your fruit. You tugged at my shirt as I passed. I give it to you as a gift. It will keep your roots moist when the summer sun is hot. You will have the sweetest fruit in the Barrens."

The sun was warm on my naked back. I stretched and felt the freedom of movement without seams. This is right, I thought, and I must do it. I turned my face to the sun as a memory warmed me. . . .

Grandfather spoke: "What are you searching for, Tom?"

I answered hoarsely, the word fighting its way up from deep within my soul, "Peace."

"Where will you look for it?"

"I don't know, Grandfather. In school? In religion? I don't know.

"You will look for it in the earth, Tom." Stalking Wolf was giving me a direction. It was something he seldom did. He taught rhetorically. I could hardly believe my ears. I had always had a desire to lose myself in the Barrens, but had discounted it as a childish wish to escape responsibility.

"Will I find it there?" I was hungry for the answer I wanted to hear. My question was a plea.

"Not in it, Tom, but through it." He said no more, nor did I ask again. He had said it all. The understanding was mine to discover, and I was excited and anxious to begin, but I knew that it would be some time before I had the courage. It would be only after I had exhausted the ways of the white man that I would turn to follow the words of Stalking Wolf. . . .

I was naked. The remainder of my clothes lay folded by the roots of a gnarled oak. I watched a tiny white spider work a miracle on the underside of a deep green leaf. A hawk screamed.

The idea of testing myself completely had been with me for some time. Stalking Wolf had told me how young Indian braves would often leave the tribe and survive alone for twelve moons. Through this experience, they would find themselves. The Indians believed that the Great Spirit would bring a special teaching to the isolated brave. Many Indian legends told of great discoveries made by these braves that benefited the entire tribe.

I wanted to experience a year in the wilderness. I wanted to survive without the aid of my civilization. I was apprehensive. Would the loneliness drive me mad? I was curious. Would I forget the art of speech? I was excited.

The symbols of civilization were behind me as I stood on the edge of the forest. All that remained was a knife strapped to my waist. I prayed.

"Naked I come to you."

At my feet were the tracks of a white-tailed deer. They led into the forest toward a cool spring. I followed.

I wandered gently through the Barrens for three moons. I had no destination, no place I had to be at a certain time. Some might say that I wandered aimlessly, but they do not understand the art of wandering. It is walking in the forest, and not through it. It is observation through participation.

Some might say that I was lost because I had nowhere to

go, but they do not understand that, when someone belongs everywhere, he is never lost. My beloved Pine Barrens was home. I belonged. I was as much a part of it as the deer. I was at peace.

The days and weeks passed swiftly by. During the days I watched as doe gave birth to fawn and the meadowlarks wove their ground nests and hatched their chicks. The nights were filled with fireflies and bats catching mosquitoes over the Barrens' swamps.

Time lost its meaning. I slept when I was tired and ate when I was hungry. I was time rich. I had no appointments to keep. I had no peers to impress. Yet I was never bored, and my time was full. I felt good about where I was and what I was doing.

Shelter was simply natural cover. A thick pine was often the roof of my home. A tangle of vines was often a room. I seldom sought these places for shelter. Rather, I used them as hiding places from which to observe wildlife.

The white man builds a shelter, and it becomes his prison. He shuts out the cleansing elements. He shuts out the sun, the wind, and the rain. He separates himself from the earth and refuses to budge. Therefore he is always sick.

I was living as the fox lived. I sought fresh air, sunshine, and good water. Stalking Wolf told me that when it came time for man to stop moving, the world would stop. I kept moving.

The summer rains refreshed me. I seldom sought shelter from them. Most people get chilled from the rain. I don't. I relax and let it flow through me and cleanse me. I found that I could even sleep in the rain. I learned that the elements were not adversaries. They were my brothers.

When the sun was hot, I would find a cool stream and spend my time communing with the water life. It was during one of those hot days that I discovered the location of my winter home.

I was following a deep stream. I had been in and out of it all day. It was late in the afternoon, and many of the animals would be coming to the banks of the stream to drink. I decided to float silently down the stream and observe. I'm glad I did.

The first visitors to the stream I passed were a family of skunk walking single file. On the bank I saw the rutted area where they had been digging for insects. I was turned upstream and floating backward. I didn't see the log, and when I floated into it, the noise attracted the skunks. When the mother's tail went up, I went down. I dived and swam underwater for as long as I could hold my breath. I came to the surface in a lake. The sun was setting. It turned the waters red. Sea gulls floated serenely on its surface. A bass broke water. A herd of deer came out of the pines and began to drink. I had surfaced in Eden, I thought.

The place seemed a paradise. Game was everywhere. The lake was teeming with life. Wild rice grew in its shallows along with cattail and reed. All could be eaten. I felt that this place could support me through the winter.

I constructed a fish trap in the stream. I gathered berries, roots, and nuts and taught the animals to trust me. The hours and days I spent by the lake will always be sacred.

Summer was giving way to fall. Another season. Another vision. Here is what I had done with my summer of gentle wanderings.

I was clothed in a breechcloth made from a rabbit hide that I took with a rabbit stick the first day I entered the Barrens. I had feasted on wild plants, roots, and berries and had not lost any weight. I had acquired a spear and had fire-hardened the point, and had a medicine pouch for all my precious possessions.

My possessions were these: a pebble from the bank of a stream that had fed me happily for a week, an acorn from an especially magnificent oak that had kept me company through a summer storm, the feather of a scarlet tanager, and a snapping turtle's egg. Such was my treasure. And I was happy.

Fall: Inner Visions

When fall came, I decided to stay through the winter months, beside the shallow lake fed by deep streams and cold springs. Its waters were alive with fish, its reeds filled with aquatic birds, its banks teeming with all manner of wildlife. It was an Eden where all that nature had to offer was present as a gift. All I had to do was reach out and accept the gift freely given.

Nearby, there was a wild wheat field, and around its

edges grew berries of every nature—blackberry, wild grape, and raspberry. It was as if they had been planted specifically to feed me. The trees were filled with the songs of birds, and game trails and runs crisscrossed the area in profusion.

The sun dancing across the clear lake hurt my eyes, and the reflection of the many colored leaves in its mirrored surface filled my heart with joy. It was a natural Van Gogh. Brilliant colors swirling from the water to meet the trees, blue, bright, and deep surrounding all. This would be my home.

Beside this lake I named simply Eden, I built a hogan. It was small. I made it of mud and rocks and logs. The walls were thick, and there was a small stone firebox in one corner. The floor was earth strewn with pine boughs. I changed the boughs periodically. In amongst them I tossed herbs and wild flowers. I hung roots to dry along the walls, as well as leaves for tea and flowers for seeds. The aroma, unlike that of most animal dens of feces and sweat, was of nature's most pleasing smells.

There were no windows in my small home. The door opened east onto the lake. The morning sun reflecting from the lake warmed the hogan and woke me early. I would rise, stretch, and plunge into the lake every morning till it froze solid. When that happened, I would run to the stream that fed the lake, striding through the snow barefooted and bathe in the clear cold water. I had very little reaction to the cold. The winter was no different from the summer. My body adjusted as I learned not to fight the cold but instead to accept it.

In the bank of the stream, I cut a smoking rack. I built my fire close to the water's edge and directed the smoke through a mud tunnel up through the fish and venison that I carefully laid on racks. I laid up a great store of smoked meat for the winter this way. The early frost, which turned the leaves such brilliant colors, the early flight south of the migratory birds, and the frenetic action of the squirrels made me suspect a long, hard winter.

I had not desire to hunt during the winter months. I did not want to compete with the local wildlife for the meager food available during a long winter. I wanted to hibernate. I wanted to meditate and dream. I wanted to observe and experience winter in all its natural fierceness and learn from it. I did not want to be bothered with survival. As the other seasons would be, so I wanted this to be a season of spiritual experience.

The geese were arriving and leaving straightaway. They weren't staying as I had observed in past years. The leaves of the swamp maple and oak were red and yellow. The wind that blew from the north was cold. I awoke to a thin layer of ice on Eden. It would not be long before the warm sun would relinquish its hold on the lake to the ice, unable in the short hours of the winter day to tug it from winter's grip. Soon I would be unable to plunge through the hardened water into the heart of the lake and would have to seek my morning bath elsewhere.

The rabbits ate fiercely, building their winter coats and layers of fat to see them through the cold time ahead. The ground-hogs searched for a winter hibernation, and the turtles began to disappear from the lake. I watched one dig deeply into the mud around the lake's edge. They were expecting a cold winter.

The blue jays followed the geese, and chipmunks scurried over the rocks full-pouched, carrying seeds to their winter retreats. Seed-eating birds remained. The sparrows and cardinals refused to retreat with the robin. The bluebird lined his nest for winter. The meadow grasses were heavy with seed. I had gathered much for winter gruel. The birches and ash were seed-heavy. Nature provided for her friends.

The squirrels chattered and squealed as they buried acorns and seeds and piled pine cones around tree stumps.

Oak and pine would spread, and there would be yet more fruit in the Great Spirit's forest for winters to come. The animals don't hoard. Nature won't allow that. Their hoarding turns to dispersion.

I watched the white-footed mouse store seeds and the short-tailed mouse search out mole tunnels that would lead to the succulent roots of plants and meadow bulbs. He would winter beneath the snow and have plenty to eat.

The skunk and the raccoon remained steadfast in their summer homes. They could hibernate through the coldest snow-covered weeks. They were capable of long winter naps.

During the fall, I hunted and fished. I constructed a fish trap in one of the streams and speared trout there periodically. I fished with bone hooks and spear for pickerel and bass. These I cleaned and smoked. I buried some near my hogan in a log-lined pit, which had a heavy flat rock for a lid. Some I put in a food box inside my hogan. This box was a deep hole lined with flat stones.

Paiute traps caught rabbit for my larder and snares caught pheasant. I hunted with a fire-hardened spear for deer and took enough food and clothing. The skins were made into breeches, shirts, moccasins, and a blanket. From the bones I made hooks and needles. The antlers made good tools for digging and spear heads. I tanned the hides with the brains and sewed them with the sinew. With rabbit sticks I gathered quail and cottontail.

The forest was good and provided well all that I would need for winter. As many times as I have taken deer, I shall never get over the sense of appreciation I feel every time one dies at my hands. White man kills with a gun at hundreds of yards. They never feel the life go from one of their victims. They do not appreciate its life nor do they respect its death. They look for the biggest rack, the strongest of the species. They take animals for pride.

I sought out the weakest of the herd and stalked it like a cat or wolf. I felt as though I was a part of nature, with a job to perform. My predatory nature was natural, not alien. I thinned out the herd and allowed the strong to live in order to build a stronger animal. I did not kill indiscriminately. I did not enjoy killing, but there was no guilt attached to the killing. I killed deer for clothing and meat. I took only what I needed, and I was satisfied to be a part of the natural-selection process. I felt as though I was relating to the forest as man should relate. I did not only take. I gave. I gave the herd a strong future.

Late one afternoon I took a large old buck. He was not large by Western standards, but in the Pine Barrens he would be considered huge. He dressed out at over 130 pounds by my estimate. I stood motionless beside an aspen by the edge of the wild wheat field for most of the afternoon. I watched the quail and pheasant run. I saw the fox catch a rabbit and a hawk field mice. I never moved. I was a part of the tree on the east side of the field. When I moved, my shadow would fall behind me and give no warning. I felt no weariness, nor was I stiff. I stood barefooted and breechclothed in harmony with my surroundings, searching the field for my prey.

I knew that he would come. I had observed his prints for a week. He was large and lame. If the snows were deep this winter, he would never escape the wild dogs' fangs. I decided that the Great Spirit had sent him to me. I would take this gift and thank the Great Spirit for the earth's bounty.

The brown buck broke through the underbrush just as the sun began to dip, red, below the horizon. It was a silhouette of former majesty as it stood against the red and gold backdrop, sniffing and searching the field for signs of danger. A cardinal sang an evening song. No animal warned of my presence. I was not there. I was an aspen.

Each time the noble beast dipped its head to graze or turned to nibble on leaves, I moved. I carried my spear directly in front of my body and stepped silently over the dry grass. I moved with the wind and the birdsong, feeling my way carefully across the meadow. When the buck lifted its head, I froze. Deer cannot discern between a man and a tree unless man moves. A deer sees movement. I stood motionless. I was an aspen.

The sun was almost asleep. The moon had not yet taken charge of the night. An owl awoke. Somewhere a fox barked. I moved in twilight, a shadow stalking ever closer to my quarry. I was three steps from his huge flank. His breath filled the cool night air. The sound of his chewing echoed in my head, reeling with the excitement of being so close to such a formidable animal. If he sensed my presence, he would be off in great bounding leaps, despite his lameness. If I were a pack of dogs, I would run him down, and he would kill one or two of us before we felled him. But I am a man and must rely on my cunning first and then on my strength.

His head was down again. I drew my spear back to one side, took two slow steps toward the deer's heart, and lunged with a twisting body motion. I drove the spear deep into his chest and pierced his heart. He fell where he stood. His eyes were wide with astonishment, and I felt gratitude as he realized how and by what he was to die. It all happened in an instant, but he knew.

I walked back to camp in the dark with the deer draped over my shoulders. What I did was right. I felt a sense of satisfaction and spoke to the Great Spirit: "Thank you for the meat and the hide of this fine animal. He must have had many good years and fathered many fawns in his time. I am happy that I could fulfill his life and that he could die honorably at my hands. I shall make a robe and wrap myself against the cold winds and think of his good life. Perhaps it will enable me to dream."

I made a robe from his great skin. I left the fur on so that it would provide added insulation.

I was looking forward to the winter. I wanted the silence its snow cover promised. I longed for its long nights and clear cold air, which would clear my mind and give me time to meditate and dream. Wisdom comes to us in dreams, and winter is the time for dreaming.

Stalking Wolf often made mention of a very special time in his life when he had spent the winter months in the northern mountains. He called it snow-cover winter. It was during those months that he had become convinced of the futility of the white man's ways. He related fondly how he sat almost naked in the snow and felt his body elevated beyond the cold as he relaxed and gave himself to the earth. He said that it was then that he was convinced that the Indian's ways were correct. They lived life as it ought to be lived. The white man lived a lie.

I had enough meat to last me through the winter. I stashed nuts and grasses and leaves, herbs and roots for soups and teas. I was ready. My moccasins were made, as were my buckskins. I had rabbit mittens and fur-lined slippers and enough deadfall timber piled around my hogan to warm my body and cook my food.

Come winter. Come dreams.

These Barrens are mine. They give me meat and clothing. I know streams and springs and lakes where fish dance and flash in the sun. The Barrens say, "Come and eat of my bounteous goodness. Come, take my game from the land and fish from my waters." The Great Spirit endowed His people with a pleasant climate and all they needed for shelter and clothing. I felt equally blessed.

I communed with the elements. I drank the rain, and I rose and set with the sun. One morning late in the season of inner vision I rose to the sun fighting through the mist that guarded the lake at night. I stepped to the water's edge, and noticed the mist swirling like hundreds of dancers moving before the wind. I threw handfuls of clear, cold water into my face and plunged in bodily.

I stood erect on shore after my bath before the advancing dawn. I faced the sun dancing dimly on the horizon. In my heart I offered an unspoken invocation filled with thanksgiving.

My daily devotions had become through the months more necessary to me than food. How I long now for those silent mornings beside the lake! A fish jumped, a bird awakened with a morning song. The smell of the sweet earth rose to greet me from beneath my feet. And the silence ministered to my soul.

I learned to worship as the Indian worshipped. Whenever I came upon something beautiful, be it a clear spring lined with lilies or a thunderhead silhouetted against the sun, a majestic hart or a warren of baby bunnies so young that they were pink and blind, I would stop for an instant in an attitude of worship. All my days were sabbaths, since they all belonged to the Great Spirit.

The wind rose steadily and blew the dancers from the lake and chased the clouds across the sun. The wind is a free spirit, I thought. Today I will run with the wind and race the sun. Many times during my year alone I would break into a run for the sheer joy of feeling the wind in my hair and the tautness of my muscles. I would give a war whoop and take off after a rabbit or break through a herd of grazing deer. It felt good to stretch my muscles hard and beat my feet against the earth with great bursts of speed. It was a celebration. My joy was so great that I couldn't contain it. It would break out in a screaming run across fields and through woods.

Today, I would run for endurance. There was an idea that I had been chasing in my dreams through the night. I had seen a young Indian boy running across a desert with a huge stone in his arms. I don't know how long he had been running, but when he came to his village, he ran to an old man, dropped the stone at his feet, and upon a nod from the old warrior he spat a mouthful of water on the stone. He had run through thirst with a mouthful of water! Why? Somehow I knew that it was tied to survival. Some day he might have to spend days in the desert with a limited amount of water and have to travel many miles to survive. But what was the dream saying to me? There was one sure way to find out. Run!

I grabbed my spear and ran toward the rising sun. I followed game trails and old roads, leaped over narrow streams and plunged through thickets. I had decided that nothing would impede my traveling east. As I loped I would trade hands with the spear. At times I would rest it on my shoulder. Whenever I came to a clearing, I would toss the spear at an imaginary target and sweep it from the ground as I ran by. I never stopped running.

I ran on through the morning till the sun was high. I kicked up game in every field and thicket. I ran quietly, loping mostly, and would be upon the rabbits, pheasants, quail, even deer before they had time to run or conceal themselves. When I ran into deer, I would take off after them and laugh as they bounded gracefully away through the pines with their white tails raised in alarm.

Midday I rested. I lay down in the leaves beneath an oak, read the mouse tracks, listened to the squirrel that chattered over my head and chewed on a piece of smoked venison. The sun was moving in and out of clouds, which told of a coming storm. The air was cooling considerably. I watched a cardinal search the ground for seeds. We must all be strong and prepared for the worst, I thought. We must all have the strength to survive. But how was the will related to the strength?

The wind kicked leaves up all around me. I will know strength if I know the freedom of the wind. I stood and began to run again. I ran with the wind. I raced the sun. I could reach my camp before nightfall or fail the test. Somewhere, deep inside, a decision had been made for me. My spiritual strength would be measured by my physical endurance. The two were not the same, but they were tied to each other. The one lent insight to the other. This was the test. My body must follow my spirit's commands, or perish.

Where survival depends on discipline and strength, a person must be able to push himself beyond the normal boundaries of physical endurance. I had often pushed myself. I would do it again. I would pass the test my soul had set, or leave the Barrens before winter. If I could not beat the sun to camp, I knew that I would never survive the winter.

I found myself driven to lengthening my stride and seeking a more direct route of travel. I broke through more thickets and refrained from chasing the four-leggeds I ran across. My body seemed to respond to the added demands for speed with thanksgiving. I felt only elation as I sped through the difficult terrain. I was a bird on the wing racing to my roost. When a branch lashed my side, I felt exhilaration, whipped on ever faster by my spirit. My body responded to every challenge with joy and agility. It sang.

The sun was sinking in a dark cloud like a ball of fire when I broke through the underbrush that separated the woods from my lake. My heart was filled at that moment as the streams are filled with water when the snow melts in spring. My strength would endure. The winter was mine for dreaming! "Whoop . . . Whooeee!" I screamed as I dived into the lake and swam to the shore by my hogan.

As I climbed from the lake, the last red rays of the sun disappeared into the night. I stood before it in silence. I offered a prayer of thanksgiving to the Great Spirit. All that could be heard in the great silence was the wild beating of my heart. The Great Spirit had smiled on me and made me glad.

Winter: Snow Cover

As I had suspected, the snows were heavy that winter. The nights were long and the silences deep. I spoke little during those months and discovered a spiritual balance of body, mind, and spirit. I became like the snow-covered forest about me. Silent.

Stalking Wolf had told me that the holy silence was the Great Spirit's voice. He encouraged long periods of speechless listening. He urged me to understand the great mystery of silence. The white man seems to think that speech is some sort of proof of superiority over dumb creation. It is not. It is but one of the many gifts the Great Spirit has given to man. To the Indian, silence is the cornerstone of character.

I sought my character through the fruits of silence, aided by the snow cover. I worked all winter in the wind and snow with bare arms and legs, and seldom felt the cold. I wore a breechcloth much of the time and bathed in the stream. The Great Spirit smiled on me and kept me healthy.

Each day I would notice the animal tracks in the snow

about my hogan. Mice lived in my woodpile. Cardinals came to eat some of the seeds I tossed outside about the door. The squirrel dug tunnels to its caches of nuts. The rabbits were always active, as was the fox. A raccoon, the eternal scavenger, came nightly to my door. The deer had a winter lie in a thick stand of pines across the wheat field and stayed close to home.

Late one afternoon, as it began to snow, I walked into the middle of the wild wheat field, and dug through the snow cover to the ground. I placed a fur rug on the exposed ground, wrapped myself in my robe, and sat. There I waited to observe the storm.

The snow fell wet and heavy. It fell in great huge flakes. I could almost make out their individual, intricate patterns as they drifted by my vision. When one landed on my robe, the pattern its outline formed momentarily made visible the beauty nature bestowed on this tiny part of creation.

A fox came to the edge of the clearing and sniffed the snow-laden air for prey. It made its way around its perimeter like a shrewd cat, soundlessly. One last foray before the storm. I had noticed some rabbit markings as I entered the field. Perhaps he would have a rabbit to fill his stomach through the storm. I wondered what he would think when he came to my moccasin prints and human scent. He would look out into the field for a man. He would see a mound being covered with snow. Would he think me a fallen deer? No, not the cunning fox. He would know the mound was a man. Yet, he would be perplexed. Man seeks shelter in the storm. The fox knew only the white man.

By nightfall the trees and bushes were struggling under the weight of the heavy snow cover. I was almost completely buried. Each pine bough carried a burden that seemed too heavy. I ached for their straining tissues. The birches were beginning their slow swing to the ground.

The forest, nature's university, instructed me. If man wants to learn, all he has to do is turn to the Great Spirit's book, creation, and read through observation. I read that afternoon and through the night, and learned much.

The hardwood trees stand staunch against the heavy advance of the snow. They gather it in their branches to see who can hold the greatest weight. They neither yield nor bend. They either stand or break. The forest was filled with the sound of dead branches cracking under the strain. They would snap loudly from their trunks and crash through the trees to the forest floor. Nature pruning her trees.

The softwood trees dipped under the snow's weight. They were content to bend rather than break. They had learned to survive a different way. They would bend to the breaking point, shed their snow cover, and spring back to gather more.

I must face the storms of life in the same manner. I learned from the hardwoods that there was a time when I should stand and not yield, a time to be pruned by experience. There was also a time to bend and yield to inevitable pressures so that I might spring back to face another day. I was the hardwood; I was the softwood. I was all of creation, and it was all of me. To separate my understanding of man and nature into different categories would be disastrous. I would never understand either.

The snow treated me as part of the landscape. It drifted over me. Covered me completely. I was a drift over a bush or rock. It became my friend. It insulated me from the cold.

Night fell. The snow continued. The silence increased, broken only by the sounds of branches snapping and crashing. The night birds were silent. The fox never barked. By morning light all was covered under nature's protective white, silent cover.

The sunlight filtered through my covering and beckoned me to reach out to her. The birds were chirping. Their calls were muffled through the snow cover. The snow softens the hard-frozen winter world. It gives an intimacy to the immediate surroundings. Sounds, unable to carry far before being swallowed up by the soft snow cover, never invade from any great distance. There is only you and the life directly about you, surrounded, protected, and blanketed by the snow cover.

I answered the sun's beckonings and dug a hole through my covering at eye level and was immediately dazzled by the bright reflection on the snow. Well more than a foot covered the ground. The pine boughs bowed to the morning, the laurel curtsied. The birch touched its head to the ground, humbled before the awesome, royal power of nature.

A rabbit dug its way out from under a laurel bush. He tried valiantly to support himself on the soft snow. The snow would hold his weight for only a moment and then begin to swallow him. After three hops, each deeper into the snow, he retreated back under his bush. There he would wait until the sun had packed the snow enough to support him. The birds were supported by the snow, but were kept from their feeding by its cover. Their wings left delicate marks when they landed and took flight.

Two doe came to the clearing and decided to cross. They moved laboriously toward me. The storm had made the snow depth almost two feet, and a foot beneath the latest cover was a crust their hoofs would break through each time they took a step. The passage was difficult and tiring for a large animal. They passed within inches of my peephole. Their sides heaved with the effort it took to move through deep snow.

There had been no dogs in this part of the Barrens for three seasons. That was due to my presence. They respected my dominance and skirted the area about my hogan and the lake. I prayed for the deer's sake that they would continue to respond to their fear of man and stay out of the area around me now. These deer would be easy prey for a wild-dog pack.

Two dogs barked. The deer leaped for the pines. They struggled through the deep snow. Two large dogs jumped into the clearing in pursuit. I looked quickly to the deer. If they could make it to the woods, they would be safe. There, the snow between the trees was easier to navigate. The footing was more stable, and they could outdistance the dogs. If they couldn't, I would have to move. I prepared myself to break out of my cocoon, whooping and waving my arms. The dogs would be startled, and I hoped the results would be that they would be sent packing. Another glance at the deer assured me of their safety, and I remained motionless beneath my snow cover. The dogs passed close by in their vain pursuit. Their tongues hung from the sides of their mouths, and the clear air was filled with the steam of their breath. In their own savage way, they were as beautiful as the doe.

In the intimacy of those snow-cover hours I prayed. I worshipped the Great Spirit that was able to create such beauty and fill it with silence. I thanked Him for the life that struggled for survival all about me—for the snow, for the sun, for the sacred wind. He had let me travel to the center of His creation and had shown me goodness and beauty. I knew that His Spirit shaped all things and made me a guardian over them. He had given me the power to let live and destroy, the knowledge of plants and herbs, and the serenity of worship. He had shown me His creation, and I had seen. I thanked Him silently.

At midday, I broke out of my igloo. I took a deep breath and pushed myself straight up through the snow and spread my arms wide, stretching toward the sun. I smiled. I laughed, my head lay back, sucking the cold air from the stark blue sky. A red-tailed hawk, circling overhead, dipped momentarily, startled at the strange sight he had just witnessed. A giant bearded butterfly had just burst from the bowels of the earth.

Snow cover had been good medicine. I was hungry.

Spring: Fox Find

Tracking in the spring mud is like following footprints across a deserted beach. My mind can wander through the forest, picking up bird calls, drinking in the yellow green of the new growth pine, and feeling the afternoon sun take the chill out of the early spring air. It is fun. It is easy. I was following a fox. He stepped lightly and quickly. He turned swiftly to follow some familiar scent, but decided not to follow. Here he dug through the leaf cover and took a shrew, tearing it from its tunnel home. There on a flat rock exposed to the slanting rays of the sun, he devoured it. Bits of gray fur clung to the rock.

I followed his trail off toward a stream. He expected to catch some small animal watering itself before it retired for the evening. He stopped by a well-worn deer trail. Here he crouched, his chest marking the ground. I could see the depressions made by his heavy breathing. He was searching for signs of danger. This cunning predator was prey for the fearsome dog packs that still roamed the Pine Barrens. They frequented the deer trails.

I stopped to check the deer tracks. The doe were heavy, pregnant with fawn. This was a small herd, accompanied by a small, young buck. A robin landed on the trail and plucked a worm from the mud and leaves as easily as I would a persimmon from a tree. Remarkable hunters. He was a deep-red-breasted male, the first I had seen this spring. A good-medicine sign.

"You're early." I spoke to him with my eyes. He looked

surprised to see a man where last year there had been only deer. The males came first. They established their territories. In a week, maybe two, the females would arrive and courtship would begin. Spring is here!

I looked again at the deer tracks and saw something among them I could hardly believe—a child's sneaker print. It was less than an hour old. I scanned the area for adult prints. None. This spot was miles from the nearest road. "Lost."

I sighted the sun. There was an hour's light left. He would keep to the trail as long as it was light, but I'd better hurry. I started to run in the direction his tracks led me. My mind raced ahead of me to what might lie down the trail. Were there any deep streams, pits, quick, and flats? No. Dog packs? I quickened my pace.

By his tracks I could tell the child was a boy about forty pounds and left-handed. His toes pointed out, and he often shuffled through the leaves and mud. He was exhausted, moving on nervous energy. He was too afraid to stop, and he had an hour's lead on me.

There was a new moon. The night would be black. The boy would never be able to keep to the trail. A crow called, and starlings flew distressed from their roosts as I crashed through the underbrush in pursuit of the little boy.

Where had he come from? There was a deepwater creek in the direction from which he had traveled. But that was a full day's march away. Had he been wandering all day? He must have wandered off from a canoeing party. If he had, he had traveled miles. The poor kid must be in a state of shock.

The sun was hanging low in the sky, about to pull the horizon up about itself and retire. Again, I was racing the sun. In the dim red light of the setting sun I saw what I feared most. I sensed them before their distinct markings registered a warning in my mind. Dog prints.

They crossed the trail. I ran by, wondering how they could have missed the scent of a frightened boy only minutes old. They hadn't. Their prints were there on the trail before me. Shadows played through the pine on the wicked prints of—

They were moving at a full gallop. How many? Five? Six? My God!

I leaped forward with a reckless abandon. I was racing over open ground, swift as the wind toward the tape and the prize. . . . Branches that whipped my face didn't exist. Thorns that tore at my flesh went unnoticed. I trampled and broke anything in my path, and saw nothing. I ran rapidly, listening intensely for a sound I didn't want to hear. My heart beat loudly in my chest. God, how could I hear? Blood pounded through my head. God, how could I see?

I moved instinctively, sidestepping the greater obstacles, leaping others, and trampling the lesser, until a low horrible bark reached my ears. It was followed by a cacophony of mad yelps and a whimpering scream. Birds cried in protest from the treetops.

The sound made by the boy was not one that anyone would recognize as human. I had heard similar sounds made by animals about to die at the fangs or talons of a predator. It welled up through a million years of civilization, carried by the fear of certain death. A prehistoric cry of futility and anger. To the civilized ear, the ear of the white man, it would not have been discerned from the yelps of the raging dogs. It spoke to my instincts, and I responded with a rage I'll never forget.

I broke madly through the pines into a ravine filled with ravenous dogs drunk with the prospect of a kill, jealous of their quarry and constructed for death. Efficient, fearless killing machines. In the darkness, dimly bathed in the red half-light of sunset, they were shadows of death.

A rock found its way into my hand, and flew just as quickly into the open mouth of the lead dog, snapping its jaw like a twig. A stick flew end over end into the side of another, cracking ribs as it struck hard and knocking it from its feet. My heel caught another in the rump, displacing its hip. One leaped at my face, and I grabbed it with both hands by the throat. Squeezing with all my strength I fell over backward and kicked up at its belly with both feet. It fell hard out of the ravine. I flung its windless body up out of the ravine and was on my feet facing the last dog.

In that tiny valley, there was no way for the dog to get behind me. I had the advantage as I reached for my knife. This one, I would have to kill. His eyes glowed demonically in the near darkness, and his snarls filled the ravine. Suddenly there was a change in the animal's eyes. Had he been a man, I would have called it doubt. Being a wild dog, I would term it understanding. He knew I was not only unafraid, but that I was ready to kill. He backed a step, then two, and turned tail and ran. I listened to their retreat, as the beaten dogs dragged their broken bodies through the underbrush.

The light was completely gone. I listened for any sound of the boy. Had I heard a scream for help or a death cry? A faint whimpering sob beneath an overhang relieved my fears. Heavy rains had washed out a section beneath the roots of an aspen, and wild grapevines growing down made a natural shelter. I reached into the blackness and grabbed a skinny leg so he wouldn't bolt. Shock makes lost children run from their rescuers.

"It's over," I said. I pulled his muddy little body out and held him close to my chest. I filled the night with soft words in an effort to slow his shallow, rapid breathing. He fought at me, kicking and slashing with his tiny limbs. He never opened his eyes. God, he must have been terrified.

"Don't be afraid. I won't hurt you," I said soothingly, surprised at the sound of my voice after a winter's silence. "Nothing will harm you now. You're safe." I petted his coarse hair and patted at his bony back. An owl hooted in the distance. "Listen. Even old man owl says it's okay." His breathing slowed.

I lifted him to my back and made straight for my hogan. He needed shelter and food. He clung to my shoulders and dug his fingers into my neck as I jogged down familiar trails toward home. His left arm was much stronger than his right. Left-handed. There I gave him meat to eat and wrapped him in a buckskin robe before a Seminole star fire. He drank some catnip tea, and I bedded him down by the fireplace in my hogan. He never uttered a word.

I knew that I would have to start out at first light and find his parents. Had it been a moonlit night, I would have attempted to backtrack immediately.

I knew that his parents must be out of their minds with worry. I asked him his name, but he would not answer. I began to wonder if he could speak. That only added to my concern. "Okay, if you won't give me your name, I'll give you one. I think I'll call you Lefty." I don't think he heard me. He fell into a deep sleep.

I returned from my morning bath and meditation to find Lefty awake. I noticed by his prints that he had been watching my every move.

"Want to take a bath?" I asked. "You sure could use one."

He wrapped his arms around himself as if shivering with cold and shook his head, no.

"It's not cold, really, unless you want it to be cold."

He looked at me as if to say, you've got to be kidding.

I motioned him to the lake. "Come on. Just your hands and face, then."

He approached hesitantly, but was soon washing vigorously.

I speared a fish in the reeds near where he was washing, and we had it for breakfast. Still, he didn't speak.

A chickadee landed on a branch overhead. He had come to beg breakfast. I held out a seed and made a kissing sound. He flew to my arms and plucked the seed from my fingertips.

"Here." I handed him a seed. "You try it."

He held up his hand, but made no sound. I wondered if he could speak. I made the kissing sound till the little black cap flew to his arms and snatched the seed.

"You're a natural," I said. He smiled for the first time. "You want to go home? He nodded.

"Get on board!" I lifted him to my back, and we were off. We backtracked his confused trail in the hopes of running into a search party.

His trail was easy to follow. He had broken twigs and branches, kicked up leaves, and recorded his movements in a manner that invited detection. Why hadn't his parents or the searchers been able to follow such an easy trail? The answer was that they didn't know what to look for. If I tried to read a book on nuclear physics, I would get hopelessly lost. That's the way it is with most people in the woods. It's not that reading the land is so difficult, it's just that it takes time and understanding, something few people today seem to have.

As we walked, I talked, pleased to hear the sound of my voice again. It hadn't changed. I pointed out the trees and plants to my little passenger. Named the animal tracks and fed him some natural foods. We munched on young clover leaves and weed shoots. I lifted him into a birch and let him swing it to the ground. The meadowlarks were returning. Hawks filled the air. Somewhere a dog barked. Lefty clung tighter to my neck.

"Don't worry. He's too far off to bother us. Besides, he's heading in another direction. See, the birds are calm. You can tell if a predator is near by watching the little animals and the birds. The mice will tell you if an owl is present."

My mind raced back to the lessons I had learned from Stalking Wolf. The phrase "Go ask the mice" rang in my head. For just a moment I thought it might be nice to have Lefty stay with me. I could teach him all I knew. A mouse ran across some rocks and under a root. Spring growth was poking green through the brown ground cover.

A flock of starlings suddenly took off from beyond some pines. Lefty pointed to them. I stopped and listened carefully. Voices broke the silence. Two people were calling hoarsely.

I lifted the boy from my back. "So your name's David. That's a good name too." He smiled. "They your parents?" He nodded. "Going to call to them?" He shook his head, no.

"Listen, they are just beyond those pine trees there. You just walk straight ahead, and you'll find them. I'm going back now." I turned to go and thought of something I had almost forgotten. I turned back and smiled. "Hey, it was good talking to you."

I stepped into the pine and heard him call after me, "What's your name?"

I stuck my head through the branches and answered, "Tom. What's yours?"

"Lefty." His grin stretched from ear to ear.

I disappeared, making myself invisible in the undergrowth. His eyes searched after me, but I could tell he had lost me. His parents came to him in that tiny clearing. They hugged and cried and called him David. Once he turned and pointed toward where I had disappeared, but the parents weren't listening. They were so happy to see their boy that nothing else mattered.

A tear rolled slowly down my cheek and onto the laurel leaf. I followed it as it flowed down the contours of the leaf to yet another and another until it disappeared into the brown earth.

The sound of a rabbit being attacked by a hawk drifted across the Barrens, and drew my concentration up from the ground. They were gone.

A chickadee called.

The warm sun of the spring day reinforced my sense of worth. Spring had arrived. The sun was embracing the earth. As the days progressed, I would be privileged to observe the results of that love. I removed my moccasins and felt the cool dampness of the forest floor bathe my feet. It was good to be close to the earth. I could almost feel its heart beating beneath the leaves.

The rhythm of the earth called to me. It beckoned me to tread its meadows and run with the deer. It enticed me into the branches of its white oak to climb with the squirrel and commune with the bird. It invited me to swim in her streams and lakes like the pickerel and bass. I was a part of the earth.

I was vested in these Barrens. I had lived with them and from them through four seasons. Earth had been my only companion, and I had not grown lonely. I had given her my love and received her blessing.

I had divined her ancient rhythm. I met it in the miraculous light of the firefly in summer, in the happy chatter of the squirrel in fall, the white breath of the deer in winter, and the song of a lark in the spring. I moved with it through the seasons. Its summer showers flowed through me, its frosts of fall embraced me, its winter snows insulated me, and its spring sun warmed me.

I was born and reborn through the seasons. I had died a dozen deaths to old values and fears proved false by the truth of nature. Each death had been followed by a new birth of understanding. It was as if my body and soul were slowly being transformed by the Great Spirit into a new being, a child of the land.

I had learned to think with my heart again. I trusted my senses and lost the capacity to worry. I was warmed by the sun, washed by the rains, and fed by the natural gardens. A seed of understanding began to sprout within my soul through the same mysterious power that wakens the seeds of the earth and calls the animals from hibernation. It had been planted there by the Great Spirit, cultivated by my teacher Stalking Wolf, and nurtured by these beloved Barrens. Now it would grow and sink its roots yet deeper into the earth and, drinking of her knowledge, raise its head high into the clouds.

I was awakened from a sleep caused by thousands of years of separation from the earth. Through the miracle of nature, I had rediscovered my roots and my purpose for being alive. I had become again a child of the land. Now, to become a man.

It was time to return to my parents' home and share my new-found knowledge. It was time to leave the womb and face the world with my ideas. I had a deep desire to travel throughout the rest of North America and learn all of its secrets.

I walked to a road after dismantling my camp. I had entered the Barrens naked. I was returning fully clothed and healthier than I had ever been since Thoreau Summer. I was also returning with a new understanding of prosperity. It was not to be measured in dollars and cents but in attitude. It was not understood through possession but through experience. Prosperity is relating, not acquiring.

I had survived a year alone in the Barrens. I had been sheltered, fed, and clothed bountifully. I was healthy and rich in new-found knowledge of the forest. Worry had vanished. I was at peace with myself and my environment. I had taken only what I needed—and I knew the forest would provide more—and had given of myself. I was in balance with nature, with the earth that sustains us all, and I was prosperous.

A crow was pecking at the remains of a road kill. I heard the sounds of a vehicle and turned to watch a garbage truck rattle toward me. It filled the air with an acrid odor. Its driver made a deliberate move to hit the crow by the roadside. He missed. Civilization.

Civilization.

A teardrop rolled down my cheek and fell amongst some broken beer bottles. A rat scurried out of a garbage ditch toward the abandoned road kill. I turned back to the womb and lived out another season alone.

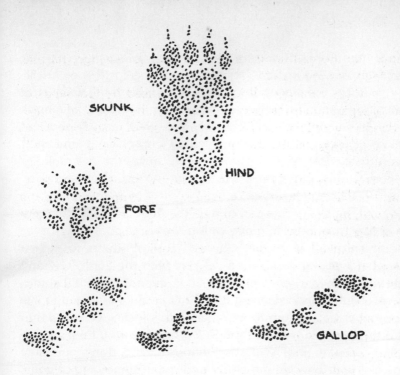

SKUNK

HIND

FORE

GALLOP

12/The Fast

Nineteen Days

The shadows lengthened, and my mind struggled for consciousness. I lay next to a game trail, praying for something edible to wander near before I lost consciousness again. Nineteen days without food had taken its toll on my body. I had never experienced such weakness and utter helplessness. I had always been able to provide for myself and had never had the fear of starving to death in the woods. What was actually happening to me had always been an impossible dream. Yet here I was, helpless, in the middle of that nightmare.

It was this attitude that had kept me in the woods, that wouldn't allow me to walk to a road and flag down a car or seek help beyond my own resources. Call it pride or call it stubbornness if you want. I've come to refer to it as "the call."

In each man I've known there is something that drives him, that moves him toward an invisible goal almost against his own will. It's what keeps the marathon runner going toward the finish after twenty miles and his body has run out of nutrients, and he is literally consuming himself. Possibly it is what drove the great religious leaders of the world as they compellingly marched toward martyrdom or triumph. It is what causes the vast majority of people unhappiness and frustration because they refuse to answer it. It's an inner voice, a "call."

"The call" is that part of man that longs to be in harmony with nature, that longs to move with it like some cool breeze over a mountain meadow. In me, "the call" was my desire to experience what Stalking Wolf called "at one with the earth." I didn't know what it meant, and yet I wanted it, even needed it. I somehow sensed that understanding it was my destiny. I wanted to live for no other reason than to experience this feeling. It was why I was born, and it looked as though it would be why I would die.

"You're always chasing ghosts. Why don't you stay home like your brother and study and make something of yourself?" My mother always said those words to me, and my answer would come almost involuntarily, sounding like the ring of a rock struck by a log, like a thud, like a hollow echo that almost groans with age and hardness and futility:

"Mamma, I don't believe in ghosts! You know that. What I search for in the woods is what Stalking Wolf calls 'the spirit that moves in all things.'"

"Stalking Wolf! What does he know?"

"Well, it's not ghosts I look for—not ghosts."

But there was something that drove me. Something I couldn't name that made me lose myself for countless days in the woods while others sought their way in the world. There was something very strong that made me give up everything the world considered valuable, to sit for hours and watch the wind work its magic on a rabbit track. Something more than adventure made me walk naked into the forest to spend a year completely alone. Something more than bravado made me face wild animals with no intent to defend myself.

"The call." It came from the depths of my being. I couldn't explain it, I could only respond to it. And if I didn't follow this mysterious force, I felt as though I would never be happy. There would always be something that was very important missing in my life. I would feel like an alien disconnected from my surroundings.

Man had grown out of the earth. Somehow he had strayed from his beginnings. I longed to return to those beginnings. To understand. To find where I fit. "It's not ghosts I look for!"

These nineteen days had begun as a fast that I hadn't expected to last more than a week. Stalking Wolf had once told me of a prolonged period of self-imposed hunger he had experienced as a young man. He had learned much in a short period of time, and I wanted to re-create that learning experience in myself.

I had fasted before and knew that I could overcome my desire to eat for at least three days. I had never experienced a prolonged period of hunger and denial or all the physical and psychological changes that go with it.

It seems that every man who has ever found himself and fully understood himself had used fasting somewhere in the process. It was one of the keys that I knew I had to use on myself if I were ever to answer my inner call.

This is where my fast had led me—through hunger, thirst, hallucination, vision, and despair. I had come to this point of total exhaustion and near extinction. It was no longer a question of whether I would find myself; now it was a question of whether I would live or die. When did this insane adventure begin?

The Bear Track

The first thing that I did was drive until I found a place that felt right, a place that I knew would be good medicine. I was driving along in the early afternoon, following a logging road north along a fast-moving stream when I saw what appeared to be bear tracks in the dust at the side of the road. I stopped my jeep, leaped out, and checked. They were bear tracks—fresh, about twenty minutes old. They belonged to a black bear about four-and-a-half feet at the shoulders and weighing 350 pounds. A good-sized animal and good medicine!

I looked around for a place to hide my jeep and soon had it so concealed that only someone searching for it could find it, and then, they'd have a difficult time at best. I turned from that task and, with only a hunting knife, headed off to track my bear.

I followed the bear tracks off the road to the west toward the setting sun. They went down the bank to the stream the road had followed up the mountain. The bear had stopped by the rushing water, knelt on its front haunches, and taken a drink.

He hadn't rested here, but had moved up the stream checking the pools for dinner. One of the pools had a rock ledge overhang where the bear had stood—his mud prints left distinct markings on the rock which would be gone with the first rain. There was some water still on the rock, lying in the indentations where it had been splashed when the bear lunged after a fish. He would only be minutes ahead of me. I lay down on the rock and stared into the pool and saw the shadow of a trout beneath the rock. The bear had missed. He couldn't have been very hungry, or he would have tried again. He turned north up the stream and then entered it and crossed after about fifteen yards. In crossing, he overturned rocks as if he were searching for crayfish, almost like his cousin the raccoon. Stealing his cousin's dinner. Bandit, I thought, and then noticed how he had lumbered up the far bank, breaking branches and causing a minor landslide.

He must be just on the other side of the hill, which he climbed after coming out of the water. He wasn't in any hurry, and if my jeep hadn't spooked him, which wasn't likely since logging trucks had used the road all summer, he should be just on the other side of the hill.

It would be good for me to wander with him for a while. I stopped and scooped some of the cool water into my mouth. I knelt there by the rushing water, listening to the music it created dancing over the rocks, and thought about what was in store. What lay ahead? What would the next days be like without food, gently wandering through the Maine woods?

The bear was just snacking before hibernation. He probably had his spot picked out by this time, beneath some overhang in a shallow cave or within some giant fallen tree, hollowed by termites. He was just passing the time and waiting—foraging for a snack before bedtime. Gentle wanderings . . .

I began to stalk as I tracked. I chose my steps carefully and watched for any sign of change in the bear's manner of walking. I would hate to look up and find that the bear had decided to have me for its final meal before it took the big sleep. As I approached the crest of the hill, I heard scratching noises. On my belly, I moved silently to the crest and peered down across a tiny meadow to where the bear had stopped at a fallen log to scratch for grubs and termites. There he sat in the late afternoon sun, rocking back on his haunches, popping grubs onto his thick, red tongue.

He was not more than twenty yards from me and totally unaware that he was being watched. What made this a very special time for me was the fact that he was cinnamon colored, and rare in this section of the country. The Cinnamon Bandit I named him immediately, and was reaffirmed in my choice when he rolled over and scratched his hide on the log. He looked like a bandit, sunning himself. A member of the "Over the Hill Gang"—fat and lazy. It was a sight that made me want to break out laughing. He rolled over in the grass, sniffed at the log one last time, and then rambled off into the woods at the other side of the clearing. I lay there, listening to him snapping branches and breaking twigs and shuffling through the underbrush and watching the sun sink through the reddening sky. "Good-night, Bandit," I whispered. "Good-night."

I rose and walked due north, looking for a place to sleep. I walked for approximately an hour until I came to a stand of pines growing closely in upon each other with their boughs hanging heavily to the ground. I crawled in under their protective arms—far in, about five yards—and gathered about me a huge pile of fallen needles. I shuffled into them, burying all but my face in the sweetest-smelling bed that nature has to offer. I lay there listening to the breeze through the pine boughs and watching the clouds ever so faintly dancing across a moon a little less than half full. The pines reminded me of my childhood in the Pine Barrens of southern New Jersey—a state that most Americans consider totally industrialized but is, in reality, over 80 percent forested. The Pine Barrens, my second home, my school, my friend, my womb.

Somewhere, the quavering song of a screech owl broke

the silence, and I had the deepest urge to watch it catch an earth-worm or a crayfish. I had never seen that. It was a mystery, one that I wanted to solve—but not tonight. I was too cozy and ready for dreaming. The pines, the gentle breeze singing a song to me through the boughs, the filtered moonlight all blended to create this good medicine for dreaming.

I felt warm and safe in this place apart from others, yet in a place where I belonged. I was more at home here than in some sterile motel bed between freshly laundered sheets. My bedfellows were ants, my music the wind, my covers the pine needles, my roof the pine boughs.

Security doesn't come from a double-locked, chain-latched steel door, it comes from within. It is the Great Spirit and the knowledge that I was where I belonged. This was a place created for me, not one man had hacked and scarred the earth to build. I felt safe and relaxed, and my mind wandered back to a campout I had experienced many years before with Stalking Wolf.

Stalking Wolf and I were waiting patiently for a rabbit to be caught by our first paiute trap. We had been waiting all day, and it looked as if we would go without dinner that night because this was the way Stalking Wolf taught us to be effective. If we caught nothing, we didn't eat. We also learned that the only reason for taking a life from the woods, animal or vegetable, was for sustenance.

"What was the longest time you ever went without eating?" I asked.

Stalking Wolf answered, "You are hungry, I know, but we will eat soon."

I wanted to ask him how he knew this, because I had been straining my eyes and ears to catch any clue of the presence of an animal, and I had detected nothing. Instead, I kept still. I knew that Stalking Wolf would teach me what he thought was important, not always what I wanted to know. And if I was patient, I would soon learn. I'm glad that I didn't ask another question because when Stalking Wolf began to speak, what he said was infinitely more interesting than anything I could have foreseen.

"We were very young, but not too young, Friendly Fox and I, when we decided to go up on the mountain and let the spirits talk to us. I was chosen to go first. We had to go separately and alone, or the medicine wouldn't work. It was the time between the seasons of summer and winter that I chose, because the coolness would keep me from exhaustion, and I would need very little water. I sat there on the mountain on the edge of a bluff, sheltered by the shade of a rock during the day. I didn't eat for a full twelve days, and I took very little water.

"On the twelfth day, the spirits tested me. I wanted to eat. I thought that I would do anything for food, even kill. I saw myself in a dream take food from an elder of the tribe. It was a fresh kill, and I devoured it raw, blood dripped from my hands. I screamed out loud, a war cry of victory. I really must have screamed, because I found myself awake and standing on the edge of the bluff. It was as if I was going to jump. I knew at that moment that the spirits had spoken through my vision, and I had learned a great truth.

"I returned from the mountain that evening with a fresh kill that I shared with the tribe along with the story of my vision. The elder I had seen in my vision said, 'Now you are one with the earth.'"

At that moment, the paiute trap snapped, and we had a nice cottontail for dinner. I was excited about our first catch, and it embarrassed me that I didn't know immediately what the great truth was that Stalking Wolf had discovered, and so I never asked. It was one of the unfinished chapters in my life that I was destined to finish on my own.

That was why I was here in the back woods of Maine in October. I came here to relive that good-medicine fast that Stalking Wolf had experienced so many years before. I was here to learn the great truth that my teacher had discovered, and I was here to become "one with the earth." I slipped off into sleep and slept soundly.

I was awakened by the sound of a junco in a nearby tree. It was a bright, clear morning with a bite of frost in the air, but the sun would soon burn that out of the air. I thought it was a bit early for juncos in this part of the country. I thought that they came just before the first snowfall. I remember a poem I wrote about them when I was very young and trying desperately to be an Indian:

The junco trilled
My heart soared

Winter is coming
Winter is coming

It was a good sign. I rolled over and crawled out of my nest into the most beautiful meadow I had ever seen. It sloped away and down gently toward the stream I had crossed the day before. There at the water's edge were two doe. The sun reflecting off the frost, the sounds of the birds and the water rushing in the stream, the bright, almost dazzling brilliance of the scene, and those two beautiful creatures drinking—and my heart soared. I was filled with gratitude and thankfulness. I wanted to laugh and cry at the same time. The beauty of this moment was overwhelming. I just knelt there by the pines that I had crawled from, and communed with the breeze and thanked the Great Spirit for being alive and for being here.

I don't know how long I knelt there watching life around me. Time was not important—only the moment and all it held.

I had learned to drink in every moment. To see everything that was around me and not worry about what I was missing. Most people race from one place to another and miss everything in between. They rush to keep appointments and complain about not having enough time—but I have escaped from that pattern. This attitude caused all time to blend with the moment, and I was able to lose myself in the detail of my surroundings. I can only describe it as what I imagine is a state of grace.

The Carpet and the Ants

That afternoon I wandered through the forest. The sun was high and warm for late October in Maine. Indian summer! Most of the leaves had fallen, and the ground was like an Oriental carpet of reds and golds. They formed a design so complex that it was indecipherable to the human eye, and yet it was real. I sensed a pattern there that should not be disturbed. And so, I moved over the forest's carpet with great care. I was careful not to disturb the combined craftsmanship of wind and tree and frost.

How beautifully the forest treats death. How beautiful death is in the wild—not to be mourned but celebrated in this breathtaking manner. The leaves brighten, then die. The tree, colorless, mourns. It's right to mourn, natural to remain colorless, but only for a little while, a season. The leaves will brown and decay, and their nourishment will enter again into the earth to feed the tree that gave them life. So natural, so good, and so very simple. Yet most of us miss it. We rake the leaves and burn them, we put them in piles and put them out for the trash man. Rather, we should let the wind work its magic and weave for us a beautiful carpet from its leaves.

We are so locked into order. Everything must have its place, and we fail to see the natural order of things. Leaves are untidy and must be raked. Their presence on our lawns broadcasts neglect and laziness. Their absence reflects order and control and pride. If only all people could join me here, not physically but where I am spiritually, and relax and gently wander through creation and realize its order and beauty. If only, I thought.

I stopped and watched a colony of red ants work the sap from a dripping maple that had been scarred by a bear, which had decided to use it to sharpen his claws. They marched by the hundreds up and down the maple trunk. They looked to me like veins, red and swollen, a never-ending stream of life, carrying that sweet sap home to their colony.

I felt good and was content to stand there silently and watch. Awe-inspired, the Oriental rug beneath my feet, a ceiling of clear, cool blue—I was in a mansion not made by hands, majestic and life-sustaining.

I eventually followed the ants' trail, leading away from the tree. It wound about over and under leaves and rocks and branches. Objects of that size would be enormous roadblocks to a man, but they were hardly that to this army of determined ants. They crossed them as if they were not barriers at all and made their way directly to a miniature cave they had excavated at the base of an oak.

I watched them until dusk. Their activity never slackened. A constant vein of workers carrying sugar from the maple to the colony. Their energy was amazing. Digging a home from the earth and letting the forest feed them.

The path the ants followed, like a road, was not cut out of the earth, but a part of it. Barriers were not blasted but overcome. There would be little trace of the ants' presence after their pilgrimage was completed, no litter left to mark their way, only a faint path across the forest floor.

Man in his desire to make the earth better for his survival has managed to scar, to deface it to the point where it now threatens him with extinction. Man takes from this earth but fails to replenish. He is afraid of the earth; he sees it as an enemy that wants to compete with him for supremacy. Why, he even encloses himself in metal and concrete when he is placed in the earth to rest. "Ashes to ashes," should read "Ashes to concrete." Fear? Or is it greed that drives us to destroy the basis of our existence? "Ashes to metal, dust to concrete!"

What makes us deny our beginnings and avoid our natural end? I have read that the Egyptians denied death through embalming. Even then we had strayed far from the truth. The Indian saw death as a very real part of life, not to be avoided but understood. Some were buried naked in the earth from which they came, free to decay and become one with the earth.

Is that what Stalking Wolf meant when he mentioned understanding what it meant to be one with the earth? Did he mean that I must understand death? Was he referring to our mortality? I didn't think so. What he pointed toward was not so simple as that. It meant more, because it dealt with life, I was sure of that. It concerned the living and the understanding of life. Perhaps it was connected with the understanding of death, but it was more than that.

A cool breeze ran across my neck and made me realize that the sun had almost retired behind the mountain. I raised my body up off the forest carpet and stepped carefully toward the stream, making certain not to disturb the ants' thoroughfare.

The water was so cold that it almost burned going down my throat. I hadn't realized it, but I hadn't had a drink since early that morning. Almost twelve hours. I would have to be more careful and remember to drink more often. I didn't need to become dehydrated. I knew that I would weaken over the days without food, but I didn't want to get sick and have to postpone this fast, for I felt that this was the appointed time. I'd just have to be more careful.

The next few days blended into one long warming feeling. I experienced some stomach cramps that second night and a headache on the third day, but I knew that they would pass and largely ignored them until they disappeared. It was as though time had stopped and I were suspended in eternity. All time was now, and I was flowing with it in an almost indiscernible motion, slower than slow . . . floating.

The Owl and the Hare

Across the meadow I noticed intersecting paths, like some intricate causeways that were depressed below the higher grasses. On these runs were the droppings of a varying hare. I felt good that one of nature's most vulnerable creatures was sharing this place with me. I wanted to meet this hare and tell him that he had nothing to fear from me.

In the evening as I lay at the edge of the pines watching the meadow in the ever-increasing moonlight, I would see him. He would feed his way up the meadow and toward me. His ears were constantly turning to pick up the sounds in the forest about him. He would feed to within inches of my face. I would remain very still and study his coloring and eyes. Here was a shy and cautious animal, built for speed and maneuverability, but with no other defenses from every carnivore in the woods.

The first time he came close, I wondered what he would do when he scented or saw me. To my surprise, he did nothing. Perhaps my spirit more calm than at other times because of my fast. I don't know. What I do know is that that hare was not afraid of me. He sat there and chewed grass and then, in one hop, was next to my hand, which he sniffed and then hopped over. This was incredible. A hare unafraid of a human! I felt very good about that. I felt very close to that hare and was thankful that he could understand me. He sensed that I meant him no harm, and he trusted me. It was something I had experienced with very few people, and I wondered why humans had lost this ability that animals have of sensing danger and safety?

This varying hare was with me for most of the rest of the time I stayed at the pine camp. I gave him the name Rabbit. It was a small incident, probably long forgotten by Rick, my childhood friend. We were identifying animals one day and I identified a varying hare as a rabbit. Rick laughed and said, "No, it's a hare."

"What's the difference?" I said, "It looks like a rabbit to me."

"The difference is the hair," he said, still laughing.

I was getting annoyed and sternly asked, "What do you mean?"

"Rabbits are born blind and naked, and hares can see and have fur . . . or hair."

"Oh," I said embarrassed. "The rabbit's no hare."

This memory caused me to name this hare Rabbit. I whispered, "Be careful, Rabbit. There's an owl, a barred owl that works this meadow at night. I've heard its call, and I've seen its shadow. I'll bet it has a four-foot wing span and can carry off a hare even as large as you. Be careful, Rabbit."

Through the days and nights that passed, I came to expect Rabbit's presence. He was like a balm, a calming spirit. He was life, vulnerable but totally free. If I had to define my feelings toward Rabbit, the word would be "brother."

The barred owl was a beautiful bird. I first heard its song, eight notes. I next saw its shadow in the night sky. The third time I encountered it, it was hunting the meadow, and it was then that I saw its full size and power as it swooped down and caught a mouse in its talons only yards from the pines where I lay. It flew at an improbable rate of speed when it dived, and I watched it come against the moonlight and rise to a roost high up in a maple. There once again, it gave its eight-note call. "Who cooks for you? Who cooks for you?"

The owl and the hare. The hunter and the hunted were living so close, and yet there was little fear and no hatred. These creatures have found their natural positions and live gracefully within them. We can't do that, because we have yet to discover what our position is in the world. Or perhaps we once knew, but we lost sight of it?

Every evening I would talk to Rabbit and the owl would talk to me. The "spirit that moves in all things" made sure that I was never alone. I have never been lonely when alone in the wilderness. There's too much life to be observed and to take part in. If we can sit for hours and watch a colony of ants work a maple, we will never be lonely. If we realize that the spirit that moves in the hare also gives us life, then we are never isolated. If we stand in awe of the constant movement in the earth and the sky and the plant life that surrounds us, we can never be lonely.

I have often been alone, but the only time I have ever felt loneliness was at a dance in high school. I didn't know how to dance and found myself envious of the boys who could. I ended up sitting alone in the bleachers, lonely because I had nothing in common with the other kids. But I have never felt that way in the woods. Perhaps I shouldn't have felt that way at the dance, but I did. Today, I don't feel as though I would ever feel lonely again. Today, in life, I realize my relationship to nature and to others.

These animals came to be my companions, constant and reassuring. They were always present, and the realization of their presence told me that I was still alive and aware and real. They made me realize I was awake and not dreaming. Their reality and companionship was a strong gift for, as the days passed without food, I found it increasingly difficult to discern dream from reality.

The Thirst

I woke one morning to a brilliant hoary frost. The sunlight playing through the frost-laden branches acted like a kaleidoscope forming shapes and reflecting colors. I had to shake my head for fear I was hallucinating. But this was no hallucination, it was real and lovely. There is an awful silence that comes with frozen fog. It's almost as if the very air will crack and fall to pieces if you speak. So I thought quietly, in a whisper.

Peace overcame me when I looked across that frost-covered meadow, alive with the glistening sunlight. It looked like someone had sown diamonds about. There, by the stream, I could see the warm breath of a doe as it raised its head from the water to look and listen. She seemed as responsive as I to the sounds of the junco and the bobwhite as they echoed through this crystal garden. This was a vision of what heaven would be like. God, I was happy! There in the frost that would rapidly disappear were the tracks of raccoon, deer, mouse, hare, and chipmunk. Momentary tracks, I thought, quickly burned by the sun, whose only immortality lies with my memory. They were placed by nature for my consciousness alone, an intricate, transitory pattern. In that moment of great joy, I experienced a sadness that I alone could witness this beautiful work of nature, which my sensitive state had transformed to art.

Tracks. I thought that this would be a good day to try my hand at some difficult tracking, to test my skill after seven days without food. I decided to follow the bear tracks that were made a week earlier by Bandit, which had led me to this paradise. I wondered how far he had wandered. I know that bears have territories, and I would test my guess that this old boy was making his final rounds before his hibernation.

I began at the edge of the meadow where I had last seen him lumber off at his breakneck, two-to-three mile-an-hour pace.

I enjoy tracking bear because they are so whimsical. They can eat almost anything and find food almost anywhere. They can sleep wherever they lie down. I remember watching one take an afternoon nap between two saplings. He never stirred, even though another bear passed close by. They don't have to go anywhere or be anywhere, and are never in a hurry unless they are in danger. Their natural curiosity leads them to some very interesting and amusing situations. When unmenaced they are gentle wanderers like myself, and I feel a certain affinity toward them. Following them lends itself to my style, because it leads me on so many interesting side trips. A bear will change its course if it smells an interesting odor or hears an unusual sound. Where most animals will move away from anything strange, a bear will turn and investigate, and nothing is sacred to him.

I was looking forward to this track also because it would be a challenge. Six days of wind and frost would make the track very faint, and I would have to be very alert not to lose it. I had no idea that I would be so challenged and so engrossed that I would meet the unexpected.

From the log where he had snacked on grubs, he wandered down through a gully and up the bank and hill on the other side. He seemed to have no regard for bushes. He pushed right through them. On the bank at the far side of the gully, I was given a treat. The angle of the bank was so steep that the bear left marks of its claws in the earth.

Usually a bear pads along, heel striking first, and seldom does it leave a mark of its nonretractable claws. In fact, the hind paws leave large marks that have sometimes been mistaken for a man's moccasined footprint. But there they were—five small indentations just above the digit marks as though someone had stabbed the ground with a tapered stick.

Just over the hill, I found where I thought the bear had spent the night. It was a a huge thicket patch. Some brown fur was caught on a thorn where he had crawled in to curl up for the night. He came out the same way and headed off at a 90-degree angle to the direction he had been traveling when he had come over the hill. Now where could Bandit be headed? He was probably headed toward some water. I was thirsty, since I had forgotten to drink that morning, and I was looking forward to quenching my thirst at a mountain spring. However, I didn't get the opportunity, because I hadn't gone a quarter of a mile following the tracks when I came upon a field of rock. I lost his tracks in that field and was forced to follow the edge of the enormous field and hope to pick up his track again.

I tried the downhill side, figuring that if he were heading for water it would naturally be at the bottom of a mountain. I was wrong. I searched all day, forgetting to take the time to find some water. By late afternoon, I found where I thought the bear had come out at the uphill side of the field. There were some broken branches there and what looked like the remains of some bear feces. I looked up at the sky and knew that I had only about a half hour of light left, and so had better seek shelter before nightfall. I was thirsty, but I didn't relish the idea of stumbling around in the dark searching for a drink. Besides, it had begun to cloud up and would possibly rain. That would solve my thirst problem. Now, I had better find a dry spot for the night.

I found a shallow cave. It was more like a rock overhang. I gathered leaves and pine needles for my bed and some boughs to cover the mouth of the cave in case the wind tried to blow rain into my sleeping quarters. As I was going to sleep, the thought went through my mind that I had been at least twenty-four hours without water. Bear tracking would have to wait in the morning while I searched for water.

It didn't rain during the night. I was hoping for some puddles to drink from. I considered the terrain and decided to head straight down across the rock field and into the valley. It was during my descent that I fell. It must have been my weakness, for I don't remember if I slipped and was knocked out, or if I blacked out and fell.

When I woke up, I was wedged between two large boulders and very dizzy. I had a nasty gash and bump on my forehead, and it took me quite some time to free myself from the rocks. It would have been a simple task had I not been weak and dizzy. My left leg was twisted and wedged under one of the boulders, and I had great difficulty freeing it. I was sore, and my ankle was beginning to swell noticeably. It was very painful to put any weight on it.

When I finally climbed out, I was exhausted. I would have to crawl to the woods and cut myself a crutch if I wanted to travel any distance. What should have taken minutes took hours. I was tired and frustrated and very thirsty. I passed out at least three times in that short crawl. One thing began to concern me greatly. As much as I struggled and panted and strained, I never sweated. My mouth was very dry, and I knew that the dizziness I was experiencing was caused by dehydration as well as by the accident. If I didn't get some water soon, I might pass out and never wake up.

I finally managed to crawl to a fallen branch at the edge of the rock field. I hacked at it with my knife until it resembled a crutch. I wrapped my bandanna about the Y at one end, placed it under my arm, and with all my strength raised myself up.

Pain shot up through my leg, and I started to black out. I fought back the nausea and tried to deny the pain. I had to get to water! My thirst was greater than my pain, so I moved. But it was impossible. Before I had gone fifty yards, the light failed. Cloud cover negated the moonlight and the steepness of the grade along with my terribly weakened condition forced me to halt.

I lay down exhausted in a pile of leaves and fell off to sleep. Forty-eight hours without water.

In the morning, I licked the dew from the grass and put some of the grass into my mouth and limped down the hill. I moved from tree to tree, slowly and laboriously. The swelling had not gone down in my ankle, and it was still painful to put weight on it. Everything was spinning and it took every ounce of my willpower to keep going. I would fall and lie spent, then force myself up to go on. It seemed as if I would never reach the base of the mountain.

Finally, at the base of the mountain, I fell—I couldn't call it letting myself down. Lying there in the dry leaves, I heard the faint sound of water trickling over rock. Thank God! I crawled through the underbrush and put my hand in the cold water. I was thirsty beyond belief. It had been fifty-six hours since I last tasted water. Yet, I didn't bury my face in that spring. Something told me not to. Something from deep within began to groan and fight its way to my conscious mind. It fought through the nausea, the weakness, and the pain, and it cried out to be heard above my physical needs.

I knelt beside the spring, cupped my hands, filled them with water and raised them, dripping, above my head. Then I turned slowly and let that water fall on the dry leaves about my exhausted body. It was a grateful libation to the Great Spirit that moves in all things, to survival. It was simple. I was glad to be alive.

After drinking my fill and resting for the better part of the day, I made my way back to my pine camp, where I rested and nursed my ankle for two days.

I was getting noticeably weaker each day and was on the verge of giving up this impossible quest. Was it worth my life to discover what it meant to be "one with the earth"? I doubted during these days of recuperation and would have packed out if it wasn't for some mysterious force that caused me time and again to forget my doubts. Each time I was ready to leave, a junco would sing or Rabbit would appear, and my spirit would be calmed.

Stomach cramps began to reappear during these days, but they only lasted the morning. A drink of water and a little grass would usually settle me.

How long would it go on? What was going to happen to

me? Surely the short hallucinations I experienced were not all that I would see? I was disappointed and somewhat discouraged. I calmed myself by thinking over and over, It won't take much longer. I did not know what lay ahead.

The Vision

I was twelve days into my fast. The hunger pains had ceased, and the headaches had passed. It was amazing that I couldn't remember when the pain had left me that day since it had been so intense that morning. I only knew that as I approached my camp and saw its familiar surroundings that this night would be different from the previous eleven.

The forest was silent, different from any way I could remember. But I had learned that nature's ways are so infinite that I should never be surprised, only grateful.

The owl I had grown to expect after sundown did not come, and my friend Rabbit was also missing. What was present in the forest that was keeping my friends in hiding? I closed my eyes and listened intently for any sound that might give me a clue.

Perhaps the fox whose tracks I discovered when I returned to camp had not left the area, as I had assumed. I was excited when I found the fresh tracks of a fox because I always consider them good medicine. My mind wandered back to the time I spent snow blind in the Pines because I was so intent on tracking a fox. Good medicine?

My eyes were closed tightly and my ears were straining for any clue, when it hit me and knocked my senses into another dimension. I didn't know then what was happening to me, but afterward I knew that I had experienced that strange and wonderful phenomenon called a vision.

My head began to spin as images appeared and disappeared in rapid succession in my mind, as if I were on a high-speed train rushing through my past. I was traveling over every path I had ever known as a boy, and I was following at incredible speed the tracks of a large and powerful but older man. They were familiar tracks, and yet I couldn't place them, so I found myself compelled to follow them and find their maker.

On and on I traveled, realizing every camp and every track I had ever known or seen, until I found myself in an unfamiliar land that was different from anything I had ever experienced. It was different not in texture, but in spirit. It was a desert place, and out among the rocks was the old man I had been following. He was making his way through the rocks toward a distant mountain. There was no sound whatsoever, and the beating of my heart pounding from the chase sounded like a tom-tom in a closed room.

It was as if the old man heard my heart, for at that instant he turned to face me, his pursuer, and I saw that the man I had been tracking was my old friend and teacher, Stalking Wolf. His eyes were the same intense, accepting eyes I had always known, but they radiated a new image of a sad peace which beckoned to me, almost pleaded with me to come . . . come . . . come.

And then, as suddenly as it had begun, it ended. But his eyes were still there, burning with an intensity in my mind that I had never felt before. The owl rushed overhead, and its sound made me aware of where I was. I looked around and a chipmunk and Rabbit were about on their nocturnal forage as if something had called them back.

I did not understand what was happening, but I realized that it was good medicine, and I knew then what I had to do. I must find Stalking Wolf! There was something about him that I didn't recognize, but I knew that he wanted me with him on his desert walk.

That meant that my fast was over. I would have to find food immediately in order to have the strength to hike out of these mountains.

I had prepared a rabbit stick for just such a time, and I knew that I must kill Rabbit now before my sentiments talked me out of it. As I reached for the stick in the corner of my lean-to, I noticed the bright eyes of a small animal watching me, and I knew instinctively that the fox whose tracks I had discovered earlier was back. And if the fox was there, the chipmunk and Rabbit would soon be in hiding.

I moved quickly and silently toward where I had last noticed Rabbit and knelt to feel his tracks. They led off toward some heavy brush, and I knew that I had lost my chance for a kill. The strange thing was that the tracks told me that Rabbit had not been in a hurry or frightened. They were not the tracks of a worried animal fleeing a pursuer. They were the normal tracks of a rabbit foraging for food, and they went directly into the heavy brush as if he had been led there.

Seven Days

It's difficult to relate just how the next seven days passed, because it was as if some force were at work warning the animals I tracked and stalked of my presence. Each time I was about to strike or throw or trap, the animal would lift up as if it were receiving some message on the wind and would bound off in the opposite direction. I would sit by the stream where the raccoon came every night to drink and wash its food, and the raccoon wouldn't come. I would set traps on the rabbit runs in different places, and the rabbits would not appear. I would stalk a deer and know that if I waited in a certain place that the deer would pass and I could fall on it and kill it, but it would not pass.

The days passed as if I were in a dream. Nothing seemed real except my hunger and weakness, and nothing worked. I walked miles looking for game. I spent hours fishing, but there was no food. Here it was fall, a time when food is most plentiful in the woods, and I was starving to death. I couldn't understand it. Something beyond anything I understood was in control. But yet I fought to survive. I ate grass, grazing like a deer, at times on my hands and knees for hours. But it wasn't enough. Often I would dig a root or eat some bark, and my stomach would reject it. This had never happened before. Nature and my body were conspiring to destroy me or drive me from the forest.

I didn't feel as though I were in control. My life was being guided by a force both within and without that I neither understood nor accepted. I continued to hunt, and I continued to eat the roots and grasses and even grubs I could find. I would not surrender. I would not be defeated. I knew that I could survive in these woods, and I would. I refused to let the idea of walking out and seeking any help beyond my own instincts and resources enter my mind. When it did, I would push it out with a giant effort of my will.

I began to stumble and forget where I was or from where I had come. I would slip in and out of consciousness, and had countless hallucinations—some so wild that I could never describe them, and some so real that I thought they were just that. In one, a rabbit jumped into my arms and invited me to kill it. Falcons and hawks flew in droves like crows. Snakes crawled about my body, and the sun at times filled my entire conscious vision so that everything was hidden behind a blinding light.

At times I thought I was going insane, losing my mind. But always my mind would clear, and I would shake back the fears and go on.

I don't know how far I wandered from my camp or how many times I had failed to attain food. Those things were unimportant to me now. The only thing that was important was survival. I was nervous, tired, weak, and very close to panic. I was doing everything I told myself I would never do in a desperate situation. I was acting defeated. I was acting scared. I was uptight and I couldn't relax.

Days passed into night and back again into day, and each day found me weaker and weaker. I must walk out of this place, get to my jeep, and drive to safety! Why couldn't I admit that I was beaten? What was holding me in this wilderness? Was it my time of testing? My trial to see if what I believed was really important to me, important enough that I would risk my life?

Did I really believe that I was indestructible, that I could live in the woods and never be in any danger because my relationship with nature would insure my survival? Or was I afraid that my home was rejecting me, as if I were an alien? "Leave or die," it was saying. "There is no place for man in the forest." NO! I couldn't believe that. I was not being rejected, I was being tested. The question was, Would I measure up?

I had become so weak that, whenever I stopped to rest,

I fell asleep or blacked out. I would sleep for minutes or hours, I was never quite sure. My one concern was that one of these involuntary sleeps would last a very long time indeed.

I had to make a decision. If my mind was not playing tricks on me, I figured that I had been without substantial food for nineteen days. I was literally on the verge of starvation. My weakness was becoming dangerous. I don't know how many times I had stumbled and fallen. One of these times I would fall into a position from which I would be unable to climb, or I would strike my head and never wake up. I was just too weak to move quietly in a stalk. I was discouraged, to the point of despondency.

What should I do? Use my last reserve of strength and make for the jeep, or stay and face the inevitable? I must make the decision immediately, or it would be made for me. I knew my body, and I had never felt it so vulnerable before. I felt as though I could just lie down and die. It was not a scary feeling, and it didn't invoke fear. I was just tired, and I wanted to sleep forever.

I wandered through the woods, searching for some sign of animal life, pulling bark from the pines as I passed them and chewing on some wild grasses. It was hopeless. I would have to find my way back to my jeep. Just then, a cool wind blew through the trees and a bird sang:

> "Winter is coming
> Winter is coming. . . ."

Looking up, I noticed the thin cirrus clouds as they raced ahead of the west wind and across the sun. The faint shadows they cast on the mountains and meadows broadcast the warning that snow would follow.

I thought of Bandit, whom I had tracked, and how he must be heading for his winter home. It was then I noticed the bear tree—a hardwood tree with bark scarred about six feet from the base. At the base of the tree there was something very unusual: the remains of a bear's kill. The skull and some fur and bones of a varying hare lay there. I thought it unusual that a bear would carry its kill any distance before devouring it. Perhaps another larger bear had been in the vicinity, or perhaps there was an active hare run very close to where I was.

That was enough. The decision was made for me. If

there was life so close, and if a bear could find it, so could I. It may not seem like much of a sign to anyone else, but to me it was good medicine.

I backtracked the bear who had been there perhaps a day before, and didn't have to travel very far before I came across an active game trail. It was not only used by hares, but also by deer.

I searched the area until I found a place where I could lie undetected and concealed and wait for something live to pass within my reach. I would have to be very careful to remain awake and alert. That would take all of my willpower, because already I was beginning to feel faint. The walk and short track had exhausted me.

This place I had chosen for my concealment—would it be my final resting place? These and similar thoughts walked slowly across my mind as I found my way into position behind some brambles and lay face down to wait.

The Call and the Kill

An ant, small and black, began to wind its way across a leaf in that fast staccato way ants have of traveling—stopping and starting, exploring, and retracing his steps to begin where he had wandered from his original trail. It was coming toward me in its never-ending search for food. It was up and over leaves as if they existed for no other purpose than to act as obstacles to slow his search. Yet he traveled undaunted, alone, from shadow to shadow, ever searching among the leaves and decaying undergrowth for something to take back to his colony. Searching in the decaying leaves, among the dead, for sustenance.

I must have lain there for hours, drifting in and out of consciousness and waiting for something to move and praying that when it did, I would have the strength to pursue it and use it to nourish my depleted strength. Suddenly the dappled sunlight began to move against the wind on my face, and I heard the sound of a bird light on a branch just above my head. Would it fly off, or would it land to feast on that ant who had become my friend and companion these past hours? If he noticed the ant, surely he would notice me. But if his hunger was great enough, perhaps he would risk the ant, and then I would take him. It all seemed so natural—the ant, the leaves, the bird and myself. Waiting. Each an integral part of all that was happening around us.

Then it was on the ground just before my face, hunting for some seeds among the grass and leaves. It was a slate-colored junco with a slate-gray hood and back and a beautiful white breast. I stared intently at its dark brown eyes and noticed their complete peacefulness. The head moved as he searched for food.

In a man the eye moves, in this bird the entire head jerks and bobs, like a boxer avoiding a jab. There was a marking on its sandy beak. A chip was out of the forebeak and had turned dark. It must have pecked at a seed too close to a rock or tried to take a seed too hard from rocky soil. I studied that bird, the stripes on his legs, the dark outer edges of his wing feathers that give the impression of stripes and the white tail feathers that framed its long narrow tail. I named it Chip after the marking on its forebeak. Chip, I thought, I must take your life now, though it will give me no pleasure. I must or I'll die.

There it stood, inches from my face, unafraid, unaware that a predator lay so close and could, at any moment, snatch from it the breath of life. But can this predator take that bird? That had always been the question. I had never enjoyed a kill, even though I killed only what I needed in order to survive.

I must reach out for that bird, or risk the chance of starving to death. Yet the bird senses nothing that denotes fear. Is it because the bird knows that I am not going to take it? What is going on? I've always been in control before, and now it all seems to be slipping through my fingers. I'm losing control. What does this bird sense that I don't know? I must kill this bird or die! It's as simple as that. It is what I've been trying to do unsuccessfully for the past week. Why the hesitation? "Take it, Tom! Take it or die!"

I closed my eyes and tried to move my right hand and arm toward the bird. They would not move! It was as though I had no control over it, as though it were a separate entity. My mind was telling it to move and move swiftly and silently, but it was not obeying. Something, some other force, was in charge of my limbs. Or was it? Perhaps there was a deeper level of my own consciousness that was now in control of my body, that knew, that realized more than my logical, trained consciousness could ever understand. And that was that I had nothing to fear. That what I must do is wait and surrender myself to the earth around me. To give in to what I was and had always been—and that was not a conquering pioneer. I did not have to give up, only give in. To flow with the spirit of my surroundings. To be different from, and yet a part of the earth. Give *in*. Give *in*. Become . . . You are it, and it is you, and we are all one entity. Like the ant and the bird. Like the leaves and the mulch. Like the earth.

I began to tremble. It was an inner trembling that was not goose flesh but a shaking, beginning at the center of my body and radiating out. It was as if my soul were shaking with an inner laughter and joy that it could feel only upon being discovered and realized. Like a child who is discovered in his hiding place. It was a shaking, but my body didn't move. The trembling came from somewhere deep within my body. It was a deeper feeling than I had ever before felt. My soul was bursting with joyous laughter, and its movement was rocking, moving my body in a strange rhythm unlike the normal movements one would expect from the body. It was the trembling I would expect to feel from an earthquake. I was moving with the earth, an integral, living part of the earth!

There, face down in the moist dirt, I had the experience that Stalking Wolf had told me about. I was one with the earth, both physically and spiritually. We were one. I opened my eyes to share my joy with my friends, but couldn't see them because my eyes were so full of tears. Everything was blurred. I blinked hard twice to clear my eyes. But the bird and the ant were gone, as if they had never been. I searched the dirt before my face and saw the faint, almost vague path the ant had made between two leaves, the distinct prints of the junco intercepting those of the ant, and a faint mark of a chipped beak where the ant's trail ended.

My heart felt a sad joy. At the very moment of my personal revelation, this ant was feeding a starving junco, and somehow that said more to me than anything I had ever learned. I was on holy ground. This moment and this place were sacred, as were all places that had given and received life.

My eyes blurred anew with tears of sadness and joy, and

I had to close them. Again the trembling began. It had the same rhythm as before, but it was not coming from within me but from the earth. The same rhythm that I had experienced as the laughter of my soul was now being realized outside my body. The earth was trembling as I had trembled. At that moment, I knew that the spirit that had commanded my arm to remain still had sensed this vibration long before my body sensory system could pick it up. I knew that my soul sensed this vibration of the earth long before and had told my arm to remain still. It was sound and movement together in the earth and in the air. It was a deer, not too large, moving down the trail in my direction, and it could not be more than twenty feet from where I lay.

My body suddenly came alive, and every muscle tightened, ready to spring. I knew that this animal was my prey, as the ant was the junco's. There was no hesitation on my part to take it if I could. I opened my eyes and watched it carefully and silently move down the trail.

It was a yearling. It had been born in the spring of this year. It looked to be about 110 pounds. Its ears were cocked and alert for any sound out of the ordinary. I could see the lashes, black above its brown eyes, and the moisture about its nostrils and the white and brown hair on its chin that forms its almost invisible mandarin beard. The yearling stopped directly in front of me and lowered its head to graze on a clump of wild grass on the other side of the trail.

I sprang through the undergrowth that separated us with no concern for eyes or flesh. The brambles caught at my clothing and ripped at my face, but I felt nothing but the pounding of blood in my temples. Where my strength had come from I don't know. I had one thought, one objective, and my adrenalin supplied the strength I needed to reach that goal.

I was on the deer's back before it could react, and I felt the momentary surprise as its muscles tightened, and it began to raise up. But there was no time for a struggle. My hands found its muzzle, grass still between its teeth. I lunged back, twisting and pulling, and I heard a snap, definite, and the yearling went still. It was a clean kill. The deer felt nothing more than momentary fear.

I did not feel a sense of happiness after the kill. I felt only an understanding and the deepest humility. He died that I might live. It was as simple as that. It didn't involve any complicated philosophy or rationalization. I was just like that deer, only it was not yet time for me to die. There was much yet that I must do.

Yet, as I looked down at his wide staring eyes, I wondered if he had sensed the end. There was a peacefulness in his eyes that made me wonder if he hadn't known that this was his final walk.

I unsheathed my knife and cut some flesh from his thigh. I ate the flesh, warm and raw, blood dripping from my hands. It all happened as if it were a dream that I was acting out in someone else's mind. I lay down next to my kill and fell into a deep sleep. In the morning, I woke to the sounds of vultures screaming overhead for a chance to come down and feast on my kill. I moved to do what had to be done, to use the animal completely.

I don't remember having done it, but I had apparently gutted the animal before I had fallen asleep. I skinned the deer, sliced the meat, and set it to dry on some logs that I could watch from where I worked. I scraped the hide and took the brains of the deer and saturated the leather. I had too far to go to save all the bones, so I took only a few along with the hoofs, and tied them together with some of the sinewy tendon from the deer's foreleg. Then I packed most of the meat in the hide and cooked what was left for breakfast and felt even more strength return to my body.

I repaired my campsite, doused and buried my fire, hoisted my pack and turned to walk back to my jeep. As I turned to look one last time at that sacred spot, I realized that there was nothing there that would ever belie my presence. My kill was cleaned and whatever remained would soon be carried off by the birds and the other small scavengers of the forest. The signs of my lying-in-wait and my struggle would soon disappear as the wind and rain melted the tracks of my presence even further into the earth. I was leaving this place as I had found it, still whole. After all, it was a part of me, and I of it. That demanded respect and concern.

I made no attempt to mark the spot where all this had occurred. It wasn't necessary. If I ever had to find it, I could. Any mark would change it. It had to remain natural. Only then would it remain sacred and capable of working good medicine.

I found my jeep late that afternoon, undisturbed. I climbed in and before I could start the engine, I heard the sound of a bird high above my head in the pines.

"Winter is coming
Winter is coming. . . ."

I looked up, and directly above me was a junco singing its evening slumber song. The light was fading quickly as it does in the north at this time of year, and I can't be certain, but it seemed to me that there was a small chip in the beak of that bird. "Sleep well, Chip," I said and drove south down the mountain to find Stalking Wolf.

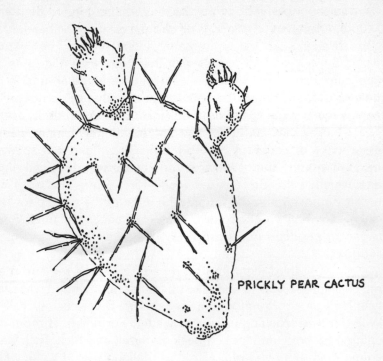

PRICKLY PEAR CACTUS

13/The Final Walk

When Stalking Wolf left New Jersey to return to his ancestral home, he prophesied concerning Rick's and my futures. He said that Rick would take a journey with the spirits, and I would journey and teach men the old ways. We pressed him for a prophecy about his own future. He said that he would take a walk to the mountain.

During my fast in Maine, I had a vision that I felt was Stalking Wolf calling me to come to him. I had decided, before I left the Maine woods, that I would travel to the Southwest and find Stalking Wolf. I was anxious to know why he might want to see me, and I wanted to share my fast experience with him.

At the time I did not know, although I suspected, that Stalking Wolf had taken his prophesied walk to the mountain.

Fall would rush into winter. The leaves were almost gone from the quaking aspen in the Pine Barrens. It was good to be home. I could reflect here. Stalking Wolf called it clearing the head. I had gone through near-disaster in Maine. I almost died. I had experienced a vision and a oneness with the earth. It all had to be put into perspective. The experiences were swimming around in my head with no direction. I wanted to know what to do next. Perhaps a few days at the good-medicine cabin would do it for me.

The day was spent foraging for dinner. Dinner was an assortment of water plants and fish. The night was spent in meditation and sleep. I relaxed this way for two days and nights and watched the Barrens get ready for winter. The frogs and turtles dug deep into the mud at the edge of the swamp for their winter hibernation. The squirrels gathered cones and nuts. Geese began to populate the swamp, bringing with them their unique sound.

The third night I had a dream that woke me and made me pack that very night and take off for the Southwest. I was sitting with Rick on a rocky mountain in a desert. Before us sat Stalking Wolf. He was teaching us spirit tracking. For one brief moment I entered his body and looked back at myself and Rick. Rick was a young man, but I was old, as old as Stalking Wolf. I woke with a start and went straight to my jeep.

It took two and a half days of hard driving to get to the Southwest where I expected to find Stalking Wolf. I took the canvas top from the jeep in order to stay awake. The wind in my face was far more effective than caffeine. I can't tell you how much I thought of my dream of Stalking Wolf during the trip. It haunted me.

The area was arid. The vegetation was dry. The mountains were huge mounds of rock and sandy soil. Small, trickling, shallow streams crisscrossed the land. Their courses were marked by cottonwood and willows that lined their banks. The plains were covered with sedges, sage, and cactus. Giant saguro stood sentinel at the edge of the Indian village I found to be the home of Stalking Wolf's tribe.

Stalking Wolf did not live there. He was too independent to live on the reservation. They directed me an hour's, maybe two hour's drive over some low rugged mountains to an arid valley.

There I find a tiny pueblo made up of three small adobes and some lean-tos where they kept their animals.

Two children were sitting in the dust playing a game with broken pieces of pottery. An old woman sat under a canopy made of woven cottonwood branches and rolled out corn tortillas for the evening meal. A dog ran to greet my jeep. I called it to my lap.

"He told me you would come." The old woman spoke to me before I came to her.

"Grandmother," I addressed her with respect. "Where is he?"

"You are Tom." It was a statement, not a question. She ignored my question.

"Yes . . . listen, I had this dream, and I must find him to explain it to me."

"He has taken his final walk," she answered.

"When?" I was disquieted by the fact that he had gone.

"Two weeks, maybe less."

My apprehension was well-founded. It had been two weeks since I had the vision in Maine. That was Stalking Wolf beckoning to me in the desert.

"Which way, Grandmother? Did he say anything? Did you see anything? Can you help me?" My anxiety was evident in my stammering voice. The urge to find him hadn't waned.

"He said you would need no help."

He had taught me. He had faith in me. I would need no help. All I had to do was track the wisest Apache who ever breathed across rocky, arid terrain after the weather had had two weeks to deteriorate the trail. I would need no help.

The words "walk to the mountain" raced through my mind as I surveyed the surrounding country. There were mountains on all sides. Which one? The beauty of the area began to impress me as I scanned the hills and plains. The setting sun made the rocky hills to the east burst alive with dazzling reds and grays and rusts, while the shadows on the western hills made them appear almost black. Long shadows were cast across the plains, and the first howl of the desert coyote reached my ears.

West. To the black mountains of the setting sun. That is the way he would walk. Back to the reservation. Into the setting sun completing his circle of life. To Stalking Wolf, the circle was sacred. Pink and gray light streaked the black hills. The sun was giving up the earth to the moon.

I walked to the edge of the pueblo. There I found a branch of an ocotillo bush bent to the ground and pointing west. I fell to my belly and pressed my cheek to the ground. There was the mark of his moccasin. The edges had deteriorated and the sole had almost completely filled up with sand, but the shadows made the sighting easy. It was his mark, and it was two weeks old.

I stood and looked toward the mountain, now gray instead of black as the sun retreated ever farther westward. "You made it easy for me, Grandfather." But then, the beginning is always easy. A distant rumble came across the desert from the mountain. It sounded like the drums for a hunting dance Stalking Wolf taught me.

"Tom, come and share our meal." The old woman was dishing black beans from a fire-blackened pot and handing tortillas to the children. It was a good meal. Afterward the old man of the pueblo offered me a draw on his pipe. We didn't talk, but he spoke to me through the silence we shared.

I had experienced this many times in the past with Stalking Wolf. I would be excited about what the morrow held and would want to talk. Stalking Wolf would cut me off with "Shh, listen to the night. It speaks to us of tomorrow." Then he would sit without stirring for what seemed like an awfully long time and then he would say goodnight. At first this filled me with dissatisfaction, but eventually as I relaxed and listened, the experience took on meaning. The owl's intermittent hoots told of an approaching storm. The smoke from the fire staying close to the ground told of a low-pressure area that could mean rain. The cricket chirps told the temperature. As I discovered each sign, I would look to Stalking Wolf, and he would nod his approval. That way I learned to speak to him through the silence.

The smoke from the old man's pipe rose straight and disappeared into the darkness. The coyotes howled at the new moon. A mouse skittered in front of our feet and under the porch. The signs were fair. Tomorrow would be my final test. Intuitively I knew that Stalking Wolf would not go straight to the mountain. And I knew he wanted me to follow every move of his final walk.

Every move had something to teach. Every mark would be a lesson. My final lesson from the master. If I learned it all, I would be immeasurably richer. If I missed it, I would be as I have always been. I prayed to the Great Spirit to make my senses keen and my memory strong for the ultimate track.

I accepted a cup of chicory coffee from the old woman at first light. I was ready for the search, dressed in loincloth, moccasins, and the beaded headband Stalking Wolf had made for me. My only tool was a handmade steel knife Rick had made and traded to me.

"I'll be going. Use the jeep if you have the need."

"Young brave has no water."

"No. He would have anticipated my thirst."

The old woman looked at my headband and motioned, no feathers. She was surprised that the young brave that was expected to follow Stalking Wolf and receive his blessing had no trophies of accomplishment.

The beginning was easy. I knew where I was going, so I wasted little time. I took off at a trot across the desert toward a line of cottonwoods that marked a river bed. I slowed only to check my location and reassure myself that it was Stalking Wolf's print I was following. It's true, the track was two weeks old, but in many places the soil was sandy and the impression had deteriorated little. Some tracks were protected from the wind and seemed almost fresh. I could tell their age only by the marks insects or lizards had made in them.

On I ran for some time until I realized that I had lost his track. At first I thought it was the rocky ground I had entered, but something told me that wasn't the case. My sixth sense had registered two depressions that were slightly deeper than the others had been. Why hadn't I recognized what that meant? Stalking Wolf had used one of the oldest tricks known to tracking. He had backtracked. He had simply stopped and walked very carefully backward in the depressions he had just made, and then cut off at an angle to the trail he had been traveling.

I went back and found the deeper tracks and backtracked till I came to the depression that looked as if he had jumped from it. He had taken six steps backward, and it was hardly discernible even to the trained observer. How could he be so good at his advanced age? He had to be in his nineties! I expected to look up and see him laughing at me from the shade of a cottonwood. He had often done this when I was learning to track.

When I was first learning to track, I would become so absorbed in the individual tracks that I would forget the animal I was tracking. I would forget to take into account its personality, its habits, its purpose. He often told me that when I was tracking a fox, I must be a fox. Well, I had forgotten, if even for an instant, that I was following my teacher, and that he would teach me, till he could teach no more. To follow him, I must become a teacher.

Okay, I thought. I will remember your tricks, Grandfather. Up to this time I had been trying to avoid any thought of the man who had made the trail I was following. It was my own attempt at denial. If I didn't think about him, then he simply wouldn't be at the end of the trail. This would all be just an exercise in two-week tracking over arid terrain, a mere exercise. But Stalking Wolf would not let me deny the reality of his final walk. He forced me to think like him and thereby think about him.

He had hopped north off his original trail through some willow and sage and down an embankment to the shallow, rocky river bed—although it could hardly be called a river now. In the rainy season it was probably a wide rushing torrent, but now it was hardly a trickling stream. It was all rounded river rock, the most difficult terrain to track over save solid rock. The easy part is past, I thought. What would Grandfather do next?

Drink! I went down on my stomach to sip some of the cool water that watered this arid land. Stalking Wolf said I drank like an animal on my stomach. He would never lie down, but would crouch and cup the water in his hands. He said that was the way a warrior drank. He had better vision and could move from the squatting position more swiftly. He said it was the one thing that separated him from the animals.

My argument for lying on my stomach was that I could feel the movement through the earth before I could see it from a crouching position. Besides, it made me feel closer to the animals. If Stalking Wolf had stopped here for a drink, then he knew that I would also. I pressed the side of my head hard to the stones and closed one eye. I was searching for disturbances. Any stone that might seem out of place. A depression amongst the smaller stones. Stalking Wolf had taught me this trick of tracking on hard-packed dirt. He walked softly across a hard path and asked what I saw. I strained, but could discern no depressions or scuff marks. He told me to lie down and put my head close to the earth and look again. I did, and as if my magic his trail appeared, showing the depressed dirt and pebbles where each print was located. By closing my top eye I could see the marks where the first print was located. When I closed the bottom eye, the position changed, and I could see the tracks farther down the trail.

I closed my top eye and covered every inch of rock and gravel for 180 degrees. Nothing. I closed my bottom eye and covered the same area. I saw it instantly. There was a heel mark in some gravel next to some larger stones. Now at least I knew the direction in which he was traveling. Had he slipped, or had this been a deliberate sign? A Texas horned lizard skittered across the stone from the river bank and hid under a large rock by a small pool of water.

I moved along the river bed and scanned the banks for any disturbance that might give a clue as to where Stalking Wolf climbed out. I looked for tumbled stones, trampled grasses, broken twigs, or branches bent. He would not make his next move an easy one to discover. The heel mark was a gift. No more gifts, I thought, from now on it would be hard tracking. That was my clue. Stalking Wolf would not leave the river bed by any route I could possibly discover by vision. He would take a hard route, and that meant wherever solid rock met the river.

I came to where a red rock abutment made the river bend. The rock was twenty-five feet high and as smooth as a concrete wall. How could he ever have climbed that? I surveyed the rock with the trained eye of a rock climber and found some fissures and chips that just might support a climb. I decided to try and reached for the nearest fissure and instantly withdrew my hand. The rock was as hot as a live coal from the desert sun.

What was I to do now? Should I go around an easier way and pick up his trail on top? Was I to wait until the sun set and the rock cooled? Is this where he would have me spend the night? I was in a quandary as to what I should do. What would Stalking Wolf do? He would find a way to climb the rock. He often taunted me on our long treks when I tired: "Young brave too weak to keep up? What will happen to tribe?" It was usually enough to make my adrenaline flow to keep his pace. I wasn't shamed by his taunt. He never degraded anyone. Rather I was challenged by it and the sense of responsibility I felt to someone else. I wasn't keeping up to prove that I was a better man than he. I was struggling for the survival of others. If I gave up, who would carry on?

I stripped some bark from a willow. I wrapped my knees and forearms and formed pads that would protect my palms. I soaked the pads and splashed my body with water from the stream and began my ascent. It was a difficult climb. The first handholds were deep, and I was able to find a shallow depression for a toehold. I lifted myself effortlessly five feet up the face of the rock. The next move was more difficult. There was a chip in a fissure that ran diagonally up the rock face, but it was three feet above my hands. It would mean letting go and pushing off from the shallow toehold. It would be like jumping, only it would be straight up the face of the rock, and there was room in that fissure for only one hand. If I made that jump, what would be my next move? I couldn't hang from one hand indefinitely. There was another toehold, but it was seven feet across the rock. I jumped, caught the fissure with the fingers of my left hand and swung to the toehold and planted my right foot securely in place. It was a difficult move, and my position was far from stable, but it wasn't as dangerous as one might think. After all, I was still only ten feet from the river bed. Fifteen feet to go. My respect for Stalking Wolf was growing literally by leaps and bounds.

I inched my way up that rock and got some pretty nasty burns in the process. At times I had to hug the rock and use its slight natural roundless for leverage. I didn't want to expose my body to the burns, but I had little choice. It was pain or jump. I chose the pain. "What will happen to the tribe?" kept flaming up in my conscience. Its meaning burned my soul more than the rock burned my body. In the white man's society it seems that everybody is out for himself. White men have forgotten their responsibility to the community. They ignore the brotherhood of all mankind. Stalking Wolf taught me that I lived for myself only when I lived for the tribe.

When I finally pulled myself over the top of the rock,

I couldn't believe my eyes. There for as far as I could see was a field of giant boulders. He could travel over them in any direction for a mile, and I would never know which way he had gone.

"You make it very difficult, Grandfather. How can I follow you over rock?" I spoke to the wind. And as if it heard me, a shadow glided across the rocks giving the illusion of a fish swimming through water. I looked up and spied a golden eagle soaring out of the sun toward the mountains, looking for snakes among the rocks. Perhaps if I climbed a tree. Perhaps a different perspective was all I needed.

I climbed a cottonwood and shared the branches with a western tanager. I think he was surprised to meet a human in his roost, but he didn't fly away. They are traditionally tame around people. I made a weak attempt to speak to him in his own language and failed miserably. I asked him to stay, and he flew straight away. I think my *pit-ik* sounded more like *git!*

This was the highest vantage point in the area and afforded me an unobstructed view across the boulder field. If Stalking Wolf traveled across those boulders in the heat of the day, he would be very thirsty. It would take him an hour, maybe two to cross the rocks. That would take him late into the day. He would head for water and a good-medicine spot to spend his last night on the plains. The idea that Stalking Wolf could have a last night was abhorrent to me. I shook my head to clear it of such thoughts, but they refused to go away. I was forced to face them. Each teaching from Stalking Wolf was a gift—this one, no less than the others. However, I didn't want to accept it.

Far off on the plain stood a lone mesquite tree, surrounded by cactus and sage. I remembered the stories Stalking Wolf told of gathering the pods from the mesquite when they ripened to a bright yellow. He delighted in the lonely journeys across the desert. He would often spend the night beneath some lone mesquite and nibble the pleasantly sweet raw beans for dinner. The beans allowed him to dream clearly. From this distance, I knew the tree was substantial, though it appeared small. There was no sign of water near the tree, but that didn't matter. Perhaps he licked the dew from the rocks in the morning to sustain him till he could reach the river again? I decided to make for the mesquite. It was as if his spirit beckoned to me.

It took me two hours to cross the rocks. I picked up his trail after a short search and headed in an almost direct line toward the mesquite that I knew was west, but was not visible from the ground level in the slightly rolling terrain. I thought for a brief time that the track would be easy, because I knew he had to make the tree by nightfall. I was mistaken. He seemed in no hurry to reach the tree. His tricks continued; he stopped twice to follow the tracks of a gray fox that was crisscrossing the area. He backtracked again, and when he came to an area of extremely hard-packed ground, he circled in a wide arc and brought me back almost to the place where I had started. I had to track over the hard ground on my hands and knees and forgot to check the surrounding landmarks. When my shadow appeared before my nose, and I finally noticed it, I looked up and discovered I had made a full circle. I could have sworn I heard him laughing at this mistake that it took him years to break me of.

"You do not make it easy, Grandfather." I couldn't seem to keep from talking to him as if he were within earshot. "You leave no scent. You trick me. You laugh at me, and my loneliness makes me anxious." I longed to find Stalking Wolf more than I had longed for anything else in my memory. More than I longed to live. The urge to find him was primal, as if to lose him would be to lose myself.

I lost his track twice and had to cross-track the area in order to rediscover the trail. "See with the eye of the spirit and see as Stalking Wolf sees." He had told me that years before. Actually he didn't say it exactly that way. I think he was referring to a rabbit I had been having trouble tracking, but as years passed, I substituted his name for the animal's. Whenever I lost his tracks, I would sit and study the terrain and my memory to decide where he might have gone. Had he deliberately walked on branches or stones to hide his trail? Did he choose the easy or more difficult path? Was he playing the mule deer or the porcupine? We would often sit, each playing the part of a different animal. I would be a fox and he a rabbit. I would verbally try to catch him, and he would flee. But once his rabbit fought, and my fox did not know what to do. This way we would learn to think like the animals.

His movements led me to believe he was playing my

childhood game with me. Would he ever get to the tree before dark?

It was a full hour past sunset when I felt my way into the camp Stalking Wolf had made under the mesquite tree. He made no attempt to hide the mound that buried the ashes from his campfire, and the place he had slept still yielded up the shape of his body. He knew I would find this spot at night. Perhaps he thought the sure knowledge on my part that he had been there would afford me clear dreams. If that was the case, he was correct in his assumption.

I woke with a tremendous thirst and hunger. I had been too exhausted the night before to worry about food. A quick scan of the area led me to a barrel cactus and the gratification of my thirst. A rabbit stick was easy enough to find as was a jackrabbit in this open country. Patience and a practiced throw provided a filling jackrabbit breakfast.

I felt wonderful. I was in my element. I had been here before through the stories and songs of Stalking Wolf. This was not a strange land but familiar territory, and I belonged. The sparrows had come from their roosts by the river and reminded me that it was time to begin again. Already the better part of the morning had passed. I checked the sun and the distance to the mountain. It would be a race with the sun to reach the mountain with enough light to find where Stalking Wolf had ascended. My body was nourished and my soul refreshed. I was ready to finish my quest.

Before I left the mesquite area, I restored it. That is, I removed all traces of my presence. I brushed the ground and buried my fire and what remained of the rabbit. All I left was the impression Stalking Wolf's body had made in the red earth beneath the tree. Somehow, I felt that it would be wrong to erase that last sign from this good-medicine area. Grandfather could rest there under his beloved mesquite till the wind carried him away.

The day flew swiftly by. I ran. Like a wild horse for the sheer joy of feeling the wind in my face. The trail was not difficult. The earth, softer and more impressionable, revealed her secrets with less coaxing. Stalking Wolf, as if in final celebration for his glorious life, ran much of the time. Imagine, if you can, a man in his nineties, on his final walk, running like a pony through the sage. As I ran, I became Stalking Wolf. I breathed deep the dry air and catalogued all the sweet desert fragrances. I noticed the eagle catch the warm updraft from the plain and soar to great heights in search of food. I heard the numerous bird calls and caught their constant darting flights, picking insects from the sky. I talked to the yellow bird with the red head and black wings and tail. "I have passed this way before. Do you remember me? I fed you a fly and we talked of your enemy, the western rattler." He swooped from a cactus and caught an insect so close I could have reached out and touched him.

I stopped, not to rest, but only when the trail told me Stalking Wolf had stopped. Each time I looked for the attraction that had slowed his journey. Once it was an unusually large coyote track over three inches long. The animal must have weighed over sixty pounds. Another time it was a mule-deer trail, and yet another it was a fox-kill area. He squatted and re-created the entire scene in his mind. The fox came from behind a rock and caught the rabbit browsing. He leaped on its neck. It kicked once —no, twice—wildly before it yielded its spirit. The gray fox ate part of its kill on the spot, and carried the remains off to the south. All this had been recorded in the earth. I read it and smiled.

My spirit was in tune with his. I moved as he moved and observed what he had seen. His trail seemed to jump out of the ground at me. The impressions seemed engraved in the landscape. As if they would always be there. I had little trouble following his footprints. They led back across the winding river bed and up to the base of the mountain. *Wert-wert-wert*, a prairie falcon warned of the coming night from its perch high in a cottonwood. A cool shiver ran down my back. I was nearing the end. I stopped and sat by the tree from which the falcon had called. There in the sand were grasshopper tracks. Stalking Wolf had taught me to track even the grasshopper, and eat them as the falcon did. The light was beginning to fade and the shadows lengthened. I knew that I had to continue, but I couldn't.

I sat under the cottonwood and wept. A loneliness that I hadn't felt all day began to overtake me, as though I had kept ahead of it by running. *Wert-wert*. I looked up at the falcon staring down at me and remembered how Stalking Wolf would comfort me during the difficult periods of change throughout my youthful years. He told me it was okay to cry as I tried to hide my tears. "Cry when you are saddened and let the tears fall to the earth. Share your sadness with your Mother, and she will comfort you." The sand beneath the cottonwood was wet with my sorrow. Will I ever be happy again? The sorrow seemed to permeate my entire existence, to the very roots of my soul.

Another phrase came to me through the sobs. It was given to me by Stalking Wolf just before he left the Barrens and walked back to the Southwest. I had been confronted by some friends who had attacked my life-style as an evasion of responsibility. They intimated that I would never grow up or contribute anything to society. That I would always be a little boy and play Indian in the backwater swamps of the Pine Barrens. This questioning of my values depressed me. He comforted me.

"Your preparation is different from theirs, and it demands discipline and patience. When your spirit is low, look up and take heart. Someday your spirit will soar with the eagles." The eagle to Stalking Wolf was the essence of life. Its predation kept the flow of nature in balance. It had the greatest purpose— the care of the earth. I looked up toward the mountain and rose from my sorrow, or rather through it and forced myself to place one foot in front of the other—the way the Indian walks.

A feather stuck in amongst the rocks caught my eye. There beneath where the feather had been placed I discovered Stalking Wolf's medicine pouch. The feather was an eagle's, a symbol to mark my inheritance. I stared at the pouch, unable to move, yet moved by the sacredness of the moment. I was not to go any farther. It was not time for me to climb the mountain. My head reeled with the thoughts the moment produced. I was overcome with humility and fear and gratitude. Some force moved my hand to lift the pouch from the bush over which it was draped. Thunder rolled over the mountains, or was it drums? The sun set.

The moment I touched Stalking Wolf's medicine pouch, my sadness left me. It was as if it were lifted by the wind and carried over the mountain. I lost the insatiable urge to find Stalking Wolf, because I knew that this was the end of my journey. He had willed it for me. He told me with the feather that I had accomplished a great task. I had learned to spirit track. My eyes had become his eyes, my ears his ears, my hands and feet his. I had thought like him, moved like him, and discovered his joy. The feather was my trophy, the pouch my destiny. I must carry on from here and teach as he taught. I was responsible for the earth. I was liable for the old ways.

I did not sleep but kept vigil about a teepee fire. The night was full of ghosts. They danced in the shadows and rode the rising sparks to the treetops. A great horned owl called from a willow. The crickets chirped. I sat in that ancient land amongst the memories made possible by Stalking Wolf. Apaches passed the pipe of peace and told stories of great hunts. They danced in the firelight and sang to me from the desert. I let him go that night. There were no more tears. All night the thunder pealed, like drums.

"Hello, young scout." I was greeted by the old woman as I walked into the pueblo. She looked at the feather I had placed in my headband and the pouch over my shoulder. "Now you are the medicine tracker."

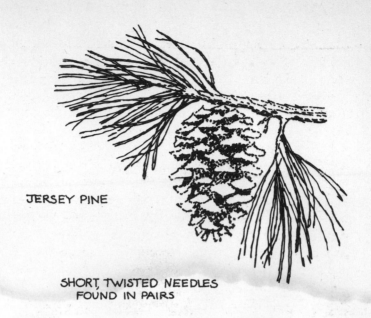

JERSEY PINE

SHORT, TWISTED NEEDLES
FOUND IN PAIRS

part four

AFTERWARD

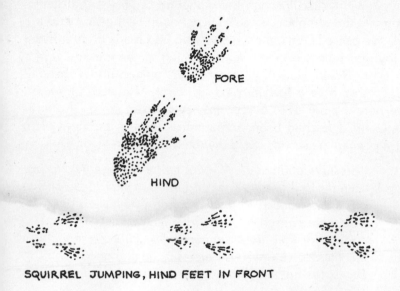

FORE

HIND

SQUIRREL JUMPING, HIND FEET IN FRONT

14/The Nature of Love

There is an oak in the Barrens behind Judy's home that is over five hundred years old. Legend has it that the Indians had met beneath its branches for sacred ceremonies. Years before, Stalking Wolf had told me of an oak's significance to the Indian, and the tree had taken on a special meaning for me. I vowed then that if I ever married, it would be under the sacred canopy of a great oak.

My vow was about to be fulfilled. Judy and I were moving toward an open field and a great oak where we were to be married. It was a great spreading white oak with branches as broad as a man's body. Its leaves were bright reds and yellows. They reflected the sun and bathed the field in a kaleidoscope of colors. Its branches were filled with birds and squirrels. Behind it stood an old split-rail fence and a small woods filled with our friends, the animals of the forest.

We walked through the gathering of family and friends listening to the symphony of sounds provided by the birds and the wind. We passed Doris, the woman who had made Judy's dress; her joy was reflected in the tears forming at the corners of her dark eyes. Robin, Judy's younger sister, waited under the oak wistfully shy; a very special maid of honor. We were all meant to be here—every tree, every bird, every person—as if everything in our lives had been preparing us for this moment. The minister began the service we had written.

> "Brothers and sisters. We are gathered together in this sacred place to join Tom and Judy in marriage. This place was chosen for its beauty and hallowedness. You were chosen for your friendship. They were chosen for their love, and welcome your presence at this blessed ceremony. Enjoy the beauty about you. Digest the colors. Listen to the bird and wind songs."

He began to recite our favorite Psalm, the hundred and fourth, the Creation Psalm.

> "Bless the Lord, O my soul!
>
> O Lord, how manifold are thy works!
>   In wisdom hast thou made them all;
>   the earth is full of thy creatures.
>
> These all look to thee,
>   to give them their food in due season."

I was listening to his words and wondering if the red squirrels that inhabited this great tree would understand the words of the psalmist. Would they know that the God who made them and provided for them brought Judy and me here today? They were there. I saw them as we walked in. It was surprising that they weren't chattering in competition with the minister. By my feet were the tracks of a raccoon. That's how this all began, I thought. . . .

It was late summer, and I was following the trail of a raccoon, which had caught a brown trout. I followed his prints along a stream and saw where it had climbed an old dead tree. Maybe there were some young in there. I climbed the tree for a look.

Judy, who had been hanging out wash, had also been watching me. She saw me crawling on my belly beside the stream. She saw me come up over the bank, paying no heed to the brambles that stood between me and the tree. She thought I was crazy.

"What are you doing?" she called.

"Shhh." I put my finger to my lips in the international sign for silence.

She couldn't believe her eyes. "What?"

"Shhh. Come here." I motioned with the silliest grin on my face.

Judy took a few very hesitant steps toward me, then stopped abruptly. "Do you know you're trespassing?"

By this time I had a baby raccoon in my hand and was petting it. I pointed to it and smiled a broad grin. I must have looked like an inmate at the state hospital.

She repeated her warning. "Do you know you're trespassing?"

"Huh?" I finally heard her and tried to explain myself. "Oh, no. I'm sorry. You see, I was following this raccoon down the stream. That stream there. And—uh—he caught a brown trout. Good little fisherman. I mean fisherwoman, or person. That's it, fisherperson." I tried to laugh, but she just continued to stare at me defiantly. "Anyway, he—I mean she led me here."

"Right, Tarzan, and just where is this big mother you were following?"

"Gone." I shrugged.

"Gone?" Judy was giving no ground. "Where?"

I began to climb down from the tree with the words, "Here, I'll show you."

"Oh, no, you won't!" she said firmly. "You won't show me anything. You'll just march off my property the same way you came. And I'll thank you to stay out of my trees."

"But I was only—"

She cut me off. "The last guy I knew who climbed trees did it in order to look in windows. Following raccoons! Couldn't you think of something that might make sense?"

I was turning toward the tree and the stream, gesturing

about the baby raccoons in my defense, when I noticed the mama raccoon's trail and blurted out, "Look between your legs."

She raised a handful of clothespins as if to throw them at me. "Now that's enough!"

"No, I mean it. Look at your feet." And I pointed.

"What are you talking about?" She questioned as she looked at the ground about her feet.

"The raccoon went off toward your shed. There are her tracks."

"Where?"

"Here, I'll show you." I began to walk toward her, then stopped. But she motioned with a nod of her head that it was okay, so I knelt by her feet and pointed to the tracks in the sandy soil.

"They could be cat tracks" was Judy's comment.

"With claw marks?"

"Cats have claws." She thought she had me.

"Retractable."

"Oh."

"Do you put garbage in that shed?" I asked her.

"Yes, why?"

I cut her off this time. "I thought so. Raccoons are as good at scavenging as they are at hunting. Here, let's follow the tracks." As I walked, I pointed out each set to Judy so she would know that I wasn't trying to hustle her. When we got to the shed, the door was open, and we caught the raccoon scrounging for some morsels. When she saw us, she took off in the opposite direction from her babies. Smart mother.

"You *were* following a raccoon!" Judy was astonished, and I think a little startled by the animal in her garbage.

"That's what I told you. Sorry to have startled you. I'll ah—be going." I backed off a few steps and turned to walk back toward the stream when I heard her call.

"Say, what's your name?"

I looked over my shoulder without breaking stride and yelled, "Tom."

"Tom? How about a cup of coffee?"

I turned and looked toward her and answered, "No thanks."

She shrugged and smiled, so I went on, "Tea?"

"That's better. Come on." She motioned to me to come up to the house. I stood and watched the deliberate way she walked, like someone who was very sure of herself. She stopped and looked back, noticing that I hadn't moved. "What are you waiting for? Want me to disappear so you can follow my tracks?" She smiled.

"What's your name?" I was curious by this time.

"Judy."

"You're very pretty, Judy—but a little skinny."

Judy raised an eyebrow and walked into the house. I followed. . . .

"I will sing to the Lord as long as I live;
I will sing praise to my God while I have being.
May my meditation be pleasing to Him,
For I rejoice in the Lord."

The sun hung low in the western sky. The shadows lengthened. A hawk made its final run over a timothy field behind the wood. Somewhere an owl awoke.

The minister directed me to turn to Judy and make answer to his question of intent.

"Tom, will you take Judy to be your wife?

"Will you pledge to her your love, devotion, honor, and tenderness? Will you live with her in this holy union, and cherish her in this holy bond?"

"I will."

Judy's eyes were reflecting the golden light coming through the oak. They were misty, but smiling. A breeze caught her auburn hair and raised it from her shoulder. Kelly immediately stepped to her mother and fixed her veil and brushed the hair from her face.

The kids were both there. They were a part of the ceremony. After all, it was their idea. . . .

Judy and I had been sitting over our cups of tea for about an hour when P.J. came home.

"Hi, Mom."

"Hi, P.J." P.J. was twelve.

"Hi, Tom." P.J. greeted me as if I had always been there. I was surprised to see who Judy's son was. He was one of my scouts in the troop I led. His recognition of me made both Judy and me realize that we weren't complete strangers, for we both said simultaneously, "So you're the one he's been trying to fix me up with!" Then we laughed.

P.J. had been trying to get me to come in and meet his mother for weeks, but I had thought better of it. I frankly expected someone much older. I wondered what impression she had of me from P.J.'s description.

"Where'd you come from?" P.J. asked.

"The woods—where else?"

"Oh, yeah, I should have known. Tom, did you see the raccoon family in the old tree out back?"

"That's what brought me here." I smiled and looked at Judy.

"Pretty cool, huh?" P.J. and I were communicating on the same wavelength. Judy realized it and was just a little put off.

"You never told me about the raccoons, P.J.," she said.

"I just discovered them yesterday when I had to pick up the garbage you thought some dog had dragged all over the yard."

Judy looked at me, and I just shrugged my shoulders. "I'm just passin' through, ma'am."

"Okay, P.J. Where's your sister?"

Kelly was standing silently in the hallway, listening and watching. She was a smaller version of her mother, except for long blond hair and what seemed to be a permanent pout. Kelly was fourteen.

She spoke to me from the hall. "You're P.J.'s scouting instructor, aren't you?"

"Yes."

"What else do you do?" It was a loaded question. She knew that I didn't do anything that she would recognize as a legitimate job. Oh, I chopped wood to keep gas in my jeep, but most of the time I wandered the Barrens. . . .

Judy turned to Kelly and handed her the bouquet of wild flowers we had gathered that morning. Kelly was crying, but was trying valiantly to hide the tears and smile. Judy took her hanky and wiped a tear from her cheek, then turned to me.

We held hands and a nightingale began to sing.

Tom, I take you to myself to be my husband.
I promise this before God, family and friends.
I will be your loving and faithful wife through all the
seasons. When there is plenty and when there is little.
When we are joyful and when we are sad. When we
are ill and when we are well. Forever you will be
mine, and I yours.

Judy and I had done a lot of thinking about our vows. We didn't want to recite something from the book of common worship which neither of us understood. We wanted them to reflect our deepest feelings for each other. After all, we both felt that our love was a gift from the Great Spirit, that our meeting was fateful and my acceptance by the children a miracle. . . .

Judy made a statement. "You're staying for dinner."

"I can't do that. I haven't contributed anything." When I said this, Kelly's eyebrows raised slightly. She didn't know what to make of that statement.

P.J. implored, "Please stay. Come on. You can pick some tea."

Kelly piped up, "You don't pick tea, silly!"

"Yes, you do," I answered quickly. "It grows all around here."

"No, it doesn't. It grows in China." Kelly was trying to defend her point, but I could tell that she was curious.

"Come on." I started for the door, holding out my hand to her.

"Where are you going?"

"China."

We walked through the backyard and to the edge of the stream. On our way a number of black-capped chickadees and a male cardinal flew over us and into the thick growth that bordered the woods.

"Well, what kind of tea strikes your fancy? Sweet, mild, tangy, or mellow?"

"Mellow." Kelly almost whispered the word.

"See that plant over there? The Indians ate its roots the same way you eat cucumbers. It's called Indian cucumber. See those cattails? You can boil or roast their roots. The Indians dried them and pounded them into meal. Shake the pollen into a dish and mix it with flour and water, and presto—pancakes."

"You mean you can really eat those weeds?" Kelly didn't know whether to believe me or not, so I continued to point out the numerous edible plants in and about her yard. Dandelions, wild mustard, burdock, milkweed, chicory, nettle, pokeweed.

"If all these plants are edible," Kelly asked, "then why do we bother to cultivate and have gardens?"

"Kelly, there wouldn't be enough to feed all the people if we did that. If we just took from the land and gave nothing back, we would soon starve. The Indians were beginning to cultivate when the white man came to these shores. They had maize or corn, tobacco, cotton, fields of roots. But mostly they were gatherers and not planters. But they never gathered more than they needed. They always recognized the balance that was needed to sustain life. How about some hemlock tea?"

"Isn't that the stuff that killed Socrates?"

"No, that was from the hemlock plant. This is made from the hemlock tree. You steep the needles. There are dozens of teas. The mellow tea is made from catnip. It makes me sleepy. I could make you a sweet tea from sassafras, or the world-renowned New Jersey tea, but that means drying the leaves. How about a little pine-needle tea, laced with catnip and wild mint?"

Kelly liked that idea, so we set about gathering the ingredients. As we gathered, we talked about school, the woods, Indians, and boys. It was, all in all, a good conversation. On the way back to the house she noted, "I guess if you can keep yourself on weeds and stuff, and if you don't grub off people, you don't need a job."

"The gatherers have returned with lots of good stuff," Kelly proclaimed as we entered the kitchen. "Did you know you could eat the bark of those old pine trees out back if you were really hungry?" Kelly was sharing all her newly-discovered knowledge with the rest of the family. Judy gave me a quick glance as if to say, "What have you been telling my daughter?" I shrugged again.

"You're going to get rounded shoulders if you keep that up!" Judy threw the remark at me like an old dish rag. I shrugged again. "Get out of this kitchen till the cooking's done. Go! Shoo!" We all retreated before her motherly advances.

"Tom, place this ring on Judy's left hand."

I took the ring from my brother and placed it on Judy's hand and recited, "Judy, the Great Spirit that moves in all things brought us together and will keep us as one forever. I love you."

Judy took the ring from Kelly and placed it on my hand with the words, "Wherever you go I will go. Wherever you live, there will I live. Your people will be my people, and your God, my God. Where you die, there will I die. I love you." For the first time during the ceremony, Judy cried. Somewhere a cricket sounded its fiddle.

We sat about the fire that evening and talked of the woods and the Spirit that moves in all things. I told them of Stalking Wolf and his concept of family.

"The family is made up of more than mother and father. It is made up of all living things. We all have a human mother and Mother Earth. We all have a human father and the Great Spirit. Everything else is our brother or sister."

Finally, I made an overture to leave, making some excuse about the late hour. Really, I didn't want to go. I belonged in that home even as I belonged in the woods. I felt a part of that tiny family. But I knew I had to go, and so said, "It's getting late. I'll be going now."

To my pleasant surprise, both the kids pleaded, "Don't go." They looked at Judy and implored her to let me stay. "Tell him not to go, Mom." Judy looked at them for a long time. The silence was uncomfortable, so I moved toward the door, expecting Judy to say it would be impossible for me to stay.

"Tom," Judy called after me, "stay."

I stayed.

The minister was praying. "Lord, your birds are singing a song of joyous love. Your sun warms us as your magnificent day draws to a close, and its deep red rays reach through these autumn leaves and touch our hearts. This place is truly a holy place. Here we feel your presence in the love of Judy and Tom. Be with them, Lord, and walk with them along the trail you have set before them. Amen."

We kissed beneath the sacred oak, as if for the first time. I didn't hear the red squirrel scold or the owl's call or the evening songs of the birds or the west wind's mellow tune. All was still for that moment we kissed. The world stopped for me then. This love was greater than any other force in the world.

Rice poured over us as we ran for our jeep. The kids were screaming, and everyone was laughing and crying at the same time. Through it all the nightingale sang.

We didn't speak on our way home. We watched the sun set and listened to the evening concert played out by the nature about us. It was our marriage symphony. Frogs and crickets kept the rhythm. Owls and nightingales carried the melody. A symphony of sound rose from the Barrens. It was as if it had been composed for just this occasion. It was conducted by the Great Spirit.

The night sounds have never been the same since. That symphony was played but once. We were lifted by the music and transported to another world. We were one with each other and the world of nature about us. Everything else ceased to exist.

We spent the first night of our honeymoon at the good-medicine cabin deep in my beloved Pine Barrens.

"Here we are, Judy, the good-medicine cabin I told you about."

"Tom, you told me we were going to spend our first night out under the stars." Somewhere a wild dog howled at the moon. Judy moved closer.

"Don't want to shock the animals, do you?" I promised we could sleep out the next night.

Judy whispered as we unloaded the jeep, "Maybe you'll forget."

"What was that, Judy?"

"Nothing, just that I don't mind sleeping inside."

We talked that night of what had transpired at this place between an old man and two young boys.

"Do you miss them?"

"I did. Not anymore. Not with you here."

"That's not what I mean, Tom. You'll never take the place of my grandfather. I mean, is it hard being here without them?"

"They are here, Judy. That's why I don't miss them. I carry them with me and feel their presence in everything I do that we ever did together. Besides, the Great Spirit has given me another family." I hugged Judy close. Closer than I ever held anyone and prayed that we would never be separated.

"I do miss someone, though, Judy."

"Don't tell me, let me guess. Mother?"

"No."

"Your teddy?"

"My what?"

"Your old girlfriend?"

"Close."

Judy hit me in the stomach.

"That hurt."

"You deserved it. Okay, this is my last guess—the kids!"

"Right."

"We'll just have to go back and get them in the morning." When Judy said that, I knew I had someone who completely understood me.

"I was hoping you'd say that."

It may seem odd to spend a honeymoon with stepchildren. It didn't to us or the kids or the dog. We had a great time at the good-medicine cabin, basking in the sun and swimming in the good-medicine creek. We fished, gathered, told stories, and barked at the moon. We made bow-and-drill fires, fed chickadees from our hands, and P.J. almost touched a deer. My new family brought me new joy, and a day didn't pass that I didn't thank the Great Spirit for my good fortune.

The final night of our honeymoon we had a pipe ceremony. P.J. and I had been whittling one all week just for this occasion. They all wondered what it was, but thought it would be great fun.

"Listen, this is a very serious ceremony. The Indians

never took it lightly, and neither do I. I'll explain what it means. The smoke is the spirit. By sharing the pipe, we are offering the goodwill of the Great Spirit to each other. We are also mingling our spirits with each other's, recognizing the brotherhood of all living things. It is a way of saying I trust you, I honor you, I wish the best for you. It is a way of sharing love."

There was no laughter during the ceremony. I offered some tobacco to the earth and scattered it to the four winds. I sang an ancient Apache song, lighted the pipe, and passed it to Judy. "The pipe of peace and brotherhood." That phrase was repeated three more times about our family circle that night. We were one with each other and with the world about us. We sat and listened to the night talk. The bats catching insects over the swamp. The owls searching for mice. The dogs calling to a spirit wild and primitive.

Later that night, after we had said good night, Judy offered, "Tom, you should share yourself with more people."

It was a pleasant thought on which to end a honeymoon. I smiled and fell off to sleep wondering, "How?"

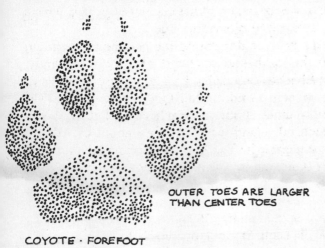

OUTER TOES ARE LARGER
THAN CENTER TOES

COYOTE · FOREFOOT

15/The Evolution of a School

Stalking Wolf had given me this injunction: "Teach." Judy urged me time and again to trust my dreams and teach my skills. But I was afraid. I hesitated. I did not feel that anybody would be interested.

In the spring of 1978, Judy persuaded me to try. I began a modest school for survival and tracking. My first class had two students. Today, I teach three thousand students a year. My first classes were weeks, even months apart. Today, they run continuously on both coasts.

This chapter is about the evolution of the school and its content. I want to tell about it because it embodies so much of what I am and what I believe. The uniqueness of my school is that I teach the way Stalking Wolf taught me—through participation. This chapter will explain what I mean by that.

Roosters crowed to the rising sun on a neighboring farm. I was excited about the school and had been awake listening to the hunting antics of a resident barn owl. In the barn where the owl lived and worked, there were twenty-five students from all parts of the United States and Canada. It was my first large class on this new site in Asbury, New Jersey, and I was nervous.

Less than a year before, two friends asked me to take them into the Pine Barrens of southern New Jersey for a weekend and teach them some of the survival skills I was always talking about. I agreed. We had a great weekend living off the land. As we parted at the end of the weekend, they insisted on paying me.

"For what?" I asked.

"We learned more this weekend than we learned in all our botany and zoology courses at the university. And there we paid $348.00 per credit hour. Take the little bit we are offering. It's worth much more."

I took the money but felt guilty. Stalking Wolf never expected anything for his teachings except gratitude and reverence for the earth. How could I sell something that was so freely given? How could I charge for doing the only thing I ever really enjoyed?

These were hard questions. Judy helped me through them.

"Tom, remember the legacy Stalking Wolf gave to you?"

"You mean his prophecy?"

"Yes, he said that you would teach the old ways."

"I know, but he never mentioned my receiving payment. It seems almost sacrilegious."

"Tom, did you ever bring Stalking Wolf gifts out of gratitude? Didn't you share the meat from your hunts? Didn't you build the medicine cabin so that he might have a place to sleep? Didn't you scrimshaw and whittle and tan and sew him numerous gifts?"

"Yes, but he never asked for those gifts. They came naturally." I could see the point Judy was trying to make, but was not ready to let my pride be pierced by reason.

"If you can't accept the gifts, then you can never teach."

I was confused. I didn't understand what Judy was trying to say. "What do you mean?"

"You have told me time and again that the circle is sacred, that the life of a man is a circle, that everything comes back that is given. If you won't allow your gift of teaching to come back to you, then you are breaking the circle. If you don't accept the gifts, then you don't allow those you have taught to express their gratitude and fully learn what you have taught."

I wanted to reject what she was telling me. I wanted to tell her she was wrong and didn't understand. But the truth was that I was wrong. I taught gratitude. I taught reverence for everything received. I taught that everyone must return all that he has received in order to feel a sense of fulfillment and a oneness with his surroundings. Then I was denying my teachings by trying to refuse the gifts of gratitude offered freely by my students.

Judy continued: "Your students can't give you buffalo robes or wild ponies. You have to adapt yourself to the society in which you live, Tom. This is a money society. Don't reject its only way of showing you gratitude. Don't be so proud of your rejection of the 'white man's ways' that you cut off your ability to teach."

I was really impressed with her sincerity. "Judy, I'll try to see things your way. Maybe this is the answer to our dreams. I can stay close to the earth and provide for my family. If it is meant to be, it will happen."

And happen it did.

After the *Reader's Digest* condensation of my book, *The Tracker*, appeared in November 1978, I began to receive letters by the hundreds, asking about the school I alluded to in the book.

Quite frankly, I am a woodsman. I know nothing about this monied society. But as I have always been cared for in the past, so I was sent a friend who does understand business. Bob helped me plan and set up a full-time school on a farm in Asbury, New Jersey. We had moved in a week before my first class—the class that was waiting to be led.

I walked into the tiny bathroom that was filled with steam from Judy's shower. I couldn't see a thing in the mirror, so I doused it with some cold water and what I saw startled me. The droplets of water streaking down the mirror gave my head and face the look of an ancient red man. Feathers hung from my braided hair and wrinkles told of years of wisdom and exposure to the wind and sun. I blinked hard, thinking I had seen a vision of Stalking Wolf. When I opened my eyes, Tom Brown was the image reflected. I smiled.

The farm in Asbury is a naturalist's dream. It is set far back from the road in the middle of five hundred acres of fields and woods. There is a pond, a nearby river, and a profusion of animal and plant life. An enormous barn graces the property a hundred yards behind the one-hundred-year-old farmhouse we now call home.

The students sleep on hay in the barn, and we all cook in a fire pit constructed in the barnyard. We consider ourselves just another group of animals. We do not mean that in any derogatory sense, since we consider the creatures of the fields and woods as our equals, and indeed in many ways our superiors. That is meant as a compliment. Our reverence for life depends on our understanding of the brotherhood of all life.

The first night my students arrived, I gave them an outline of the course they would receive and the reasoning I used for picking the things to be taught. I also shared with them the unique method of teaching they would experience. I call it observation through participation.

We had spent hours that first evening talking, and I found myself lecturing about things I had never planned to say outright.

Thomas Carlyle stated that "The tragedy in life is not what men suffer, but what they miss." We are so locked in to our "civilized" life-styles that we no longer understand who we really are or where we come from. We walk around with little machines on our wrists that tell us when we are hungry or late. Our heads are filled with sounds from machines that dance unreal pictures of life before our tired eyes and blare false prophecies in our ears. We define who we are, not by what is in our hearts, but by what is in our heads. We think with our heads. The Indian taught that we were to think with our hearts.

We come from the earth. It sustains us, it nurtures us, it provides for us and shelters us. But how many of you have ever tasted it? How many of you have ever wrapped yourselves in her cool moistness and smelled her? We are so removed from our roots that we have lost touch with our beginnings. "The farther man's feet are removed from the earth, the closer he comes to doom." I believe this to be true.

The danger within our society is not starvation, but isolation. Our concrete and asphalt have removed us from the ground. We have constructed shelters unnaturally. We cut trees and blast open the earth for stone. We crush it, mix it with water, and build unhealthy square shelters. The Indian marveled at our reasoning. He couldn't understand why we went to so much trouble when nature had provided all we needed naturally. There was plenty of dead wood and grasses and mud for wickiups. Plenty of stone for hogans. Why destroy the earth to create a shelter?

Stalking Wolf often told me of the Plains Indians' attitude toward the white men's dwellings. White men's dwellings were so permanent. Everything changes; why should the white men fight the change? Why should he fear the change? The Plains Indians lived in tepees that moved when they moved; they spent most of their time outdoors and were healthy. Somehow they felt there was some connection between the permanence of the white men's dwellings and their seemingly constant illness.

We have come from the earth, but have denied our dependence on her. Therefore, we are isolated and confused. "I hope that through this course," I told the students, "you will begin to see your relationship to the earth, which sustains you, and find yourselves and your roots. It won't be anything mystical or magical or religious. It will be the simple truth understood."

I said, "I guess that is what we will be searching for throughout this week. The truth. I hope you find it. I hope you discover your kinship with the earth and its inhabitants. I'll try to give you the tools for this search. You will have to supply the desire. This is a survival course, but I see it as more than personal survival, I see it as the survival of all mankind. We must begin to treat our earth with respect if we are to continue to expect her to support us, and we can't do that unless we understand our relationship to her."

The class was made up of twenty-five individuals from all parts of the country. There was a woman from California, a French Canadian, a couple from Washington, some friends from the

Midwest, a rebel, some cosmopolitans from New York City and Washington, D.C., and some students. Men and women from every conceivable walk of life—teachers, doctors, lawyers, business persons. By the end of the week, their personalities would be described by Indian names that would grow out of their experiences. One would be called Dull Knife, another Spring Hawk, Deeper Vision, and so on. It would be a week of confrontation with nature and observation through participation. It would be an experience of intense learning and hard work, but it would also be a time of dreaming.

I walked to the barn beside the pond. A bass leaped after a minnow. The red-tailed hawk that inhabited the woods on the south side of the property started his first pass at a newly-sown alfalfa field. The sun was warming the April morn and promising a beautiful day. The ground was covered with tracks: a snapping turtle whose home was the pond, deer, fox, rabbit, domestic cat, and dog; a variety of beetle and worm markings and bird tracks too numerous to count.

The remainder of this chapter is divided according to areas of study rather than into days. We studied continuously throughout the week, slept little and talked much. It is almost impossible to discern one day from another in such an environment.

As we began to function more and more like a tribe, time began to flow. We lost track of time as the white man knows it. We lost ourselves in our surroundings through participation and became time rich.

There was darkness and light, morning and evening, surely, but they were related to what the wildlife did during those times. We ceased thinking of morning as breakfast time or noon as lunch break or evening as dinner time.

In the morning we observed a fox sneaking back to its den. We listened to the owls roost and the day birds awaken. We sat silently and petted the deer as they walked by toward their day beds.

At noon, when the sun was high, we worked on our skills.

In the evening we observed the reawakening of the night creatures and the roosting of the day birds. In the dark hours we would be enlightened through vision seeking or sharing. Vision seeking is simply being alone with the earth, observing all sounds and movements. It is listening with your heart as well as your mind to what the earth is saying. It is a time of introspection.

Sharing is what happened around the fire among the members of the class as they related their newfound wisdom and feelings.

So I invite you to continue reading what transpired in the hearts and minds of the students, who lost track of time and became time rich, and found themselves in the process.

Survival

Survival is simply staying alive. It's easy. Nature has provided everything we need. We live in a garden of Eden and think we are in the wilderness. All we need to survive is the knowledge of where to locate three things: water, shelter, and fire.

Most places have water. If not, then you can find it. Don't be afraid to soak up the dew from rocks with a piece of clothing and wring it into your mouth. Lick it from the stones and grass. Water is more important than food. You can eat plants and bark and roots and stay alive indefinitely as long as you know what you're eating, but you can't last very long without water. Make water your first priority.

After you know you can find water, think about shelter. The simplest and, I've found, most effective shelter is a leaf hut. It can be made with discarded waste and, according to the thickness of the walls, can protect you against heat, cold, and moisture. Rick and I made one with walls three feet thick! We leaned a pole against a tree, covered it like a tent with branches, piled on leaves, more sticks, more leaves, and it kept us warm as toast in the coldest weather. You can do the same.

Fire is needed if you want to stay warm in subfreezing weather and if you want to cook. You won't always have matches, so I taught the class how to make a fire with a bow and drill.

We did, and we kept at it till every student could start a fire with one.

An entire day was spent learning the basics of survival.

We built a wickiup that could house a half dozen adults warmly and dryly indefinitely. We made it from deadfall poles and long grass tied in bundles. It took the class about two hours to construct one. They were amazed that they could make such a permanent structure in such a short period of time, with just the materials at hand.

We practiced with rabbit sticks—sticks about two feet long that can be used for killing rabbits and other small game and game birds. They are easy to come by. You can pick up any stick. They are easy to learn how to use, and they are an effective way of acquiring food. We threw them at targets and got so we could hit the targets that were set up behind the bushes.

Each skill learned brought the class more confidence. I taught them how to construct traps and work with leather. We brain-tanned the hide of a deer that had been killed on the road by the farm. We worked with stone and made hand tools. We made fire-hardened spears and did scrimshaw work on dried bones.

By the end of the week, the class was assured not only of survival but of the possibility of prospering if they were ever lost in the wilderness.

One student from California stated that she hoped she would have the opportunity to get lost—because if she were ever lost, she would be very difficult to find as she would probably enjoy it so much.

Observation

The first concept I teach a class is that of observation. Most people miss 90 percent of what happens right before their eyes. They don't notice. It doesn't register, because they live not in the present, but in the future. What am I supposed to do next? Where will I have to go next? We insulate ourselves and fail to see things or relate them.

Stalking Wolf taught that every movement meant something and was related to every other movement. His was the original domino theory. When we learn to see through the eyes of the Great Spirit and notice everything, not as humans, but as every animal and bird and insect might see it and hear it, we are *participating*. Through the two actions we are able to obtain the truth. I call it observation through participation.

First, we will observe, then we will participate. The first is physical, the second spiritual. However, the two are so closely related that you will be unable to separate the physical from the spiritual.

I taught the class two techniques. The first was splatter vision. In this you scan the horizon looking for movement and color. When you catch some movement, then focus. It's the way animals observe. The second is varying vision. Look out at a 45-degree angle to the ground. Look far out, and then come down slowly, focusing on everything. Look for horizontal lines. Everything stationary in nature is most likely to be vertical. If you see something horizontal, it's liable to be animal. When we look out, we should be huge receptors of everything we see, from the minute to the majestic.

The participation is a bit more difficult, but is very satisfying. I begin with observation through the eyes of a rabbit. We crawl as a class through the fields and notice everything a rabbit would notice. Things look different when you're looking up at them. We lick the dew from the grass and nibble at twigs and young shoots of edible grasses. We experience the largeness of our natural surroundings and also discover fears and abilities we never realized a rabbit might have.

My French-Canadian student was especially impressed with this exercise. He said that now he knows why it is so difficult for the English-speaking majority in Canada to understand the French-speaking people. They have never been in their situation. "Now I know how big a man must look to a rabbit, and I also know how easy it is to avoid him."

The next exercise was one I call "a closer look." It enables us to understand the interconnectedness of all things and to appreciate that interrelatedness better than any exercise I know.

We spread out over a field. Each student had a paper and pencil and was instructed to study a piece of land one foot square. They were to name or draw a picture of every moving thing in that square. When they were finished, they were to stand up.

A man in Green Beret fatigues stood first.

"Let's see how many things you noticed," I said as I walked over to him.

He showed me a list of twelve items and two drawings.

"Okay, Mike, let's take another look." I motioned him to the ground with me. We observed all those things Mike had mentioned, and I then took a stick and pulled back part of some decaying grass to expose a layer of all new little creatures. Mike wondered how I knew that they existed down there. I told him the same way I know a mouse is in a field when I see a hawk dive. "Many of those bugs you described from the upper layers feed on these little guys under the dead grass. Remember, everything is related."

It is no exaggeration to say that the class spent hours with their noses in the dirt. They tasted the ground and smelled it. They noticed every insect and every plant. They could be found at any time during the week checking and rechecking their little patches of ground. They came to know that ground and every insect and worm and beetle that inhabited it. They could discern the slightest change. They knew the effects of the hot sun on the bugs and the effects of the rain. They could tell when a bird had fed on seeds or insects from their land.

Mike took one last look before he left for his home in Pennsylvania. He said he discovered more about himself and life in that square foot of earth in one week than he had discovered through sixteen years of schooling and four years of service. I believed him.

Stalking

"How many of you hunt?" I asked and saw most of the hands in my class shoot up.

"How many use guns?" They all laughed at this question. It's amazing to realize that an entire race existed for thousands of years on this continent and prospered as hunters, and didn't know what a gun was. When we think of hunting, we think of shooting.

"I'm going to teach you a way of stalking that will make the use of firearms unnecessary. I'm going to teach you to walk silently and invisibly across an open field toward a deer and make it possible for you to touch that deer before it knows you are there." The class was astounded. They were hearing a claim they believed couldn't be substantiated.

"The white man walks with his toes pointing out left and right, and his feet cut a wide path. He clomps and swings, grunts and moans across the landscape like a bull elk in heat." I demonstrated. The class laughed.

"The Indian walks with his toes pointing in the direction he's headed. He cuts a narrow path and registers one foot in front of the other. He walks with his thighs and uses far less energy." Again I demonstrated. They didn't laugh.

The secret to moving silently is how you place your feet. Touch the ground with the outer part of the ball of your foot and roll slowly toward the arch, carefully noting the presence of rocks, twigs, dry grass, or anything else that might make a noise. When you are assured of a silent step, then shift your weight and carefully lift your back foot with the toe pointed toward the ground, careful not to catch on any grass or bush. Repeat the process again and again till you have moved silently across an area. It is very possible.

I invited the class to practice the technique. They complained of how hard it was on their upper legs, but they were pleased with the way it felt. By the end of the week they were stalking each other and tapping one another on the shoulder before being discovered.

"Stalking Wolf could run across a bed of dry leaves without making a sound. Someday you'll be able to do that." The easy part of the lesson was finished, and the difficult part was to begin.

"This stalking walk is fine, Tom, but animals are constantly looking around. Won't they see us tiptoeing across the field toward them?" Eric, the man who would be known as Touch Deer before the end of the week, asked this question skeptically.

"Do you remember what I taught you about observation?"

"Yes," Eric answered, "look for movement."

"Exactly. Ninety percent of an animal's defense is camouflage. An animal detects movement. If there is no movement, and the wind is right, he won't see you and he will go back to his grazing or whatever."

This is the difficult part of stalking. The first, knowing how to walk silently, is physical. This part is spiritual. In order to do this, you must be in tune with everything—the animal you are stalking, the wind, the sounds about you. You must be able to flow with the spirit of your surroundings and become a part of it. I demonstrated by moving across the barnyard toward a robin; when it looked toward me, I froze. My arms were in front of my body, and I never smiled or blinked an eye. When it fed, I moved. I knelt and reached toward its back and felt the touch of its wing as it took flight, startled by my closeness.

The class was amazed, but not half as amazed as they would be later in the week when they would be re-creating this scene in their own lives. Throughout the rest of the week, whenever I looked at a field, I noticed some of my students stalking deer or rabbit or birds. The stories began to circulate among them of how close they had come to different animals. They would be up before dawn in order to position themselves for a chance at touching a deer.

The excitement could not be contained. It radiated throughout the group and built as the week progressed. The class began to experience what it would be like to be a spirit and be able to flow with the wind over the land, observing all things. Think what it would be like to be invisible and move through a crowd listening and observing, and yet unobserved. It would be like being a part of the wind, or the wind itself. It would be a totally freeing experience. Invisible and silent. Able to move like the wind in and around all things.

By the end of the week, Eric had touched a deer. We named the camp skeptic Touch Deer. He liked it and still signs his letters that way.

Tracking

The secret to tracking is patience. I know that sounds too simple, but that's the whole of it. If you can find a fresh print, identify it, and then watch it for a month and memorize the changes made by the weather. . . . If you can find that same track in a hundred different soils, then watch each for the same amount of time. . . . If you have patience, you can track.

I took my class out into the woods. First, know the animals. Read about their habits. Know what they eat and when. Know where they live and how many young they have. Know their sizes and their tracks. Be able to recognize their track and its changes through the seasons.

Secondly, have patience. When you come upon a track, study it. Touch it and determine the direction the animal is moving. Determine the age of the track and decide if the animal is traveling to or from its home. Is it eating, running, walking, fleeing? Ask yourself questions and then seek the answers.

Thirdly, begin the track. Follow the markings, and with each step notice everything that is around you. See where the deer chewed the tender buds of a sapling or the rabbit hid on a run from a fox or cat. Constantly check the terrain and surrounding animal and plant life. Notice everything. It is all speaking to you. It is like a giant puzzle. When you put it all together, you will have the picture of what transpired on the spot you are on.

I took the class into the woods and stopped by a drainage ditch. The bottom was covered with soft sandy soil. It was also covered with animal prints. I asked the class to notice all the prints that were visible. They named two animals and guessed at two more. There were eleven, not counting the dog.

When I ask for prints, I'm not just looking for clear sharp markings of large well-known animals. I'm searching for an explanation of every mark on the ground. I pointed out the fox and deer, dog, cat, rabbit, raccoon (which was a week old), possum, and groundhog. I also pointed to markings made by a turtle, a beetle, and a worm. As I study the markings a picture begins to form in my mind of what passed the spot I am checking before I arrived. My mind begins to place animals in space and time.

Something began to take shape as I noticed the age of the different tracks.

"What are you thinking, Tom?" Touch Deer tried to break into my concentration with a question.

I shook my head and motioned for silence as my mind

raced back in time and developed the picture from the negatives of tracks.

"Wow!" I yelled. "Look at that." It had all come together, and I began to explain the scene to the class as I pointed to the markings that were the tracks of a dog and a rabbit, which had been on this spot at the same time.

"Dog came down, saw the rabbit before it smelled him. Maybe a cross wind. He jumped after the rabbit. Here is his first set of four running prints." I pointed. "Here, here, here, and here. Here is the rabbit moving up the side of the ditch to that sweet new grass." Again I pointed to markings that looked almost as if someone had scraped the dirt with a branch. "The rabbit sees the dog, does a boogie here, and races down the hill. He made two gigantic leaps. See where he jumped? See where the dog leaped for him and missed? Skidded here, regained his balance, and followed up the other side, there."

I looked up and could tell by the smiles on the faces of my students that they were beginning to see what I had seen. They were excited by the possibilities. Imagine being able to read the earth like a book and picture what had happened.

"How did you do that?" Kay asked.

"I sat for days on the edge of a field and watched rabbits feed, breed, bear young, and avoid danger. After each happening, I would study the marks that had been left in the earth. I can tell when a rabbit is sitting or standing, agitated or calm. Whenever a dog came through the field and happened on a chase, I would follow its every marking, remembering what my eyes had seen just moments before. After a great amount of time, I began to recognize those signs as I happened onto them."

The explanation was an honest answer, but I could sense that it had discouraged the class. They were looking at the impossible nature of the task. They felt as if they would never be able to master the art.

"You're thinking like the white man again," I cautioned. "There's no schedule to keep out here. You've got all the time in your life to learn this. If you want."

"Time rich?" Dull Knife offered.

"That's right!"

I took them through the field and into the woods, building their confidence as we moved. I pointed to some obvious signs and asked questions. They answered, delighted to be able to recognize the deer trail, a rabbit run, a deer's night bed and day bed. Then they began to notice markings and signs, stopping and studying and calling to the rest of the class when they made discoveries.

Eric found a hole in the side of a knoll with fresh dirt piled about it. He studied the tracks and came to the conclusion that it belonged to a groundhog. He was right!

Kay discovered an owl pellet at the base of a tree and searched its branches for a roost till she found one. We were all excited to pull the pellet apart and discover the owl's diet. An owl has a very effective digestive system. It swallows its prey whole, its system uses what it can, and discharges the rest through re-gurgitation. The result is a pellet of fur, feathers, and bones of the mice and birds and animals the owl has eaten. It all holds together and is an excellent indication of the many forms of life that in-habit an area.

I led the class into an area that was filled with deer tracks. I directed the class to disperse and find a clear print and follow it as far as possible forward or backward. I demonstrated on some tracks at my feet. Then I circulated among the students and assisted where it was necessary. One thing I had to remind them of constantly was that, though the earth recorded everything that happened, it was sometimes hidden from our view. We had to search for it.

I would part the grass or lift a leaf to reveal a partial print. I would skip over rough ground to where the deer would probably have moved and regained the trail. It is much like reading an an-cient religious text that is faded and full of errors made by some tired recorder centuries before. Always remember that the truth is there to be found. Discover the mistakes, lift the leaves, part the grass, understand the symbols—the turned rock, the scraped twig —and the message is clear.

The message began to be read by the class as they stud-ied and worked at tracking. All else was forgotten as they found themselves following trails through the woods. I watched them move carefully on their trails and was pleased to see how they took the time to observe. Mike reacted to a squirrel that bounded through the branches, and searched to find what had startled it. Deeper Vision was diverted by a raccoon's trail that crossed the deer's path he had been following. He checked every turned stone and bent branch as he started off on a new adventure. However, he was careful to mark where he had left the deer trail. He would come back when he had exhausted the raccoon's trail.

The owls were hunting before the class returned for their evening meal.

The last night found the class sitting around the fire sharing stories of their adventures in the woods that day. They had become integral parts of the land. Some had crawled all day to experience life through the eyes of a rabbit. Others had climbed trees, and some had followed a single trail all day. They were into what they had learned, and they were happy.

I broke into their circle dressed as Stalking Wolf used to dress for the pipe ceremony. The class had not seen me or heard my approach; nevertheless they were not startled. In this setting, after a week of living next to the earth, a man in a loincloth stepping out of the night into the light of their fire seemed natural.

My voice blended with the crackling of burning ash. Sparks circled toward the moon. My drum beat out the ancient Apache rhythm. I sang a song in the Apache tongue that related the message. Before we talk of holy things, we must prepare ourselves by offerings. Fill the pipe. Offer it to the sky and earth. Smoke together and talk.

I sat before the fire and prepared the pipe. Tobacco was offered to the earth and sky. I scattered it to the four winds. The pipe was lighted, and we passed it about the circle in friendship. Each student took a shallow puff and passed it on. The barn owl flew from his roost in the silo. Slowly the night sounds broke through the sacred silence.

Each sound told a story that was communicated as eyes flashed knowing glances at one another across the fire. We talked.

The last of the class was gone by noon Sunday. We parted with tears and promises to correspond. One statement summed up the feeling of the week: "The threads of my life have turned into a band of steel." The class had really gotten it all together. They had found themselves in relation to the land, and they liked what they found.

From that first class on I have developed a statement that I feel shares with others my lifelong dream: "I took the time to find myself." To know what you are, you must know where you came from.

"I'm glad I took the time to find myself."

"You're happy with what you found?"

"Yes. My problem was I didn't know where to look or how. You taught me that."

"No. I pointed the way. The earth taught. Keep learning from her."

"I'll certainly try."

From that final conversation came the motto of my future classes: "I took the time to find myself."

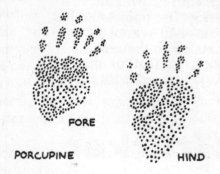

PORCUPINE

If you would like to write to Tom, you may at the following address:

Tom Brown, Inc.
The Tracker
P.O. Box 318
Milford, New Jersey 08848

Tom welcomes your letters and will make every effort to answer them.